The Moon Cottage
Cats

VOLUME TWO

MARILYN EDWARDS

WITH ILLUSTRATIONS BY

PETER WARNER

HODDER

This omnibus edition first published in Great Britain in 2008
by Hodder & Stoughton
An Hachette Livre UK company

1

A CIP catalogue record for this title is available from the British Library

ISBN: 978 0340 95453 9

Typeset in Gaudy by Avon Dataset Ltd,
Bidford-on-Avon, Warwickshire

Printed and bound in Great Britain by
Clays Ltd, St Ives plc

Hodder & Stoughton
338 Euston Road
London NW1 3BH
www.hodder.co.uk

This book is dedicated to the memory of
Peter Warner, its illustrator,
who died on 22 September 2007.

The Cats
on Hutton Roof

MARILYN EDWARDS

ILLUSTRATED BY
PETER WARNER

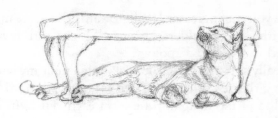

CHAPTER 1

'What do you mean, "he's gone missing"?' Michael is shouting down his mobile phone at me.

'I mean just that. As you know, we got home from Margaret's at around 5.30 and after you all left for the pub I tried to find him, but I've seen neither hide nor hair of him since then and I've no idea how long he'd been gone before that. It's now 7.30 and I'm really worried. Michael, please come home.'

'Can't a man have a pint in peace?' he sighs, but above the hubbub of background conversation and laughter, I can hear in his voice just enough resignation to allow me to relax a little, knowing that soon there will be more hands on deck to start the search in earnest. Shortly after this I hear the front door bang open and in comes Michael, followed immediately by Johnny, his son, and 'big' John, his brother. The cottage is now filled with uncoordinated cries:

'Pushkin, come on, Pushkin.'

'Where are you, boy?'

'Come on out from wherever you are.'

'Come on, you old rascal, come on.'

'Pushie boy, here boy, c'mon.'

'Puss, puss, puss, puss – what a good pussy you are, you are, you are *not*!'

As the volume increases I walk towards the three-man task force with my shoulders shrugged high and my palms upturned in frustrated apology.

'I'm really sorry to drag you back, but I'm at my wits' end. The two girls are curled up asleep on our bed, but I cannot for the life of me imagine where on earth Pushkin can be. I've looked simply everywhere and now I'm beginning to think that he must have got out into the street.'

'You don't really mean that, do you?' Michael grimaces at me. I see John's eyebrows go up and Johnny starts heading for the door. Out they all troop and I hear their voices fading away into the distance as they dolefully call out 'Pushkin' and variations on the theme of 'come here, cat' and 'you just wait till I get my hands on you'.

Moon Cottage stands on a busy road, and although we had always let our former cats, Septi and Otto, wander the streets freely, since Otto's premature death on the road outside just after her kittens were born, we have contained those same offspring, Fannie and Titus, either inside the cottage or in an enclosed yard in the garden at the back – with forays into the larger garden only under strict supervision. The same restrictions are in force for the currently errant young tomcat, Pushkin, who joined our household just under two years ago and who, in common with all his breed, the Russian Blue, is a sweet-natured but distinctly timid cat who, if suddenly released into a main road without any street wisdom at all, would panic at the first 'whoosh' of an oncoming car. As the voices of the men become indistinguishable I redouble my search round the cottage, becoming increasingly convinced that Pushkin must still be inside but, to my mounting shame, as I call out for the umpteenth time, I hear my own voice starting to crack.

'I simply don't understand how he could've got out. There isn't any way he could have broken out, or rushed between someone's legs without us seeing him,' I hear myself wailing to no one in particular. As I enter our bedroom I look across at the two female cats curled up on our bed, each in her own hollow in the squashy duvet. Fannie, a delicate tabby-tortoiseshell (torbie) with a heart-shaped face, looks up at me, her eyes large with concern at my agitation, and Titus (male name, though a female cat, because I am not very good at sexing them when they are little!), a handsome ginger (red) tabby, also surveys me, but with markedly less interest: she yawns widely and puts her head down again, flipping her tail neatly over her nose. She then lets out a long sigh that shudders through her whole body.

'Yeh, well, I know. It's a hard life and all right for some. Why can't you just tell me where he is? Why? Why? Why?' I admonish, looking down at my watch. It's 8.30 p.m. I hear the key in the door and go rushing downstairs, but I know from their silent entry that the three men have drawn a blank in their search for Pushkin. John and Johnny settle down to watch television and Michael comes upstairs and puts his arm around me.

'I know this is crazy, but I am convinced he has got himself into a wardrobe or something somewhere and has somehow hanged himself, and we will find him one day by the smell,' I whisper, because it is too awful a thought to express aloud.

'Why hanged, that is the least likely thing to have happened surely? I am more worried that he is just trapped somewhere, but he will come out, or we will hear him, I am sure,' Michael attempts to reassure me. I get a meal together and we eat in mournful silence.

As the 10 o'clock news comes to an end, I slink upstairs to my desk in the bedroom and open up the computer. Settling down intending to read email I try to shift the resisting footstool and, as I look down to determine what's in the way, to my incredulous delight I see the sleek, muscular,

panther-like body of Pushkin, jammed
underneath it, fast asleep. After hugging
him (and yes, I confess, shouting at him a
little too) I break the good news to the menfolk below, and
I think they are genuinely pleased he is alive and well –
though I get the distinct impression from them that it will
be some while before Pushkin going AWOL will be allowed
to activate a red alert on this scale again.

It is now early spring, and in the time since Pushkin as a
young kitten – he is now just over two years old – swelled the
feline ranks to three within Moon Cottage there has been
an alliance of sorts, but it is not always a comfortable one.
The two sisters, Fannie and Titus – they will be four at the
end of April – are very close and spend much time engaged
in allogrooming,* which never includes Pushkin. On the
other hand, Pushkin is clearly enchanted by Titus, whom he
appears to infuriate by his constant shadowing of her every
movement. If she wants to eat, then so does he. If she wants
to laze on the sofa in the sitting room, then again so does
he. If she wants to lie in the tiny rectangular patch of
sunlight on the bathroom carpet, then, by golly, so does he.
Titus, when Pushkin follows her, could never be said to
actively encourage his behaviour. When she is eating and he
muscles in, which he routinely does, she sighs; sometimes
she clocks him one, gently but crossly, with her front leg,
and she has recently developed the habit of filling her

---

* The grooming of each other to mutual advantage.

4

mouth with the Hill's dried food (which is all she will eat, rabbit being the preferred flavour) and dropping it a few inches away from the bowl over which Pushkin will now be lording it, so she may eat in peace. Pushkin appears serenely indifferent to the irritation he is causing his beloved, and the fact that Titus gets any space of her own at all is due to the fact that Pushkin, sleek, muscled and panther-like though he may appear to be, is also exceptionally slumberous. This trait of his calls to mind the dormouse at the tea-party in *Alice's Adventures in Wonderland*, as he spends at least an equal amount of time as that fabled rodent fast asleep. So at the point when Pushkin naps, then, and only then, is Titus free to wander on her own or to schmooze with her sister.

Pushkin's fondness for Titus appears to be constant and strong, whether Titus is on heat or not. When, however, she is on heat and lies in wait for him in order to 'present' to him, Pushkin is the master of the graceful sidestep and, having circumnavigated the obstruction without a glance, he will then sidle off to another part of the house to lie down and have a long sleep. I have discussed his mystifying reluctance to mate with Titus with our vet on a number of occasions and we are at a loss properly to understand what is the impediment, unless it is that Pushkin is so used to being swiped at by the two queens that he just refuses to believe the invitation is a genuine one when it does come.

When Pushkin first came to us I had hoped that eventually he might father one litter from one of the two girls, and then I would have them all neutered, but it now appears that this is unlikely to happen, so I frequently agonise as to whether I should neuter them anyway. As a point of interest, Pushkin's behaviour with Fannie is quite different from the way he is with Titus. Most mornings around feeding time he will try to befriend Fannie, but as his initial greeting always comes in the form of a strong head butt (endemic to the breed) which she detests, she invariably hisses back at him, and even Pushkin, who in a touchingly amiable way can be slow on the uptake, recognises that he should venture no further. I find it very sad that Fannie is so standoffish with him, as she must understand that his head butt is meant in friendliness, but her rejection of him never falters. So, having received the ice-cold shoulder from Fannie, he tends to skirt round her and, on the whole, he keeps out of her way. Sometimes they will both lie near to, but not touching, each other on a bed, but they will never share a chair. When Fannie is on heat, however, it is another matter. Pushkin is clearly attracted to her in so powerful a way that he overcomes his customary shyness and recurring rampageous pursuits take place. Fannie, unlike Titus, usually refrains from offering herself to him in any form and the chase terminates abruptly with her turning on him to hiss – and sometimes she will finesse this with a slashing of claws; or, and this is the most likely outcome, she will leap up on to the top of a bookcase or wardrobe in which domain she alone remains ascendant, being the most elfin-like of the three cats – a creature of the air – with an inbuilt yearning to climb as high as possible and with a remarkable sense of balance.

So that is the status quo at Moon Cottage at this point. I sometimes wonder reflectively if three in itself is not the problem, but I conclude that whatever awkwardness there is among these cats, it is more likely to be caused by the introduction of a strange male into the midst of a true sorority rather than three as a quantity, and Pushkin is for life, so we will all have to make the best of it!

CHAPTER 2

As I look up from my desk I find myself mesmerised by the tension I see in Fannie, in her body language and her facial expression, as she stares out of the bedroom window, head tilted upwards towards the roof line of the cottage which juts out above her at right angles, where a plump, round woodpigeon is perched on the tiles with its back to us, nonchalantly preening. Initially my attention has been drawn to Fannie by the sinister chattering of her jaws clacking together.* This has now stopped. The little cat's eyes are motionless, directed towards the bird in total concentration. Her face whiskers are standing stiffly out and the front few are curling forward in eagerness. Her ears are pointed arrow-like towards her prey, except that every few seconds – and at great speed – they flip back and forth to take soundings. Intermittently her ears quiver, violently. These shivering spasms are almost certainly involuntary, and bewitching in their urgency. The woodpigeon finishes its ablutions, opens its wings, and flies off cumbersomely across the garden. Fannie shifts her gaze to straight ahead, continues to look through the window for a few more

---

* The tetanic reaction – a rehearsal of the killing-bite. See *Catwatching* by Desmond Morris (Ebury Press, 2002).

seconds, and then casually jumps down.

It is late March and today has been exceptionally warm. The hot sun has rocketed the temperature up and, unusually for Britain at this time of year, the thermometer has registered a sultry 20 degrees Celsius. The whole afternoon long, as the heat has increased, we have been assailed by a series of seemingly unending detonations. The source of these sounds is the large leathery grey pods, hanging down from the boughs of wisteria that embrace three-quarters of the cottage, noisily exploding open to broadcast their pea-like seeds as far out into the garden as a pod can throw. This is an annual phenomenon that generally happens on one afternoon in spring each year, shortly before the new feathery blooms, which in their turn will metamorphose into pods, open to cascade luxuriantly down in those delicate mauve tresses that make them so beloved of English villagefolk up and down the land.

Throughout this hot afternoon the cats have visibly relished it. They have lain, in turn, on the table in their little yard luxuriating in the heat around them. As their fur absorbs the warmth from the rays of the sun their sides move in an almost inaudible purring. From time to time, a tail will twitch slightly in pleasure. There seems to be an understanding between all of them that each may take a go and then retire and another one take its place. As the afternoon gives way to evening, the temperature starts to drop rapidly, and with this drop in temperature the wisteria pods seem to twist and explode even more fiercely than before. This has been the one irritation to the cats throughout this hot interlude and now, with the escalation of explosions, Fannie and Titus are showing increasing restlessness. Pushkin, undoubtedly the most nervous of the three of them, finally gives up – following an especially loud report – and, jumping down from the table, he rushes indoors. Sometimes, it seems, enough is enough.

The following day it is back to the grindstone for Michael and me, and before we leave for work at our customary hour of 6.45 a.m., I ask Michael to put out some rubbish. I am always the last to be ready and it means that Michael has, by default, become the master of the early-morning domestic chores. That evening, as we enter the cottage at around 8.00 p.m., we are both assailed by a shrill wailing from outside the kitchen door. Only one of the cats has a voice pitched so high.

'I *don't* believe it. You've shut Fannie out all day!' I whinge, opening the back door to let her in and, hearing the echo of my own voice, now aware that I sound uncannily like Victor Meldrew as I do it. Fannie belts in and races upstairs like a bat out of hell.

'Well, I didn't mean to, and if you got up in time *you* could have thrown the rubbish out, and it wouldn't have happened, so don't blame me!'

'But why didn't you look?'

'She's all right, isn't she?'

'That's not the point, and anyway she might not be. It's a miracle it didn't rain.' By this time, Fannie has come downstairs again and is eating as if she'd been locked out for a week. She avoids all eye contact with both of us, so we know we are in for a spell of aggrieved avoidance, and shortly after this she takes herself upstairs and curls up on top of the bookcase for the night.

Later on that evening, in spite of the tribulations of having accidentally shut Fannie out, we leave the back door of the cottage open into the little yard as it is an unseasonably warm night. We are both sitting, unusually for us, glued to the television watching an old film filled with sentimental associations for us both. It is reaching its most emotionally charged climax when our viewing is rudely interrupted by the spectacle of Titus chasing a small brown mouse straight across the carpet in front of us. The mouse darts round the back of the television and cowers there, in a dark and inaccessible corner. Titus sits squarely and obtrusively in front of the television quivering with predatory interest and causing Michael to say unkind things to – and then about – her. Undeterred, she continues her ostentatious vigil. I try to move the television out of the corner to get at the mouse.

'Please can you help me? If I hold a jug you can chase him into it?' I plead.

'Marilyn, sit down, I really want to watch this film. We can sort the mouse out later.'

'But it might have died of a heart attack by then!' I remonstrate.

Michael mumbles and grumbles, but finally he moves the television and between us we manage to scare the small rodent into a glass jug. Michael takes it out into the garden while I restrain all three cats, who have foregathered for the fun within the kitchen. When he returns to the sitting room where the film is still in full sway, he has a grin from ear to ear.

'You'll never believe what happened when I went to let the mouse out,' he says.

'What happened?' I ask dutifully.

'Well, he just looked up at me, and in a tiny little voice he said "Thank you, Michael, for saving my life".' Michael delivers this last sentence in the highest possible falsetto. I giggle helplessly.

That was the end of March, and it is now late April. We have had a week of almost unending rain, and as a result of this the cats have been pretty solidly contained within the cottage. Over the weekend we have been away, so this morning I open all the doors and windows wide to let in the fresh air and sunlight. There is a strong breeze blowing, almost as if it were still March, but there is glorious bright sunshine, which gladdens the heart and makes the world seem joyful and as if there is just a hint of the promise of summer around the corner. Fannie and Titus gratefully bound outside and leap up on to the large garden table. It is the first time for about three days that they have been properly out in their yard. Pushkin remains firmly asleep upstairs, as is his way. I am at this time still feeding the birds, both on the ground outside the cats' enclosure and also from the hanging feeder, because I am in sympathy with the school of thought that believes that many of the birds who feed their young on worms and insects themselves need seeds and nuts in the breeding season right through to the early summer when seeds are not readily available. The feeder had run out over the weekend and I quickly fill it up. Following this replenishment, today the tally is one erstwhile derided and now rare house sparrow; one robin on his own, but who sometimes allows another one near when he is feeling less belligerent than normal – although on most days he picks a fight with one of the smaller birds, usually a finch; a pair of blackbirds; a pair of dusky pink and grey-collared doves; plump cooing woodpigeons – three for some reason; two completely stunning goldfinches; two redcrests, which are the envy of our friend and cat-sitter, Eve, who, in spite of living in surroundings close to paradise down by her canal, does not have resident redcrests; multiple bluetits;

two pairs of chaffinches; two noisy chiffchaffs; and sometimes, but not today, a magnificent bullfinch. As I am idly looking out through the lattice fencework I see the hen blackbird – lighter brown than her larger blacker partner – land on the back of the garden bench that stood for so many years in my father's garden, with her beak crammed full of long trailing grasses. She can barely take off, weighed down as she is by her burden. I watch her flap her wings labouredly, and instinctively I duck as she flies straight towards us, up over the fence of the cats' enclosure where she then lands in a knot of wisteria leaves and branches surrounded by the long pendulous blossoms just above and to the right of the opening of the back door.

Fannie and Titus, who are on the table below, watch her in fascination. Fannie especially is enthralled by the spectacle. Before I can stop her, she has leapt up off the table and sprung up on to the topmost hanging basket of a pyramid of baskets containing trailing fuchsias, which is within a foot of the blackbird who, to my horror, I now see is sitting on a large cup-shaped nest hidden among the branches. Fannie continues standing on her rear legs, swaying wildly on the unbalanced basket, clacking her teeth involuntarily. The blackbird chinks in alarm, loudly, twice, and then flies up and off the nest and out into the safer, wider garden. With great reluctance I haul out the stepladder and climb up to see if there are any eggs in the nest, praying that as she was still adding materials to it, it's just possible that she hasn't yet laid her eggs. The ladder is too short for me to see anything other than the underside of the nest, but by holding a small looking glass over the top of it, at the full extent of my arm, I establish that it is empty so I gently lift it out and place it in another tangle of wisteria in the outer garden where I hope she may find it. I suspect the truth of the matter is that birds need to select their own sites and are not very happy having these important homemaking decisions made on their behalf. Besides, when I place the nest in its new position, it is merely balanced on the branches and not cemented in by mud, as the birds prefer. This nest was still very damp on its underside where the mud was yet to harden, and she had just finished lining it neatly with the long grasses I had seen her bring to it. The blackbird flies back a couple of times in the next hour and I go out and flap my arms at her and try to scare her off. She is displaying remarkable determination as the cats are clearly in evidence, lounging around on the table outside, but after a further two hours she is no longer visible from my study window, although I can see a male blackbird regularly helping himself to the food supply.

As a cruel paradox, three days later I open the back door into the cats' yard and find two (not even just one) eggshells of whitey-bluish hue with slight speckles, almost certainly blackbird eggs, which, contents already devoured, I imagine have been dropped by the marauding and dreaded magpies. Magpies are the only birds hereabouts – although crows behave similarly in more open countryside – whose habits regularly induce in me feelings of considerable ill will. I am unable to discern a single attribute of charm they might possess in all their vile carryings-on. They terrorise small birds and kill chicks and eat eggs. They are raucous and have fights with one another when they are not plundering other birds' nests, and the very best that one can say of them is that their striking plumage of black and white gives them a smart and – happily for smaller birds – highly visible appearance, but it is a sight I would gladly forgo. One for sorrow, two for joy, seems to me a serious misrepresentation of how it actually is on the magpie front.

CHAPTER 3

April, with its tortured and shifting weather, has fulfilled its customary role of 'mixing memory and desire, stirring dull roots with spring rain'* and, having finally blustered itself to a close, May has come in full of promise, riding on the back of fresh breezes and bright sparkling sunlight; but perfidy lies around the corner. As I sit tapping at my computer keyboard upstairs I become aware that the sky has darkened mightily and there is an extraordinarily heavy atmosphere. It is clearly going to rain, but as I look up at the sky I am astonished to see a spread of the blackest clouds imaginable stretching as far as the eye can see. Unable to alter anything and feeling safe within the confines of the cottage walls, I shrug philosophically, but by now the wind has got up and the temperature has dropped significantly, so finally I stir myself to close all the windows and put on the heating. I hear a distant roll of thunder, the length of which surprises me. Then suddenly there is a hurling and clattering noise, which is deafening. Hailstones the size of small marbles are smashing to the ground, hitting the garden table and bouncing back up at the windows. A slate from the roof crashes to the ground. There is another crack of thunder

---

* 'The Burial of the Dead' from *The Waste Land* by T. S. Eliot (1922).

and everything is backlit by fierce jagged lightning. I hear distantly the plaintive contralto miaow that is the boy Pushkin's and I go downstairs to find him. It is so dark now, although only mid-afternoon, that I can barely see to walk, and very nearly tread on him because he is crawling along the floor on his stomach, something I have never seen him do before. I pick him up in my arms and cradle him. Further demonstrating his timidity in a way new to me, I feel him go limp with fear as he curls his body into a circle and buries his nose and eyes under his front legs and tries to wriggle his body into my body for protection. Unable to find the sanctuary he is seeking in my arms, with much agitation he scrambles round and leaps down to the floor where he flattens himself and tries to reverse back under the ottoman as far away from the windows and doors as he can. This proves to be so uncomfortable for him that very quickly he crawls back out and squats low on all fours in a hunched-up, miserable heap, eyes alternately staring towards the nearest window at the fearsome noise, or back down at the carpet in front of him with his nose almost on the ground.

I leave him be for the moment, and go in search of the other two cats. I find them walking restlessly from room to room as the bombardment outside continues and, as I watch them and our ears are assailed with yet another deafening rumble of thunder, they instinctively lower their torsos to the ground as they move; as they sidle out of the room, they seem to flow round the door, rather than actively walk through it. The noise is quite remarkable and the hail-stones are now piled high in little white heaps everywhere. Inside the cottage this has produced an instant steaming up of all the windows. The lightning and thunder explode twice more, with a greater pause between the former and the latter as the eye of the storm moves away. And then silence. The blizzard has abated and the clouds start to clear.

I check out the cats and discover Pushkin nestled down on a pile of blankets on the floor of our huge built-in wardrobe, which is his customary sanctuary, and the two girls are curled around each other on top of our bed. I then go out into the garden. Many of the taller plants are flattened to the ground and I find two pantiles on one of the flowerbeds, one broken and one intact, having been dislodged from the roof by the force of the hailstones. Remarkably, however, the birds have started what sounds exactly like a dawn chorus. Glorious, liquid trillings fill the air. I leave the gate open so the cats can go out, but they stay inside. There are still mounds of frozen ice in little piles everywhere, but as the hailstones melt, the volume of water swilling along the road outside is exceptional, and as I walk back into the cottage the silence is punctuated by the metronomic swish-swish of the rush-hour traffic as it wends its wary way homewards past our front door.

Two days later, on a completely tranquil sunny day which could not be more different from the day of the hailstones, I am sitting quietly at my desk when I hear the most remarkable racket coming from the garden. The bird feeder is hanging from an old-fashioned iron street lamp that we introduced into the garden to use as a garden light, and which is currently missing a screw in its anchorage, so in any wind at all it is rather wobbly. As I look through the window, expecting to see some giant bird attacking the feeder, I am amazed instead to see a large fluffy grey squirrel hanging off the lamp by his back legs in the manner of an experienced trapeze artist, while trying with all his might to extract seeds and nuts from the holes in the feeder with his front paws. His weight hanging from one-half of the crossbar of the lamp is making the whole lamp rock violently. As I watch it swaying noisily from side to side, an especially bold assault from the squirrel makes it lean over at an acute angle. Without thinking, I shout out through the window:

'What the hell do you think you are doing?' I'm completely unable to understand his reply, but reply he does, over his shoulder and chitteringly fast, just before he scarpers over the red brick wall and scrambles up into my neighbour's towering antique pear tree, from which vantage point he continues his muttered insults. I should have realised all along that it was not the delicate finches, or the acrobatic tits, or even the bombastic robin that had previously ripped off the perches, causing all the seeds to fall to the ground, or indeed gnawed through the wooden bars of the lower section that was meant to protect particularly small birds, but altogether a more wily and muscled creature, with an even larger appetite than theirs.

Later on I hear more noises coming from the same direction, but even without looking they clearly stem from an ornithological source. When I do finally look out of the window I see an adult sparrow busily flying back and forth between the feeder and two three-quarter grown chicks who are sitting idly on the bench below, fluttering their wings in that demanding manner young birds have with their hardworking parents. What surprises me is that while I know that adult sparrows will eat seeds, I thought their young would eat only insects, but these two are showing marked vegetarian leanings – or maybe they are just so lazy that they will eat whatever is put into their mouths.

~

Around this time, we take our annual holiday in France and we leave the cats to the tender and long-suffering mercies of Michael's son, Johnny. When we finally arrive at our haven in Languedoc Roussillon we discover from our hosts, Alan and Valerie, that their cat, Blossom, has died. This hugely saddens me. Blossom was an exceptionally friendly, soft-furred cat who used to keep me sane by furnishing me with a 'cat-fix' in the absence of my own nearest and dearest felines, and who always made it plain that she considered the thick carpet of lush damp periwinkle that covered the terrace of our cottage was in reality hers. She also had pretty much the same perspective on the inside of the house we stayed in, even before Alan and Valerie owned it, but very welcome she was too. This now leaves Alan and Valerie with Erin, their Westie, in sole charge.

As we share a bottle of wine on their terrace, we look out over the central courtyard of the village which is the communal 'garden' shared by all the surrounding houses and which, at different times since Michael and I have been regularly visiting the region, has been seriously overrun with feral cats, several of whom were manifestly brain-damaged. I ask Alan what is the current state of play among the wild cats of the village. He makes me laugh when he outlines a delicious piece of over-zealous feline control, which several local people have unwittingly been orchestrating. There is a new contraceptive pill for cats which is apparently very effective, and it needs to be fed on a regular basis. However, it turns out that several citizens (at least three, says Alan) with a strong sense of social responsibility have been out there putting the same pills into different piles of food, which have no doubt been eaten by the same pack of cats, so it may well be that the female and even the male cats of the village are receiving up to three times the dose they should be getting on any one day.

CHAPTER 4

On our return from holiday, Pushkin retains the disconcerting air of a cat who is not quite sure who we are, exactly
as he did last year, when first we enter the house. Who is to
say what the short-term memory of a cat might be, although
evidence suggests that this amnesia is Pushkin's very own,
rather than common to all cats. On the other hand, of
course, it may just be his way of putting us down! Fannie
assumes a sulk as soon as we walk in through the door, but
adorably cannot keep it up for very long, and typically
within minutes of our entering the cottage she comes
miaowing round to us, tiptoeing sideways and undulating
her long upright tail from side to side, shivering with
pleasure as she looks up searchingly into our eyes. I ache just
thinking about her greeting. Titus is different again. She
lurks outside the nearest room so she can hear what we are
up to, but will simply not come in; when she does finally
come in, she jumps on to the back of a sofa or chair and
avoids being touched or picked up by anyone. If they try to
cuddle her she will just jump down and move into another
room. For Titus, if we have been away for a 'long-haul'
holiday, like a fortnight, it will be a good three days before
we are 'forgiven' properly, and only after this cooling-off
period will she be back to schmoozing and climbing all over

us and shedding her white and ginger hairs so lovingly in her normal cuddly manner.

~

May has slipped into June and all danger of frosts has now passed. The garden is in its finest livery. Foxgloves in shades of cream and pink and magenta are loftily waving from every bed. The spring rains have made them very tall. That splendid, seemingly eternal flower-carpet generated by the sun and rains of late spring and early summer made up of azure-blue forget-me-nots and slightly darker bluebells has gently faded along with the once majestic heads of the common pink and more singular crimson rhododendrons, and in their place are swaggering lines of pink and red peonies, surrounded by the taller Californian pink poppies and their blousy orange counterparts. Across the lawn in the opposite bed stand proud delphiniums on the edge of opening their blue flowerheads, surrounded by the burgundy, pink and cream spikes of lupins, and at a lower level there are the wild blue geraniums, pale mauve chives, and pink ground roses. The climbing roses are in full flower, rampaging over the wooden frames of the pergola in papery pink and darker burgundian profusion, weaving themselves into a glorious tangle with three different types of honeysuckle, and adding their colour to this amazing palette are the huge saucer-sized blooms from a white and purple clematis intermingled with the more usual mauve variety. Walking under this bower is almost intoxicating as the heavy scent of the honeysuckle merges with the more delicate scent of the roses. In the heat of the June sun the dark shade is sensually welcome.

Geoffrey comes to stay, and he and Michael sneak out into the garden and sit down on Michael's 'secret' bench in one of the honeysuckle tunnels, hidden behind a wall of foxgloves where I cannot see them, drinking wine and beer and laughing conspiratorially, while I clatter pans mildly protestingly in the kitchen. I do not really mind, however, as I know mostly they are talking football, and I will hear the real news when we sit down to eat together.

The garden is more glorious in this month than any other month of the year, and although I cannot take credit for it – it having been designed with care and passion by its former owner some years earlier – I love it and tend it sporadically and wallow in the opulence of it. As we sit down to eat at the table in the cats' yard we look up at Shirley's pear tree standing behind the shared garden wall of the two cottages, which this year is supporting more magnificently than ever before a rampant climbing rose. The rose has wound its way abundantly to the very top of this tall old tree. Shirley tells me that she planted it only seven years ago in a bucket without a bottom at the foot of the thirty-year-old pear tree, and it is called Paul's Himalayan Musk. The pear tree looks like a magnificent rose bush on a scale beyond imagining.

Geoffrey is staying with us for a week while he researches information for a book he is writing, and one evening, shortly after the three of us have returned from our different pursuits in central London and are just beginning to wind down from our day's exertions, I sneakily rush upstairs before anyone else can get there in order to have a quiet few moments on my own. As I open the door into the bathroom, I discover, to my horror, right in the middle of a once white bathmat, a large yellow stain of what, judging by the characteristic pong, must certainly be male feline urine. I inwardly groan, as this is what Michael's old cat Septi started to do when he became ill. Many cat behaviourists will say that cats who have been hitherto completely clean and continent within a household will do this only if something has seriously interfered with their equilibrium. All three of the cats are in good health and are eating without any problems, so I feel I can rule out ill health as the root cause for this deviation, but I am aware that although Pushkin has shown no outward signs of full maturity, at around two and a half years old he is now well into his equivalent of late teens, even early twenties perhaps, and it would not be altogether surprising therefore if something or someone had triggered some need for him to mark his territory more aggressively than is his normal wont. As I quietly remove the offending bathmat with the intention of discreetly putting it through the machine at the hottest possible wash, I wonder if I should not make the long postponed appointment to have him neutered.

I return downstairs to the assembled company and start to prepare the evening meal, and somehow or other in the general conviviality of all that is going on I forget to mention Pushkin's lapse upstairs.

It is now high summer and Titus has been fully on heat for a whole week, and vocal withal, in a sort of grumbly, squawky way rather than calling out, which is more Fannie's line of attack. Titus is being especially insistent this time and keeps trying to wake me up by pulling at my lip with her claw and, although it is hot, the only way I can escape her attentions is to dive under the summer duvet. Tonight I see her go out on to the landing and invite Pushkin to lick her. To my surprise he does, and immediately afterwards he pulls

a strange face, and I realise as I watch him it is exactly like watching a wine taster at work. He follows this by turning away from Titus and sets about grooming his own genitalia with blatant disregard for Titus and obsessive diligence to the job in hand. Titus, abandoned on the corridor, continues to display to no one in particular, but with less and less enthusiasm. I get up and briefly try shutting them both into Johnny's room, as he is away, but soon after that I hear 'digging' under the door. I can guess without incurring any margin of error that it is Pushkin trying for his freedom. I open it up, not least to spare the carpet, and Pushkin belts out and runs downstairs. After a small interval Titus strolls out, yawns widely, and walks into our bedroom, from which vantage point she is all geared up to keep her night-time vigil over me, which she has now developed into a Chinese torture. She sits by my head, gently purring, and I, lulled into a false sense of security, slide towards sleep; but at the very moment before oblivion overtakes me, I become aware, first gently and then more painfully, of her clawful presence as I receive her 'stab, stab, stab' in my upper lip. I am probably being punished for an earlier aberration in my cat care.

At the beginning of the evening I had witnessed a small tableau involving all three cats each steadfastly doing their own thing. Fannie was on top of the dining room table (I know, I know, *hygiene*, and my long-suffering friends do try to get the cats off the table, but it is a hopeless cause!) gently patting a small roly-poly screwdriver, which – from her perspective, rather enchantingly – kept revolving within its own circumference back to the very place it started from. Pushkin, unaware of Fannie, was just sitting in a corner glaring at the skirting board in a manner that suggested something very interesting was behind it and it would only escape over his dead body. Titus, equally unconscious of the other two, had started a vigorous game all on her own with a biro that I had dropped on the floor by accident, which she kept picking up in her claws, holding it up in the air, and then dropping it again. Because I needed the biro, I rather meanly bent down and picked it up and left her without anything with which to play. Realising I had been a little pre-emptive, I bent back down to see how she had taken it. She was just sitting, under the dining room chair, with her front legs demurely crossed, trying really hard not to look hurt and staring out straight ahead as if that was really why she was there. As I continued to watch her, she finally and very slowly turned her amber eyes on to me, and stared coldly back.

'Oooh, Tites, I'm really sorry. Didn't mean to snatch it back quite like that. Will you forgive me?' She continued to stare, and I couldn't tell whether she felt forgiving or not. Well, the nocturnal stabbing is perhaps my answer.

Pushkin, as well as incessantly head-butting Titus without taking any account of her disgruntled face and forbidding body language, has little or no sense of foreplay with his human companions either. His customary manner of entering a room is to peep quietly round the edge of the door, focus on his chosen object, and then simply run at it and land on it – our bed, my desk, my shoulders – it doesn't matter. He is very agile, so although he does this at speed, usually – unless papers are very delicately balanced – he can do it without upsetting things. Sadly for me, though, Titus has been watching him and now she also leaps up on to my desk as many as two or three times a day and with the same absence of warning. The difference is that she is podgy and clumsy with it, so frequently, when she does this, piles of papers go every which way. It's a salutary lesson to me that in multi-cat households, cats actively and continuously watch and learn from one another, good and bad habits alike.

Today, however, Pushkin excels himself by his absence of inter-feline social skills. As I am making the coffee, I watch him cross the room. He approaches Fannie with an apparent determination and, as he closes in on her, to my disbelief he licks her nose, with some force. Now Fannie cannot be licked by *anyone* without a week's notice, a fact that Pushkin should surely be aware of, and yet he looks utterly dumbfounded when she not only hisses, but also slashes out at him and just misses his nose in return. Having withdrawn, blinking, out of harm's way, he slinks off upstairs for a little sleep.

Only a few days after writing the above, Fannie herself comes into oestrus and although she has visibly mixed emotions about Pushkin, tonight she crosses the bedroom towards the wardrobe from which Pushkin is just emerging. He has just done one of his enormous crocodile yawns, making a loud singsong noise of effort, and as he shuts his mouth I hear his teeth clack together. He saunters out and starts a sensual far-reaching stretch, beginning with his shoulders down, front legs pointing far forward and bum up, and finishing with a flourishing shake of each back leg in turn. Fannie waits for him to finish, and then she moves forward and gently licks his nose. He briefly stares straight ahead, and then puts his nose up in the air and walks off. This little tom will just not change his mood to suit the action; he is, it seems, entirely his own man.

'Oh, Pushkin, are you just going to remain an eternal bachelor boy, is that it?'

CHAPTER 5

It is now late July and Michael has just returned home from hospital where he has undergone a much-needed hip replacement operation. When he is first back in the house he is terrified that one of the cats will somehow get under his crutches and trip him up, but very quickly he becomes adept on the crutches and it is wonderful to watch him regain his confidence. The cats are in fact very gentle with him, and Titus in particular spends much time purrfully squatting on his knee. As I believe totally in the healing power of cats, I can only think the closer they are to him, the better. I know myself without a shadow of a doubt that when I have cuddled any of the cats I am more relaxed, calmer, more able to cope with everything, but for me it is Fannie who has this effect most powerfully, whereas Michael's healer is more probably Titus.

On the subject of healing, I have just received an extra-ordinarily moving letter from a lady in Finland, whose rescue-kitten Mushu has had a profound effect on her:

> I never thought I'd be a cat person, but the moment I laid eyes on this little black kitten, Mushu, it was love at first sight. I suffer from chronic depression and Mushu has helped me a lot. He kisses me when I'm

feeling blue, tenderly purrs when I need it, he takes care that I go shopping for food every day, and makes sure I clean our home once a week. All this improvement is because of my beautiful black cat! He has been in my life for almost five years now. Even my therapist agrees with me that it was a wise decision to make. I love Mushu to bits and am eternally grateful to him for choosing me at the rescue centre. I made a promise to take good care of him, but I never dreamt I'd get so much in return.

The moment I read this letter I recall countless occasions when the cats that live with us have helped me through bumpy and sad times. They have an extraordinary power of empathy, and although some people see feline behaviour as 'selfish', I believe, to the contrary, that they are especially tuned in to the tensions and stresses in those with whom they cohabit and for whom they have regard, and that they do have therapeutic strengths.

Returning, however, to the subject of Michael's healing, it progresses well throughout what is becoming a long hot summer, and every morning, day after glorious day, we enjoy a leisurely breakfast outside in the little yard where the cats soak up the sun. One day, as I am savouring the sight of Michael becoming stronger and more relaxed, it gradually dawns on me that he is actually enjoying this recuperation, a lot.

'This is the life,' he grins.

'You're feeling much better now, I can tell.'

'It still hurts, I'm just very brave.'

'I know that.'

'I was only joking – it does hurt a bit, but this style of living is rather wonderful. I somehow thought I would miss work, but d'you know, and this is awful, I don't at all.'

'Oh, you will when you get better.'

'No, do you know, I really don't think I will.'

And so, slowly, with Michael's recuperation begins the nurturing of a seedling that might just grow into our longed-for dream-come-true. I become increasingly excited by the thought that this might lead to the fulfilment of our desires, our precious goal, the nirvana that we have yearned for. From the time that Michael and I first recognised our love for each other, we have had – beyond needing to be with each other as much as possible – one absolute dream: and that is to return to our beloved north of England, our roots, our home, the place where we are both most at ease, where the rhythm is the right rhythm for us. That is not to say that we are not happy in the south of England; we are *very* happy here, but our lives down here are ruled by work and so we are here not by choice, but in order to do the work we do. But, and this is a serious *but*, all his life Michael has been something of a workaholic – me too – and I have always worried what Michael would do if the work-machine was removed from his life. But now, all of a sudden, I find that this beaming, peaceful, relaxed man would take to a life of ease and lack of pressure like a duck to water.

So, between ourselves, we start having angst-ridden conversations about whether and how we could afford it, and in the end the answer is yes – if we sell the cottage for its current market price, if we downscale in our future living, and if we generally draw in our horns, then we can do it. Michael will have his sixtieth birthday later this year, and after that time he can look seriously at giving the long notice that his job requires of him, so possibly by next summer we can think about moving. I keep lapsing into reveries of pure pleasure. It is such a long time to wait, however, a whole year. He laughs, indulgently, as he watches me building a myriad castles in the air. Castles that are filled with gleeful cats jumping in and out of windows on to roads that have no traffic on them, and surrounded by fields and woodlands that contain no dragons. Then he gently warns me:

'Remember that the thing that makes God laugh is people making plans.'

Through the summer Michael becomes stronger and more fit as, being grounded by default, he now walks regularly. Quite early on I discover that these walks are frequently interspersed by small get-togethers with one or more members of his little gang of local chums who are his drinking and football-watching companions. I am by now working back in my office in London and find myself mildly envious of his newly acquired 'domestic bliss', but on the other hand I'm so pleased that his contentment with everything continues and he is not showing the slightest signs of boredom.

August is upon us and the heat is phenomenal. We are letting the cats out into the outer garden more regularly, but cannot leave them unsupervised as they would simply jump over the neighbouring fence and out into the busy road where Otto was killed. But we do try to let them out at least twice a day if possible. Titus, in particular, has suffered from the heat terribly today and has been lying in an uncomfortable-looking heap on the floor. I talk to Margot, my sister, about the problem and she tells me that her friend Jacqueline, who lives in France, regularly wraps her own cats in towels drenched with cold water, so I soak some kitchen towel in cold water and envelop Titus within it. She doesn't like it one bit and protests loudly, but she does seem better afterwards – though I'm not sure she will tolerate it as a regular event. Fannie lies on the bed on her back, panting quietly but unremittingly, although generally during the day she is noticeably livelier than poor old Titus. She is of course much thinner. Pushkin is not eating much, but doesn't show his discomfort as obviously as the two queens. It has been 33 degrees Celsius today in our garden, and that is just too much. They are announcing some absurd temperature in Dubai of around 48 degrees, which is inconceivable to me and is practically off my thermometer, so it can't be real.

As always when the weather is like this, we find we need to water the garden regularly, and as soon as the water starts soaking into the soil enough to bring up any slugs or snails, or indeed enough even to produce the smell of wet earth, it flushes out a small but stalwart group of frogs, some of whom eventually work their way into the cats' yard, to the unutterable delight of its feline incumbents, of course. One such is attempting to make a bid for freedom through the big drain by the back gate. As I walk into the yard I see the rigid backs of Fannie and Titus, who are immobile with tension as they peer at a large brown frog who is unsuccessfully attempting to climb the drainpipe, and at this moment Pushkin, who I assume has just woken up, ambles out and then in turn stiffens, as he smells excitement in the air. Slowly he moves forward to see better where and what the action is, and with that Fannie turns her head a perfect 180° and, peering at him down her spine, withers him with a look that makes me laugh aloud, but it works and Pushkin drops back. The terrible thing I recognise afterwards is that I remember that putting-down look so well from school, and had assumed that it was an exclusive piece of human interchange and not one to be found in the animal kingdom.

Anyway, I spoil the fun for them all by scooping up the unfortunate frog with an empty flowerpot and gently releasing him back into the big garden. Shortly after this, I notice an exchange between Fannie and Titus that leads me to understand yet again that the power of a look, and the tension of eye contact, is of great significance between cats. Fannie is curled up on the sofa, nearly but not quite asleep and half keeping her eye open on all that is around her, as she does. (Michael calls it sneaky, but it is merely her way.) Titus jumps up beside her and quite amiably wanders along to smell her, but something on her back makes Titus sniff longer and more intensively than would be normal. Fannie turns round abruptly and lashes out at Titus, who moves back a little and turns away. A few moments pass and then Fannie puts her paw out towards Titus in what seems to me to be a conciliatory gesture, but Titus immediately lashes out at her. What now happens is that the two of them, both sitting upright, stare at each other, and they hold this intense and unblinking eye contact for at least thirty seconds, possibly longer, before Fannie jumps down and Titus starts to groom herself.

Communication between cats is clearly channelled through all their finely honed senses, through touch, hearing and smell especially; but might their emotions be declared to each other by look, as much or even more than by any other means?

CHAPTER 6

Summer fades into autumn, during which time no fewer than four people who were beloved by us die as a result of a variety of infirmities, but they are not the concern of this book or the cats, except to say that by mid-winter the human inhabitants of Moon Cottage find themselves in something of a shell-shocked condition, wondering when the next onslaught might be. During this time, in part to cheer ourselves up and maybe in part to escape from it all, Michael and I have discussed further our plans of retiring early, and we have agreed that we should put the cottage on the market in early spring, that I should prepare to hand in my notice to my boss at work, and that we should start making the cottage ready to sell from February onwards.

Getting Moon Cottage all set for sale is a major undertaking, and Stephen, the son of our neighbour, Shirley, has kindly offered to carry out all manner of projects that we hope will reinforce the obvious charms of the property. He spends many hours in both the cottage and the garden working on anything and everything that needs his attentions. On one of his visits he is talking to Michael, when Michael, who is wearing a pair of exceptionally heavy boots that he has recently acquired, steps backwards into the dining room and we are all electrified by the sound of a scream at a pitch I have never previously heard. Michael lifts up his foot quickly, but the shriek continues. The source is Fannie, whose tail was right under his great boot and who, in fear and pain as he put his weight down on it, has proceeded to make things worse by yanking it out from under with super-feline strength, in the course of which she has ripped off a substantial section of fur and skin from the top third of it.

Watching an animal in pain is quite terrible and induces in me a sensation of sickened helplessness of the worst kind. I find myself flapping and fussing as I hear Fannie run round the house, still shouting out in pain. From time to time she stops and hisses, just from the pain of it. She dashes round and then suddenly sits down and frantically licks her vulva. She doesn't yet realise that the pain is deflected and that it is in reality coming from her tail. Michael is distraught and tries to comfort her, but she is beyond consoling at this point. Stephen, with innate tact, beats a retreat and says he will come back another time. On top of all this, fireworks appear to be exploding from all around us – in this part of our county, in spite of our regular complaints to our local councillor, fireworks are detonated from early October until early December and the intermittent explosions are adding to Fannie's distress. The combination of her cries and the fireworks has already sent Pushkin slinking off to find the darkest corner of all within the big fitted wardrobe in our bedroom. I seek out Fannie and try to comfort her, but she will have none of it and eventually, with heavy hearts, Michael and I take ourselves off to bed.

The following day is a full working day and we leave at our customary hour of 6.45 a.m., but that night I manage to get home earlier than my norm of 8.30 p.m. and find that Fannie is still evidently in considerable discomfort. She comes down to the front door to greet me as she hears the key in the lock, but as I open the door, she thrashes her tail, and as she does this the pain makes her hiss repeatedly. She sits down and licks her tail vigorously. I manage to get her on my knee and I gently inspect it. Her incessant lickings have now made it very sore, so I know that the following day will find me making yet another visit to the vet's.

That night, rifling through uncharted sections of the freezer, I find a tray of frozen French snails in garlic butter close to their sell-by date, so I cook the lot of them, but keen though we are, thirty-six snails proves too many for just the two of us, and so I push the uneaten ones, swimming in their lagoon of garlic butter, to one side. After a lapse of about twenty minutes, out of the corner of my eye I suddenly spot Pushkin delicately lapping at the garlic butter with his eyes closed. I mildly admonish him and he stops, but as I return to the table I find him finishing off another couple of snail pockets.

'Pushkin, I didn't know you liked garlic? You'll get indigestion, you'll see!' He looks across at me and rather pointedly licks his lips in relish before jumping gracefully to the floor. As he hits the deck he waves his tail up and down with the pumping action that is common to his breed, shakes each of his back legs in turn, and then slowly saunters towards the chair that Fannie is lying on, from where she is watching him in a pained manner. As he gets to the edge of her chair he lifts up his head and licks her nose enthusiastically. She backs away, but when he continues to lick her she lashes out at him. A sore tail and garlic kisses is a combination of too much pain to take in one go.

'Oh Pushkin, it isn't a turn-on, except to someone else who is eating them too; you have so much to learn,' I murmur to his retreating back.

The following morning we go to the vet's and I am

horrified when the vet on duty on this particular day says to me that she thinks that in the worst-case scenario Fannie might need the upper half of her tail amputated.

'She would, after all, be perfectly OK with a shorter tail,' she attempts to console me, when I pull a face – and although I don't say anything, I find I can't bear the idea of Fannie losing her glory; it is one of her special things, her long, bendy, waving tail – she expresses her entire essence by those little flicks of the last three inches of her long tail, first to the left side then to the right as she trots around the place, and when she is being cuddled in the morning her pleasure is conveyed by the minutest twitching of it from side to side. The vet 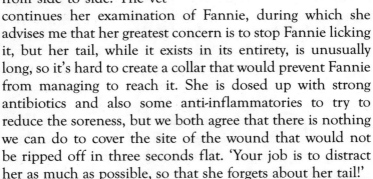 continues her examination of Fannie, during which she advises me that her greatest concern is to stop Fannie licking it, but her tail, while it exists in its entirety, is unusually long, so it's hard to create a collar that would prevent Fannie from managing to reach it. She is dosed up with strong antibiotics and also some anti-inflammatories to try to reduce the soreness, but we both agree that there is nothing we can do to cover the site of the wound that would not be ripped off in three seconds flat. 'Your job is to distract her as much as possible, so that she forgets about her tail!'

And so, for the next two days, Michael and I, and sometimes Johnny too, spend every waking hour that we are at home playing and talking and nursing Fannie until in the end she is begging for release to be allowed some peace and quiet; but, I am happy to report, the vet's ministrations of medicines do the trick and she does leave her tail alone, or enough alone for it to mend slowly and for the spectre of amputation to fade into the distance. (Sometimes, in the dead of night, I hear her licking it, and when I do, I get out of bed to try to distract her.) It is during this time of concern for Fannie that I become aware of exactly how delicate can be the balance of emotions shared between three humans and three cats in one household. It is impossible to explain to Titus, for example, why Fannie is being unceasingly nursed, and one morning Titus comes and wakes me up by quite extraordinarily insistent 'kissing'. She just sits on the pillow and keeps pushing her face into mine and brushing me with her whiskers and breathing at me.

'Tites, I do love you, honest I do.'

Tonight the most extraordinarily haunting autumnal thing has happened and it has given me a strange thrill. It is 11.15 p.m. and wave upon wave of geese are flying overhead. I have lost count of the number of arrow-shaped skeins that have traversed the sky high above the roof of our cottage, and each one has in turn emitted that honking heart-rending cry that only geese make, usually the leader to keep the discipline of the tight formation intact, and on they go, their huge wings making a loud thwacking noise as they carve through the air around them. We are within a quarter of a mile of a series of large disused gravel pits, which over many years have evolved into three large lakes, two of which are used for a variety of water sports, but the third one – the most secluded and deepest of them – is a giant bird reserve and contains the largest nesting heronry in Britain (to the consternation of all the nearby would-be fish-laden pond owners). It is home to many indigenous geese and also, to the irritation of the guardians of the reserve, to the ubiquitous and voraciously hungry Canada geese. At all times of year in the morning and at night, it is common to see two or three skeins flying out and flying back to roost as dusk draws in, and to hear that poignant sound as they call out. But tonight this happening is special and it must be some form of migration on an epic scale; also, they are flying much higher, and away from instead of towards the Aquadrome, where presumably they have been feeding. These birds are going on a much longer journey and there are literally hundreds of them. As I stand out in the garden in the dark, soft wet night, looking up and getting a crick in my neck, I feel a strange pain and sadness for all the animals and humans in the world and for the beginnings and the endings of life and love, and feel overwhelmed by happiness and grief for all that has been, is and will be, and a part of my soul takes flight with the geese.

CHAPTER 7

One of the rewards for me of writing the first two cat books
has been receiving a veritable cornucopia of stories within
letters, emails and phone calls from people whom I have
never met, who have chosen to share with me some of the
extraordinary cat experiences they have had themselves,
many of which are deeply moving. None more so than that
of Padraig, who runs a remarkable website of his own called
www.moggies.co.uk. It is a website worthy of thorough
investigation by those who are internet oriented and passionate about cats, and which he signs off as 'Moggies – Home of
The Online Cat Guide'. It contains information and
pictures and stories about cats of interest to cat-lovers everywhere. As I started to get to know Padraig better I wanted to
know more about the work he does in rescuing cats. From
the Midlands, where he lives, this is what he told me:

> I take strays in my local area, get them cleaned up, and
> either find them homes or place them in a local No
> Kill Shelter. My fastest rescue was a cat that was
> hanging around outside the backdoor to the flats
> where I live. He had been there for at least three days
> before I became aware of him [discovered on security
> cameras]. I fed him immediately and he scoffed a

whole tin of food, it seemed pretty obvious that he had no home or that he had just been dumped. I quickly got him into a cat basket and within minutes one of the flat residents came rushing around the corner to tell me that her daughter wanted a stray cat to care for. Her daughter lived a few streets away, so going from stray to finding a new permanent home took less than five minutes for this lucky feline. So far this year there have been three rescues. We have a tail-less cat that lives wild in our little outback area. Her name is Sootee, her owner died many years ago and Sootee will not live indoors any more, she gets fed and cared for by me and two others who keep a close watch on her, all vet fees are split between the three of us. When it is too cold to be outdoors Sootee will come inside to a ground floor flat, but only while it remains very cold. At present the No Kill Shelter I help at is crying out for potential homes for cats as they have just taken on in one go around twenty-plus older cats whose owner sadly died.

(An update to this, as I write, is that Padraig tells me they have found homes for nearly all of them, and there are now

only a few left unhomed.) I quickly discovered from Padraig that he currently shares his life with two cats whom he adores, one called Sassy and the other, his newest addition, Ms Tizzy. Sassy is a beautiful long-haired Norwegian Forest Cat whom Padraig met one day at the No Kill Shelter – a meeting which would never have taken place had he not gone there, following a final and heart-breaking visit to his vet with his much-loved rescue cat, Beauty (whom he always refers to as the Real King of England), who had had to be put down, to donate the redundant renal diet food that had been the mainstay for Beauty.

Sassy, no doubt as a legacy from her harrowing past, was totally terrified of everything and was contained in a large cage on her own, to give her some space to cope with her terrors. Padraig, inevitably, took one look at her and knew that she was the one for him. So home she came and, after some painstaking cat whispering and encouraging her to climb all over him as he lay on the floor, she finally adopted him graciously and lives with him to this day. He then, this year, introduced Ms Tizzy on to the scene, and Ms Tizzy and Sassy are currently working out fully how to accommodate each other, as is the way of grown cats when first introduced to each other, but Padraig reports that the signs of benign cohabitation are encouraging and getting better by the day. I confess to an especial fondness myself for Ms Tizzy as she looks like a cross between Septi and Fannie, being a short-haired tabby with tuning fork marks above her eyes and the same eyeliner markings round her nose as they have.

But Padraig nearly broke my heart when, on questioning him more about his passion for cats and what had triggered it in the first place, he finally told me the following story:

I was placed in a home for children needing care at the age of three. I found out why many years later . . . but can I just say I have a mental block on the years before the age of five and have no recollection of events before that time.

I always thought I was an orphan, no parents, no brothers and sisters, which was the way it was from the age of three to sixteen. The home I was first sent to was mixed, both girls and boys; it was a very happy time for the next four to five years. Then suddenly I was moved to a boys-only home, and that was a very big shock – and so very different. The home was a large one and didn't have full control over the children in its care. There were over 400 kids between the ages of one and sixteen in this home, and it was run by nuns and priests. It was a very tough home, no niceties like birthday or Christmas presents, just the basics to keep you going. As you can imagine, love and affection were thin on the ground.

Enter Tinkerbell, the cat. This cat was to become my link to sanity in an insane world where I was permanently struggling to make sense of what was going on and fighting to survive. Tinkerbell was a large, fluffy, black and white stray that just wandered into the home one day and sat on my lap. The people responsible for us tried to get rid of her, at which point I raised merry hell. I could be hard to control at the grand old age of five.

Eventually they allowed the cat to come and go as she pleased. Tinkerbell always had meat treats from me whenever we had meat. Other times it would be cheese or cooked bacon, which she loved. There were times when I would sneak out of bed at around two or three in the morning and raid the kitchen just to get a decent titbit for Tinkerbell. Although, if truth be known, she didn't need any food from me, she was an excellent mouser – there was many a time when she would bring prey back in and lie down under my bed for a good feast. I would just lie above her and listen to the crunching sounds of bone cracking followed by loud purrs.

On long walks in the sunny countryside Tinkerbell would accompany me and never once went off on her own. She followed me to school and was always waiting on my return. For some unknown reason, nobody bothered with me when Tinkerbell was around – it was as if they all had been warned by someone not to bother me. Often, she would sleep on top of my bed at night. Always purring and giving me slow blinks. It was wonderful having something to hold on to and to give love to in such a time when these things were thought unnecessary.

Then there came one day when she didn't turn up and I knew instinctively that she would never turn up again. It was probably one of the saddest days of my life. Tinkerbell had been with me for a grand total of ten years. Tinkerbell gave a great deal of love and affection; without her, I do not think I would be the person I am today.

When I was sixteen, I was visited by my so-called father, who decided I needed to come home, as I was now able to work for a wage. I found out that not only did I have parents, I also had eleven brothers and sisters, but by that time it was far too late. Unless you are brought up with siblings, it is almost impossible to accept them as brothers and sisters. I was so different from all of them that it was necessary for me to make my own way in the world without this newly discovered family. I have never regretted walking out on my own, as they were far too argumentative and selfish.

All in all, I was the lucky one; I had an upbringing that taught me a great deal about love and respect, and that by a single cat. Something my brothers and sisters didn't have and, as it turned out, never would have.

Because of Tinkerbell I have become a spiritual person (not in a religious way) with strongly held personal ethics, and I don't need to seek the so-called material things in life. I don't look back with sadness at my upbringing; more I celebrate what I succeeded in coming through and surviving. But it was done because of the help of Tinkerbell, a very fluffy black and white stray moggy cat who gave to me and received back from me love.

I asked Padraig a little more about his oblique reference to the way everyone left him alone when Tinkerbell was around 'as if they had all been warned by someone not to bother me', and he only slightly less enigmatically told me that he thought one of the priests in residence was protecting him, so be it, and thank goodness for it or for him.

I feel sure from having spoken and written to Padraig that he is indeed in some way a blessed person who has gained huge inner strengths from his hard times, and this is in many ways reflected on his website which was first launched in 1999 and now receives one and a half million visits a month.

CHAPTER 8

The new year dawns and with it much excitement within
Moon Cottage. I have tendered my resignation at work, and
so now there is no turning back. Following the heartache we
all suffered from those deaths last year, it is with huge joy
that Michael and I now look forward to the birth of his first
grandchild this spring and we are thrilled to hear from
Damian (Michael's firstborn) and Jo (his partner) that they
will return shortly to England and the birth will be here.
This morning on the radio a foreign correspondent recalls
the words of a Hungarian grandmother as she looks down
at her newly born grandson, holding out his tiny hands like
a small starfish: 'They bring their own love with them.' Oh
yes, indeed they do.

One night in mid-January I am awoken by a loud crashing
noise. I get out of bed sleepily, and as I turn into the landing
to climb down the steep staircase a bitterly cold draught of
air bites at my ankles. At the bottom I find Titus looking
discomfited and limping slightly, so I conclude she has
fallen off some high surface. She is the least nimble of the
three of them and the most likely to fall clumsily. In the
morning when I let the cats out into the garden I take a

careful look at Titus, and she is clearly still lame. Everywhere is white with an iron-hard frost, and as she puts her foot down to the cold ground she tenses up and, to my horror, I see her right hind leg shoot out of joint and stick out at an unnatural angle to the side and I realise that she is displaying the identical symptoms to those that affected her left hind leg two years ago. I shudder, and then find myself denying it is happening. I omit to mention it to Michael.

Two days later it happens all over again, and this time Michael is in the kitchen. I make him watch her and he grimly nods his assent.

'Sorry to say it, Marilyn, but it looks like the same trouble all over again to me.'

'I can't bear it. That operation for a luxating patella is so awful. She hated it and it is so confining and the ongoing pain is beastly.'

'Can you live knowing that she is in that amount of pain now, though, and that untreated it won't get any better?'

'I'll just wait a couple more days to see what happens.'

He shrugs resignedly and I know that he's right, but the longer I put off taking her to a vet, the better it feels to me. But of course that isn't the case because it just nags away at me, worrying me. Three days later finally finds us in the vet's, and after a couple of visits to and fro we are eventually seen by the senior partner, who quickly recognises it as a luxating patella (dislocating kneecap, more common in dogs than cats). Knowing how much I want to avoid surgery for Titus, the vet tries pain relief for some weeks to see if it will help, but I am finally compelled to go back to her and admit defeat. She then informs me that Titus will need to be referred to a specialist for surgery. When I question that, as the last time Titus had to undergo the op it was done in this surgery, she explains that at that time she had an Australian locum *in situ* who was experienced in the procedure, but this time it really does need a specialist to do it. So the poor little mite is booked in for surgery at a far distant place at the other end of the county, and it is all to happen immediately after I stop working.

Meanwhile we start in earnest with the painstaking work of preparing the cottage for sale. The bulk of the work is being done by the ever-helpful Stephen, who loves nothing better than getting stuck into projects that involve renovating historic buildings. Together we look at the whole of Moon Cottage, inside and out, including the garden, to assess what requires Stephen's attentions most pressingly. There is assorted carpentry and weeding and plastering, but the main thrust of the work to be done is painting. Stephen is one of the most meticulous workers I have ever watched in action, and although I too love things to be done well, I know that I sadly lack his almost obsessive fastidiousness. Like a mantra, Stephen repeats to me: 'It's all in the preparation, Marilyn, everything's in the prep.'

So slowly Moon Cottage begins to glow under the blush of her new clean mantle and I feel ashamed as I realise how grimy we have let the walls become in the years that we have lived here. Michael and I, separately and together over many years, have collected a phenomenal number of books and we decide that we must now take the decision to de-clutter and store as many of them as possible elsewhere, so we start to box them up. As we do a rough 'stocktake' we realise we have over 3,000 books in this little cottage, and further 'culling' is out of the question for both of us as we feel we have already jettisoned more than we can bear. We find an accommodating local firm who agrees to store the books for us and suddenly we see walls where we had forgotten they existed.

On the days that I am at home I am so used to Stephen being part of the woodwork that it seems odd when he is not present in Moon Cottage, and he begins to know every nook and cranny of this cottage as well as he knows his own next door. One day he and Shirley come to us together and suggest that it would be really interesting to have a historical adviser properly date the cottages, as when they were certified as Grade II Listed Buildings they were nominally entered as seventeenth century. Stephen, though, is convinced that they are older than that, so we all agree and a consultant on historic buildings, called Adrian Gibson, who specialises in timber-framed structures, is duly commissioned.

On the day that Adrian and his wife, who assists him in his specialisation, come to the cottage I am writing, and so I leave Stephen to show him round before taking them into his own cottage. My curiosity, however, is whetted beyond endurance – that is to say, I can no longer sit still at my keyboard, when I hear both him and his wife emitting high-pitched squeals of pleasure and excitement, and I trot out on to the landing to see what the fuss is about. He explains that many different features, including the marks on the large beam on the upper landing, indicate to him that without any doubt the building is late sixteenth century, but there are other factors too that thrill them both. He believes that the two cottages were originally agricultural in nature and were one building, probably used for the storing of sheaves of corn, and that around the year 1700 bricks were added on to the wattle and daub as a cladding to the timber frame, which is when the cottages became two, and became fully residential dwellings rather than mainly agricultural. In the report he sends us afterwards he says:

In Moon Cottage bold carpenters' assembly marks are visible, cut by a carpenter's scribe or race knife. These are of medieval rather than post-medieval type.

And then later on he says:

> This joint is typical of fifteenth-century and sixteenth-century work, but tends to be made shorter in the later sixteenth century. Everything being considered, this is probably the date of the timber framing.

It is probably the case, in fact, that these cottages are either the oldest buildings, or the second oldest buildings, in this entire area.

As I absorb this information my eyes fill up in wonder. We are living in a building that, because he reckons the date of its erection was around 1570, was built before Shakespeare wrote his first play; built two years before John Donne and Ben Jonson were born; built seventeen years before the execution of Mary Queen of Scots and eighteen years before the defeat of the Armada.

That night, Michael and I open a bottle of wine and ponder on all that we have learnt about the cottage's long life.

'Why are we leaving? We both love it here so much, and now it is even more remarkable than we ever realised?'

'Michael, don't have second thoughts now!'

'Not second thoughts, but it is wonderful here. You love it, you said so yourself. You said you have never been in a warmer, cosier, happier house.'

'I know, but you, as much as me, want to go home, to the North, don't you?'

'Yes, don't worry. Of course I do, we both do. But if only we could take this cottage with us.'

'Oh that's the agony. Now you're talking. If we could do that then we would, 'cept it would leave Shirley and Stephen and Karen needing a new east wall and feeling a bit exposed.' Johnny, who has sat down at the table with us at this point, adds:

'But hey, it would give them a huge garden – worth the hassle!'

~

And then, one day while we are still in the month of January, I receive a transatlantic phone call from my sister, Judy, which fills me with foreboding. Rod, my brother-in-law (and my second cousin, so also a friend from my childhood), has been diagnosed with a rare cancer and, having had one investigative operation, is to undergo further urgent surgery. So already this joyful new year threatens to turn into something completely other.

CHAPTER 9

LOST DOG
At Bishops Wood
Friday 6ᵗʰ Feb, 12 midday

Brindle brown Boxer/Staff
cross – white front paws
Answers to 'SOCKS'

Please help us find him, we
love him & we live in
Maidenhead so he won't find
his way home.

£100 REWARD

This notice appears under the windscreen wipers of every car in the small town and surrounding villages near Moon Cottage on the Sunday following Friday, 6 February. I have it sitting on my desk for ten days when finally I can't bear it any longer and I pick up the phone and dial one of the three telephone numbers on the bottom, and find myself speaking to, as it turns out, the owner of the missing dog. I haven't, of course, found the dog Socks; I am simply in an agony of suspense, and that melancholy Eeyore-like tendency to which I'm prone leads me to assume the worst will have happened and the dog will not have been found, and all will be doom and gloom – and yet, and yet? Anyway, I have an overwhelming need to know one way or the other.

Socks *has* been found, after an interval of just over a week but, interestingly, nowhere close to this part of Hertfordshire, but instead in Harrow, approximately ten miles south-east of Bishops Wood. The man I speak to had put posters up on every telegraph pole and every telephone box within a five-mile radius of Bishops Wood, where the dog had first gone missing; and, from his conversations with the person who reintroduced him to Socks, he has pieced together a story where he reckons some kids had found a friendly but ownerless dog (he had slipped his collar when he had gone missing) and had taken him off home with them. They then got bored with him and he landed up with the son of the man in Harrow, who took pity on him and was going to give him a temporary home until he could find out where he had come from. Where Socks was remarkably lucky was that the man who lived in Harrow, whose son had brought him home, was driving – unusually for him – close to Bishops Wood, and because he had already passed two telegraph poles in succession with a large printed sign saying 'LOST DOG' his own curiosity made him stop, as he wondered if it might conceivably refer to the dog he was caring for. The odds must have been hugely against the sign being about the same dog, but because it was, the end of this story is a happy one, with dog and owner reunited. I record this story because again and again I hear about people who have gone to extraordinary lengths to find lost animals, and so many times their energies pay off; but I recognise in myself that tendency to just give up too easily and assume the worst (I suspect it is a form of pain sublimation), and the lesson I need to learn is that having courage and perseverance pays off.

The pain of losing a beloved animal and not knowing what may have happened to it is indescribable and can only be fully appreciated by those who have suffered such a loss. One day I am sitting with Judith, my friend and publisher, in her London house, admiring her two strikingly handsome Burmese cats, Daisy and Freda, when we start talking about the agony of cats going missing. Judith, although she lives in London, has the unusual luxury of being able to allow her cats to come and go freely through their cat flap as her house backs on to a series of other houses and gardens, with no roads intervening, as is the way with some residential areas in big cities; Judith does, however, curtail their wanderings after dark. Interestingly, many cat behaviourists recommend the closing of cat flaps at night, regardless of location, 'to protect the cat from cars and creatures of the night and to protect small mammals from the cat at dawn and dusk'.* Indeed, as we are talking Judith says how she always feels more relaxed in winter, because the cats are instinctively happier to have their movements restricted by both darkness and the weather, and when they are safely within, then no bad things will happen to them.

Judith's most terrible moment with this particular pair was when they were about two years old. One hot summer's night, while she had been entertaining friends outside, she had been aware of the two cats being around in that lovely companionable way they have, and the door had remained open as the twilight had lingered on. As she started to clear up following her guests' departures, she called the cats to come inside. After a small delay Daisy appeared, but there

---

* *What Cats Want* by Claire Bessant (Metro Publishing 2002).

was no sign at all of her sister, Freda. Judith started to call repeatedly from the garden and became increasingly 'paralysed with fear and despair'. At around 4 a.m., unable to sleep and distraught with anxiety, Judith left the house and walked round the streets, calling Freda by name, but there was no response of any kind. She returned to the house, beside herself with concern and worry.

As dawn broke, a long-suffering friend who was staying the night, hearing Judith's repeated calls to Freda, tried to persuade her to go to bed and to simply leave the cat flap open on the grounds that the wayward Freda would no doubt return when she was ready. In spite of this advice, Judith, sick with worry, was still unable even to attempt sleep and it was at this point that she recognises how immensely important her friend was to her, as she simply sat her down and told her what to do, and Judith meekly obeyed. Judith thinks that it helped too that her friend was completely unemotional, and just totally practical about the cat being missing. She said 'write a note on your computer, print it off and take it round', and so she did:

> My neutered chocolate Burmese cat, Freda, did not come home last night. She may have got trapped in a garden shed. Could you please check in sheds and garages for me, thank you.

Judith then added her landline and her mobile telephone number, printed the notes out in quantity, cut them up, and started to deliver them around the neighbourhood from house to house; by 8 a.m. she had completed her task.

'The exercise was cathartic, and it made me feel that I was doing something practical to help. But I experienced all those emotions of pain, anger, irritation, despair and pessimism as to whether this would be any use, that seize

you when something like this happens
and you can only wait.'

The hardest thing in this situation is to stop the imagination
working overtime, and the
most horrific possibilities,
which are almost unthinkable,
appear in the mind's eye. For
Judith the agony was made
more acute because as the cats
were chipped, and therefore wore
no collars, anyone finding Freda
would, with the best will in the world,
have problems establishing quickly how they might track
down the human companion belonging to the cat, as with
chipping you have to get the cat scanned at a vet's. Added to
which Freda is a beautiful chocolate seal point Burmese, and
very 'steal-able', and all this is taking place in London, with
its big-city anonymity.

'So what happened next?' I ask.

'Well, within an hour of distributing the leaf-
lets Freda just sauntered in, but very hungry. Although, to
be honest, it wasn't really sauntering, more galloping up the
path. I do believe, although I will never know for sure, that
my note through those doors did encourage someone,
somewhere, who had unknowingly shut her in, to make the
effort to find her and then let her out – perhaps because of
the note, or maybe because they just found her. Being out
all night is completely out of character for both of my cats,
so I have no doubt that she was locked in somewhere.'

As an aside to this story there is also the question of the
reaction of the cat who stays at home. Judith says that Daisy
was completely laid back about Freda's disappearance and
stayed with Judith in the garden for all those hours out of

companionship rather than concern, but would this have remained the case if something either serious or long term had happened to Freda? Do cats know when their close companion is truly in trouble?

The overall lesson for me in this story is that, for Judith, writing that note and distributing it around helped her considerably at the time, as it relieved the complete sense of helplessness she otherwise felt, as it also did for the man with the dog from Maidenhead. And in both cases it may well have been the catalyst for the animal's return.

There are other ways of finding your cat too, such as simply to go out and look for him, but the trouble is that it can also be a recipe for despair when it resembles too closely a search for the proverbial needle-in-a-haystack as it did initially for Judith, and yet, sometimes, it gets results.

It was a January night and Willow (my Tonkinese) had been out all evening. He is a great hunter and there are many months in the year when he dines regularly on rabbit. (I have even known him eat two in a day!) At this particular time he had also been catching the occasional rat, but only as a trophy, not for consumption, but I should have been more curious about where he was finding them! On the night in question I was worried that I had not seen him on my return from work, but com- forted myself that whatever happened he was always in by midnight and then the door would be locked . . . but on this occasion 1 a.m. came and then 2 and then 3. By the time morning dawned, I was exhausted and seriously concerned. I dressed, determined to find him.

Jo, whose story this is, met Peter (the illustrator of this book and the previous ones) and me at Peter's local bookshop in Surrey, and talked a little of Willow to us then. Later on, I learnt more. Jo lives in a remote, rural cul-de-sac, with a fair-sized garden, and beyond that there is a large field owned by Surrey Wildlife – so a veritable heaven for an inquisitive cat – and beyond that, even more superbly from his point of view, a yard that's ostensible reason for being was for lorries to service the M25, but that was populated with outhouses and trailers stuffed with things irresistible to rats.

'The best I could do,' said Jo, 'after calling Willow endlessly, was to take a picture of him to the gritting yard. The site had a security office and I pleaded with the lady officer to ask the drivers if they had seen my cat.' Jo, unable to postpone going to work any longer, then departed with her heart in her mouth. She managed, however, to return from her place of employment at 2 p.m. in order to search for Willow in what remained of the winter daylight. She set about searching every nearby pond and waterway and all the cross-field footpaths, calling for Willow repeatedly, but to no avail. She arrived home, frustrated and distressed, just as it was beginning to get dark. As she went into the house she noticed an answer-phone message on her telephone. It was from a driver in the yard announcing, somewhat cryptically, that he had seen her cat; he then left his contact number.

Unhappily for Jo, though, when she phoned him back she discovered that he had indeed seen her cat, but this was after he had been emptying his huge container lorry at the Household Waste and Recycling Site in Caterham, some five miles distant from Jo's home and, perilously, over the other side of the M25. As the driver had opened the small trap door at the lorry's base, a terrified cat, resembling the photo he had been shown, had run out and disappeared into the middle of a town that he had never been to in his life. The driver had initially parked his lorry overnight behind Jo's house, he then confided.

'Horrified, I panicked and ran out into my driveway, not knowing what to do. I beseeched my new neighbours to help me.' Luckily for Jo, these neighbours, Denis and Hilda, had lived in Caterham until six months ago and knew it well.

'Denis said "Get your coat", and in the dark we set off for Caterham. For two hours we searched the high street and back streets, we knocked on doors, nursing homes, and even the vet's – and at one stage we even went into a pub where I spotted another neighbour of mine who has four cats of his own. I cried out "I've lost my baby" and the other drinkers looked up, aghast, as only my neighbour knew I was referring to a four-legged one. Eventually, after two hours, broken-hearted, I said we should search no more. Denis, however, knowing the town so well, said there was one more place he wanted to look, and so we set off down one more alleyway . . . and then, *I heard him!* As you will know, Tonkinese, being part Burmese and part Siamese, have a distinctive cry, and there he was, cowering in a hedgerow. I grabbed him and stuffed him up my jumper, and between us we got him into the car and drove home. When we finally got home, he did the biggest wee you ever did see! When they are frightened and away from home, cats simply stop going – and he had been missing for twenty-four hours!'

When Jo got back into her house she started the happy business of phoning the important people in her life whom she had earlier alerted to Willow's absence, and while she was doing this the doorbell rang: and there was her neighbour (the one in the pub) and his daughter, with a fistful of handwritten notices that they had specially prepared for her to take to all the shops in Caterham. Never has Jo been happier to present to anyone the physical presence of why that would no longer be necessary than at the moment she pointed down to her boy, Willow, happily purring by his familiar hearth.

In a postscript, Jo adds: 'I am pleased to say we now have new contractors on that site and the waste lorries are no more, and likewise Willow has brought home no more rats. We also have Golly [a beautiful jet-black glossy cat], who keeps us all sane – he is, however, a real wuss, who prefers to stay well within the boundaries of house and garden, and whose only failing is to destroy all the carpets!' With Willow around, she needs a Golly in her life, it seems to me.

CHAPTER 10

The day of the dreaded operation for Titus has now arrived, and I pack her up into her cat cage, having yesterday starved all three cats of food from the early evening, to their complete disgust, and the two of us set sail – that is to say, we swell the ranks of the early morning commuters jamming up the M1 – for the distant veterinary hospital. I have the wire cat cage strapped in firmly next to me on the passenger seat, with the forlorn figure of Titus within. She miaows briefly and then hunches up despondently, and stares downwards with her nose touching the bedding. Titus is always the least complaining of the cats, the most friendly, the calmest, and she is also the only one of the three to whom these awful operations seem to happen.

'I know, it just ain't fair, Tites, and I'm really sorry – it's always you, babe.' She stares up at me unhappily, but also with an expression that looks like trust on her face. I feebly poke my fingers through her cage to try to touch her, and so reassure her *and* me. The journey goes on and on, and the last part of it after we leave the motorway is long and winding and she begins to retch from carsickness; and as we turn into the car park, she finally vomits in a watery sort of way. As we enter the hospital it is still early morning, but it already feels as if the day is half over.

The vet who is to do the operation, Rob, is charming, absurdly young, outrageously good-looking and, I am fervently praying, a skilful surgeon. He is articulate and patient and I appreciate the amount of time he gives to Titus to watch her walk about his room and demonstrate her gait. He seems to be at ease with cats, which is a big plus. However, as he explains things to me, using a skeletal model that somewhat disarmingly has a vital piece of bone missing, for his demo of what will happen in surgery, I suddenly begin to have the most awful doubts as to why we are here and wonder if I might be guilty of attempting to inflict Munchausen syndrome by proxy* on her, or something akin. Does she really need this operation, I wonder, and although I know that I really shouldn't be asking him this question at this ridiculously late stage, I suddenly hear myself saying:

'I do understand what you have said, but tell me honestly, is this operation really necessary?'

At this point I have the consent form in front of me unsigned and the pen is in my hand. He looks across his desk at me long and hard and draws his fingertips together.

'Her left leg is still coming out and it could originally have been worse than her right leg, and we should possibly consider further surgery on it; but her right leg *must* be done. I am sure of it. From my examination of her I would say it is a luxating patella Grade II. I will have to deepen the groove and I may also need to tighten the tissues.'

'Rob, the aftercare and long containment is terrible. If she were your cat, would you have this operation done?' There

---

* MSBP is attention-seeking behaviour by the owner of a pet (or, more usually, parent of a child), manifested by the repeated fabrication or exaggeration of health problems in that pet, generating unnecessary medical interventions and/or procedures on the pet as a result.

is a pause long enough for my heart to miss a beat, and then:

'I hate being asked that question,' he laughs. 'But yes, if this were my cat, I would definitely want the problem to be corrected.'

'I'm sorry, I'm sorry. Please do it,' I hear myself mumbling as I sign the paper. Titus just stares straight ahead. Soon after this I leave, having watched Rob carry Titus off in her cage down a long, long corridor. My intention is to collect her either the next day or the day after that, at any rate as soon as she is allowed out.

After I return home alone, I experience that bleak sadness tinged with guilt that is endemic to the hospital visitor able to walk free. Shortly after I get back, at around four o'clock in the afternoon, Fannie lets out a small squawk, and I am so galvanised by her utterance that I phone the hospital. They tell me that they have just this minute taken Titus down to surgery for pre-operative investigations. At 5.40 p.m. exactly, Fannie, who is on the bed behind me, screeches out really loudly, and then jumps up on to my lap to be comforted. I know I have to wait for the phone call, so I just stroke her and pray. At 6.30 Rob, the surgeon, phones me and I ask him:

'What exactly were you doing at 5.40?'

'Oh, manipulating Titus's leg to see how bad it really was', he replies. So Fannie's telepathy was not for Titus's safety, but in reaction to her comfort, or lack of it – if, indeed, that is what it was. Anyway, the operation has been performed, Titus has regained consciousness and is now sedated, and they are keeping her pain under control, and as for the rest, time will tell.

In the two days that Titus is at her special referral centre, Fannie in particular is rendered wholly distraught by her absence. I can hardly bring myself to look at her face. It is showing utter, naked grief, and Pushkin too looks most discomfited. They are both restless and walk around the house endlessly. So Titus, the great bonder, whose many talents may well go unrecognised by some, if not all of us, we badly want you home. I cannot wait to collect her, for all our sakes.

When I make the return journey with a light heart to collect Titus, I discover from Rob that she has undergone 'sulcoplasty and tibial tuberosity transportation and lateral imbrocation of the right patella'. He is happy with the changes he has made to the alignment of her leg and expects her recovery to be a good one. I am given a piece of paper by the hospital, which reads:

- Titus needs pen confinement for a further six weeks.
- Supervised exercise but confined to one room.
- Suture removal in ten to fourteen days' time at your own veterinary surgery.
- Return here in six weeks with a view to examining the other leg for surgery.

When I get Titus back – with her right leg four-fifths shaved (the only fur remaining on her leg being a white sock topped by a small ginger frill at the very bottom, making her look poodle-like), so her skin is exposed, naked, from her lower joint right up to her belly, and on her upper flank up to her spine with a long deep sutured scar dissecting the front of the top half of her leg – her would-be-euphoric homecoming is marred by Fannie's absolute rejection of her. One sniff at that anaesthetic-laden breath and the erstwhile grieving sister turns into a scolding dragon. Fannie spits and hisses and carries on as if the devil himself was in the cage in front of her, and Titus sinks to the ground, dejected and in pain and looking more miserable than I ever remember seeing her. Michael shouts at Fannie for being awful. I shout at

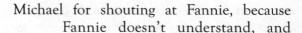

Michael for shouting at Fannie, because Fannie doesn't understand, and Michael shouts back at me, saying neither does he! Pushkin runs away and hides.

On our behalf, Shirley from next door has borrowed a metal fold-down puppy cage from her friend Cindy, and to begin with we put the cage on the coffee table in the sitting room, near to the log fire, but after Fannie's disgraceful behaviour we realise that Titus needs quiet and rest so we take it up to our bedroom. From then on I spend as much time as I can with Titus in the peace of that room, which in any case is my study. After two and a half days, Fannie finally stops hissing at Titus on entering the room. Pushkin, on the other hand, has at no point hissed at her, although he does sniff at her as if she is altogether a different cat from his best buddy. He often sits outside her cage and just stares at her. Titus hates this, so I have rigged up a blanket as a partial curtain to block out staring cats and also draughts, so if she wants privacy she has it. She has to spend the majority of each day in the puppy cage, so to give her more room I have fixed on to the end of it another cat cage in which she has her litter tray. I have purchased a large squashy dog duvet for her to lie on and, under Rob's strict instructions, I take her out of her cage three or four times a day for restricted exercise (no jumping whatsoever – and that is something of a challenge, I have to say), and also for much needed cuddling and stroking. Whenever I take Titus out of the cage both Fannie and Pushkin immediately climb inside it themselves and eat her food, use her litter tray, and lounge around on her duvet, clearly trying to work out why on earth she chooses to spend so much time in there. Fannie has become amazingly sneaky at stealing the food out of the bowl I have in the cage for Titus, even when the cage is closed, and it becomes increasingly difficult to stop her from hooking her paw in and fishing out food, which anyway is freely available to her at all times down in the kitchen. I put books and small pieces of cardboard to prevent the theft, but still she continues.

The regime for Titus's recovery must include this restricted exercise (which is different from my instructions following her previous operation, when I was told she must be contained at all times, except for cuddling), and also Rob agrees that her morale needs consoling and we should all spend as much time stroking her and talking to her as possible. To this end, as well as taking her on my knee as often as I can, which she does seem to love as she purrs deeply while there, I also let her and Fannie lie together on the bed, and sometimes Fannie grooms her and is surprisingly good at avoiding her operation scar; it seems the bonding is good for the pair of them. This is, however, slightly fraught with danger as it is absolutely essential that at no point does Titus get up and jump to the floor. I find that I can sit at my keyboard with a mirror rigged up so that I can watch the two of them like a hawk, wherever they are on the bed behind me. As I sit there, anxious in case I am unable to cross the room fast enough to stop Titus jumping down from the bed, I suddenly recall with awful clarity:

> She left the web, she left the loom,
> She made three paces through the room

followed, with unseemly haste, by the dreadful:

> The mirror crack'd from side to side;
> 'The curse is come upon me,' cried
> The Lady of Shalott*

(And oh how we girls giggled when, as eleven years old at school, we were learning that line!) But there are some really bad days in the long process of recovery. Sometimes Titus seems almost comatose with pain and/or boredom and I am at a loss to know how to make her more comfortable. What she wants, of course, is her freedom, and she looks up at me out of her cage with a yearning in her big eyes that breaks my heart. When I try to get her to exercise she is clearly in a great deal of discomfort, and I know well exactly how tolerant cats are of pain so I begin to wonder just how much pain it is fair for her to take. Added to this, Michael is beginning to lose patience with Fannie, and I too am having problems concerning her demands. Fannie is finding what she sees as an unnecessary amount of attention being devoted to Titus as unfair and uncalled-for. However, in her prison cell Titus watches everything and she makes it abundantly clear to Michael and me that she is hungry, nay starving, for love. And so the long days creep by, and if the time drags in this way to a human witness, I dread to imagine how long it must seem to an imprisoned feline. It is now just over three weeks since she had the operation, and today Michael says to me that he feels that Titus's limp is getting worse and that she will never walk properly again, and that I should take her to our local vet to get her checked out with some speed, and this I do.

Pat, the local vet who had removed her stitches twelve days' post-operatively, is impressed with her recovery and doesn't think there is anything wrong at all, but reminds me

---

* From 'The Lady of Shalott' by Lord Alfred Tennyson.

how very serious the procedure has been and that there are internal wires and also, in spite of the restricted exercising, Titus will have lost a lot of muscle power in the period of her incarceration, so her limping is bound to be severe. In other words, we are just being neurotic parents.

CHAPTER 11

Jo and Damian have now returned to England and are living only a few miles away from us in a relatively remote cottage that a friend of theirs has kindly lent to them, and I find myself becoming surprisingly broody on Jo's behalf. In the role of stepmother-out-of-law, one is not properly allowed the indulgence of claiming grandmother-hood, but nevertheless I find that I am instinctively drawn towards this tall, young, elegant woman who is being very brave, and very positive, but who is experiencing all the anxiety of a first-time pregnancy, combined with the difficulty of being in a foreign country and away from her own mother and father in far-off Sweden. I long to give her as much comfort as I can. Their baby is due in under a month's time and Jo is carrying him, for *him* they know it to be, high and proud. Damian and Jo are both extremely conscientious about healthy dieting and healthy living for Jo (though Damian is not so strict on himself) and I am hugely impressed with Jo's own resolve. We go on a couple of shopping sprees, which are huge fun for me, and we buy all manner of baby things. In the evening after one of these shopping trips, as Michael and I sit down to have a meal together, I find myself saying:

'Michael, when we finally find a house and have moved in and settled down, the cats will obviously have more freedom and be able to go outside. Do you think that Pushkin at that point might actually get his act together and mate with Fannie or Titus?'

'Uh, uh! What's brought this on, eh?'

'Oh just, you know, the girls are getting on a bit and it would be so lovely if they could have one litter each.'

'I thought you told me that Titus wasn't supposed to have any kittens, and she's certainly in no state right now to be getting pregnant.'

'No, that's true, but when I asked Rob if he would neuter her at the same time as sorting out her patella, he said it was too much to inflict on her in one go, which made sense, so I suppose that is the next blimmin' hurdle for the poor old thing. But Fannie, maybe?'

'Marilyn, I think we should concentrate our energies on buying and selling houses right now.'

'Yup, maybe you're right – oh well, just a thought.'

Within the confines of Moon Cottage there is much coming and going. We have put the house on the market with a local estate agent, and quite quickly a couple of appointments with would-be buyers ensue. I begin to worry, as people come to view the house, as to what sort of perverts they might think we are when they come into our bedroom and find Titus cooped up dejectedly in her cage. A rather defensive pitch becomes the norm as I try to explain exactly why she is in the cage, and that really she is there for her own good.

While this is happening around Moon Cottage, Michael and I have been internet surfing to find properties in the north of England, which should ideally be:

- Away from any lethal roads so that the cats may have their freedom at last.
- Surrounded by hills, or in an oasis of peace and quiet and with far-reaching views.

- With a pub within decent reach for Michael.
- Not *too* isolated – being able to pick up the paper in the morning being an issue.
- Most importantly of all for one of us, within an hour's drive of Ewood Park, which is, I am led to understand, a piece of hallowed ground in the environs of Blackburn.
- Close to where Michael's mother is and close to several of his siblings.
- Close to Wensleydale where Geoffrey lives.
- The house itself must be an old building, preferably a farmhouse or cottage.

It all proves more difficult than one might think within our budget. Our chosen counties are North Yorkshire, Cumbria and Lancashire. Each of us spends hours fantasy-shopping in this way; it truly is the stuff that dreams are made of.

Meanwhile, Johnny too is busy looking around nearer to home for a place of his own. Michael and I have both felt hugely guilty that our proposed move means that he now needs to find himself his own home, but Johnny, with his characteristic generosity of spirit, replies:

'No honestly, I needed a kick up the arse. If you hadn't both decided to do this, I would have been living with you till I was middle-aged.'

'Johnny, you are very welcome to live with us in the north of England; it would be wonderful if you would come,' I protest, and Michael of course endorses this fulsomely.

'No, sorry. Can't do *North*, just can't!' he retorts, omitting all explanation, although he is in a good job where he is in the south-east of England, which is reason enough, but I remain unsure if that is the sole basis for his reluctance. One night, soon after this, Johnny comes home very excited. He has found himself a property that he loves, and although it is more than he was budgeting for he is sure that it will be a good investment. The three of us go off to see it together that weekend and it is sweet. It is a tiny cottage down a quiet mews with one huge room downstairs and a kitchen and a utility room, and one bedroom and bathroom on the next floor, and a further bedroom on the top floor – it is like a teeny version of Moon Cottage in some ways, and it has an adorable walled courtyard behind, which is completely splendid for container plants. Michael and I are really happy for him. He will be able to exchange and complete in a couple of months, so we joke with him that he will be gone long before there is any movement on our front. But then, to my delight, Michael suddenly says:

'Look, I think we should start to physically recce now, because until we really start actually looking we are fumbling in the dark.'

'I agree, oh I agree, but what if we find somewhere really quickly?'

'Let's cross that bridge when we come to it.'

So we start our search in earnest and we distil down to eight properties, but sadly they are spread all over the place between the Yorkshire Dales, Cumbria and Lancashire.

Michael does an advance recce of three further properties during a business visit to the North, and one of them in particular, a farmhouse near a lake in a secluded valley in Upper Wensleydale, I have high hopes for. Sadly, however, he gives it the thumbs down, and before I can see it for myself it has gone 'under offer'; but it needs us both to be on board, so I am content enough that it doesn't pass muster and we must 'move on'.

Our allotted weekend for the big excursion arrives and it is possibly the wildest and certainly the wettest weather forecast for the north of England that I have heard for a very long time. Michael remains undaunted and off we go. Our very first property, where we are to meet the agent, Richard, is just outside a remote village in Swaledale. The rain is completely horizontal and the wind must certainly be close to gale force, if not actually at it, and as we drive up the dale from the eastern side of the country, we have to negotiate our way round one fallen tree after another. We eventually discover the tiny single-track zigzag road that will lead us up to the farmhouse. As we start to ascend, we meet a large white van coming down, and although the accepted rule is other, the driver makes us reverse for him.

'I can't believe we're meeting white vans here, I thought we'd left all that behind in the commuter-lands of the South, and he's driving like a white-van-driver too,' Michael grunts crossly.

We continue our journey upwards and then, to Michael's incredulity, one of the several hairpin bends is so acute in its angle that it is necessary to reverse and go forward twice to get round it. We climb some more and finally arrive on the top of the hill where we find the building we have been looking for. It is a butty stone farmhouse, squat and low and very solid, and will clearly withstand many gales yet to come. It has a conservatory clamped on to the front of it, which is square and ugly and looks just like a reinforced glass box, and inside there is a row of six empty chairs all next to each other, for their potential occupiers to sit staring straight through the glass front at the view. The view today consists of solid cloud, which is enveloping the hillside in a blanket of thick dank fog, and the only visible movement is the driving rain mixing with the swirling cloud and some forlorn clumps of straggling brown grasses blowing wildly in the wind, and nothing else – not even a single sheep.

'This reminds me of an old-people's home, but less cheerful,' Michael observes, staring at the chairs in their regimented line. I try not to let him hear my despairing giggle.

'Michael, I know this part of Swaledale really well, and the view out there is breathtaking honestly. It's just the weather today.'

Richard hears my plea and does a sterling job as we walk round the rest of the building, finding a selling point here and another there, but it is quite clear that Michael cannot wait to get out, so there is little point in delaying our departure. Our descent is considerably easier, although there is no escaping the tortuous back and forth manoeuvre on the worst hairpin.

Thrown by our first joint foray I am now fearful of what lies ahead. We then see four different houses, all of which have several charms, but none of them has enough of our required ingredients, although we do see a house from the outside in a village called Thornton Rust in Wensleydale, which is close to where I used to live with Geoffrey. This house is charming, albeit on the small side, and it gives us hope. The saddest house of all, though, is in a village too far east to be practical for us, close to Richmond. The house is a large elegant Georgian farmhouse and looks tremendously attractive, but as we get close to it, to our horror we discover its frontage is on one of the busiest dual carriageways in Britain, the A66. People die regularly on that stretch of road, never mind cats.

Dales friends of ours, Thomas and Doreen, tell us about a farmhouse near the renowned Ribblehead Viaduct that has suddenly come on the market in the last twenty-four hours, and so with that and the Thornton Rust property in mind we talk to an agent in Hawes. I am having trouble concealing my excitement as I long to be back in this part of the world, and I so want one or other of these to be the one for us. We drive out to the Ribblehead farmhouse on the Sunday evening, just as it is getting dark, and again the wind is up. It is wild and very empty around there, but the views are magnificent and the skyscapes spectacular. We park the car and we both climb stiffly out, but the jacket Michael is wearing is only lightweight. As the wind tears at the back of it, he hauls it more firmly round his body and I can hear his teeth chattering; I too am pretty chilly, it must be admitted. I look at the expression on Michael's face. It is all screwed up against the wind and his teeth are clenched, but I detect an additional firmness in his jaw line that does not augur well.

'Getting a paper in the morning could be a bit of a problem.'

'Yes, but look, there's a pub only fifty yards away.'

'But what if we got snowed in and couldn't use the car, we would be completely trapped, and anyway it's too small.'

I know in my heart of hearts that this property isn't going to work and that he is right; it is blissfully secluded but also, paradoxically, the road could be a problem for the cats because remote though it is, it is the main road into Hawes from Settle and Ingleton, which produces its own weight of local traffic, added to which there is a great deal of tourist traffic for two-thirds of the year, and also bikers in their hundreds use that road. I know for a fact that the farmers who draw on the grazing that surrounds us, which is split into two by this largely unfenced road, are in despair at the number of lambs – and even sheep – they lose in collisions with cars every year.

My persistent concern about the cats being run over is

both reinforced and dissipated by Richard telling me, when I raise it with him yet again, that when he and his wife lived in a village called Bampton, they were three miles down a track which had no traffic on it at all, and to their horror an oil delivery lorry filling up their tank for their central heating ran their cat over. They put food out that night as usual, and when the cat didn't come back they went looking, and found its squashed body the following day. They assumed that the driver didn't even know he had done it. So where on earth is actually safe? Inside a house I suppose.

The following day, Monday, we are due to see just two more properties, both in Cumbria, and then drive back south to Moon Cottage. We set off early in the morning and the first property we are to see is one that I initially found on the internet, but which then disappeared, and then I found it again being handled by a different estate agent. Technically, therefore, it is one of our properties, but Richard, whom I supplied with a list of our favourites, has offered to see it on our behalf in advance and has reported back to us that he thinks we should see it, but he is concerned that it might be too small. We say our farewell to Geoffrey and to Hawes and drive out past Ribblehead and out on to the main Kendal to Skipton road at Ingleton and turn up towards the little market town of Kirkby Lonsdale.

'Marilyn, the traffic on this road is awful.'

'I know, I avoid going on this road whenever possible, and it seems to be bad at all times of year too. The trouble is that the trans-Pennine routes are in short supply and this one goes south-east towards the industrial cities of West Yorkshire and cuts off a whole corner, so it's a really useful link road.'

'Humph, well I'm not impressed, is all I can say.' Soon, however, the signs for Kirkby Lonsdale are visible and we know we have to start looking for a side road to the left, which will lead us to the village where we have our first appointment. I have studied the map and can see a more direct road than the first turning and, mindful that first impressions are all important, I reckon we should go for the second turning. As we make the turn into my chosen route, to my amazement we find that the road is single track, but neither of us says anything. We drive slowly round a right-hand bend and go up a hill, past a little copse on the left, and suddenly there is grass growing out of the tarmac. Neither of us says a word and the grass continues its triumphant march down the middle of the road. After we swing round the fourth completely blind corner along this narrow road bordered by a mixture of dry stone walling and high hedges, Michael asks quietly:

'Was this the only way into the village?'

'No, but it looked like the most direct way on the map. We're nearly there now, honestly.'

'Good, glad to hear it – but it is very beautiful round here, look at those views.' We arrive at the end of this long, winding little road and turn right as we get to the main village street, passing the post office on the left, and start to climb up a steep hill. As we near the top, on the left we pass a grand-looking Victorian house standing back in its large garden, which we can see only in tiny snapshots through small gaps in the hedge. As we pass the end of the sweeping curved driveway into this large house we see an enormous ancient copper beech, with a breathtaking spread of branches growing from it, standing in the very centre of the driveway. This is the Old Vicarage and next to it is a very strange-looking building which is, it turns out, the Coach House – and our destination. In the details we have acquired from the estate agents, we know that this building was the original coach house to the vicarage, for whomsoever was the current incumbent of the church that stands higher up the road. Michael says:

'Let's just drive on a bit further and get a feel for the place.' We drive on up to the little church and stop the car there. The church is a charming Victorian sandstone building with a turreted square tower, surrounded by ancient yews and equally ancient-looking headstones and it announces itself boldly as St John's. We turn our backs to the church and gaze out across the valley to the distant hills. I squeeze Michael's arm:

'I think those are the Howgills, not sure, but could be – and look, that nearer one is probably Whernside! The brochure said you could see two of the Three Peaks from the house, and also Barbondale.'

Michael laughs with pleasure and squeezes my hand back.

'It certainly has a most "agreeable aspect", I must say, Mo, but wait until we have seen more.'

We get back into the car and drive back towards the Coach House. The most imposing thing when looking at the house is in fact the group of massive Scots pines (probably about ninety feet high), which are gathered together at one end of the garden. The house is high up and behind a thick evergreen hedge, so it is quite hard to see it fully from the road. We walk in and introduce ourselves to the owner, Pamela. Richard is yet to arrive. She shows us round the house with enthusiasm and clearly loves it herself. As we walk around it I become slightly mystified by it. It has two staircases to two separate bits of an upper floor, which are not connected to each other. We discover that this is because it has grown with each successive owner, who has added a bit on as they were able to afford it, so it has become an organic building; but there was never enough land to build another room at ground level to make it work like a normal house, room on room.

As we walk into what Pamela calls the guest suite at the southern end of the building, she walks us through a large bedroom with windows in three of the four walls, facing north, east and west, which makes it very light and airy, and then we are led into the large guest bathroom. This has a pair of floor-to-ceiling French windows with a balcony outside and one long high window down the other side too, so it is lit from the east and the west. As Pamela pulls aside the curtains and opens the French windows, she invites us to step on to the balcony. She laughs as she does this, admitting that all her life she had wanted a Juliet balcony and has had to wait until her middle years before she finally achieved it. At this point, Richard arrives and she goes down to greet him, leaving Michael and me alone. Michael is staring transfixed through the French windows at the view across the valley below and up to the high hills beyond.

'Well?' he demands urgently in a low voice. 'Well?'

'Yes, it's lovely, but do you . . . ?'

'Surely, this is it?'

'Just like that?'

'Don't you agree?'

'Yes, I do agree, but I'm just surprised that you have committed so quickly in this way.'

'But this is how it was with Moon Cottage, don't you remember? It was exactly the same.'

In fact, Moon Cottage surprised me because Michael fell in love as he walked through the front door, but it took me slightly longer. I didn't love it *completely* body and soul until I was in the dining room. But I am thrilled that he feels this way about the Coach House and I find I share his feelings. Interestingly, when the moment comes, all the things on the 'must have' list of requirements become suddenly less mandatory if the house is right, so neither he nor I discuss any of those at this stage. One thing, however, that has pleased me hugely during the time we have been here is the absence of traffic. We have seen one lorry and one tractor go past in something like an hour. The garden is small and interesting and there is a way round the back, over a fence, into an enormous field and beyond that is a wood, and hanging above that, we learn, is an outstanding limestone pavement known as Hutton Roof Crags, so there are endless possibilities of good things for the cats to do.

As Richard walks into the room on his own, Michael tells him quietly that we are about to cancel the next viewing appointment, and Richard beams happily at the prospect of a done deal. We go downstairs and ask Pamela as many questions as we can think of in connection with the house and the garden. There is a room downstairs, which Michael has already nominated as his study cum library, but which is currently set up as Pamela's studio where, we discover, she works on her sculptures. There are several hand-carved boxwood miniature animals and birds on one of the tables, and when I ask her about them I discover that she is about to exhibit in London at the invitation of the Royal Society of Miniature Painters, Sculptors and Gravers, for which she subsequently receives one of the Society's most prestigious awards and is presented to HRH the Prince of Wales. Her sculptures (technically okimonos rather than netsukes, because they are miniatures in their own right, rather than toggles for kimonos) are truly beautiful and it is motivating to contemplate living in a house that has been inhabited by someone who cares about the natural world and has such obvious artistic talent. Pamela is also a skilled nurseryman and has grown a range of extremely interesting perennials for sale for some years, which has hugely benefited the garden.

As we somewhat breathlessly take our leave and cross the road to the car, Pamela suddenly calls out over the hedge:

'If you do want it you'd better hurry up, there's another couple coming this afternoon, they have just been on the phone now.'

'Don't worry, we're off now to start things rolling,' Michael calls back.

CHAPTER 12

When we are alone and finally able to talk freely to each other, Michael and I find we have no doubts at all that the village of Hutton Roof and the Coach House within it are where we would love to spend the rest of our days. On our return to Moon Cottage, therefore, there is much to be done. We have to set in motion the raising of money to buy the Coach House. One young couple who have already seen Moon Cottage once are clearly interested in it, but openly admit that the price is out of their bracket; our hopes are high, though, as they have asked us if they might send round an independent valuer, which we interpret as good news. Meanwhile, we know from both Richard and also from Pamela herself that there is not much time to play with, as Pamela has already bought a property in France and has a moving date organised – and is therefore compelled to sell to the first buyer she gets. The French system for buying and selling houses is similar to the Scottish one, which means that once you have committed, that is it, and the date for exchange of monies is set in stone. We are terrified that our newly discovered earthly paradise will slip through our fingers and so, without more ado, Michael goes into action and, with the aid of a helpful broker, we manage to raise a second mortgage, commission a solicitor recommended to us by our agent and make our offer for the purchase of the Coach House. The sale is agreed and the ball starts to roll.

Back at the cottage I am beginning to let Titus out of her cage for longer and longer periods, but am increasingly frightened of her jumping up or down. On three occasions now she has jumped down from the bed before I could stop her in spite of the 'Lady of Shalott' mirror arrangement; and I have been severely warned about the dangers of her undoing her surgery, which would be dire. Her spirits are so low, though, and she clearly doesn't understand why she is incarcerated in this way; I really fear what her interpretation must be of the treatment she is receiving at my hands. Six weeks' imprisonment is a long time. In part to try to compensate for this 'cruelty', I spend long periods of time with her on my knee, or, as a variation, with her lying on my desk, where I will stroke her and talk to her, to try to make her feel loved. I have also noticed that she and Fannie seem to be almost closer now than ever before, even taking into account that they have always been devoted from early kittenhood (Fannie's nastiness to Titus post-operatively excepted), but the fact that they can't sleep together seems to have reinforced their bond rather than severed it, by providing them with a form of yearning for each other. As an experiment, for the sake of Titus's morale, I tried putting Fannie in the cage with her, but had to abandon it due to the fuss (from Fannie, of course, not Titus, who was clearly up for it).

And now, at last, the day has come when I can take Titus back to our local vet, Pat, to get clearance to allow her the liberty she craves. I am a little concerned in case some of the jumps have caused irreversible damage, but Pat gives her the all clear and feels that her recovery is on the right track, and that we just need to be very careful with her, especially when we let her outside. I am more concerned, knowing the cottage, about the stairs as they are so very steep. When we get home and finally fold away her cage, 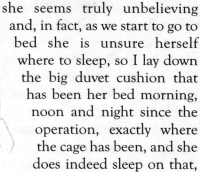 she seems truly unbelieving and, in fact, as we start to go to bed she is unsure herself where to sleep, so I lay down the big duvet cushion that has been her bed morning, noon and night since the operation, exactly where the cage has been, and she does indeed sleep on that, although after about half an hour I hear her jumping up on to the low armchair that she and Fannie consider their own piece of furniture. Indeed, the following day, for the sake of her peace of mind, I reinstate the cage with the door open for a couple more nights until she is properly ready to re-enter the 'real' world. Later on, in that first night of freedom, I hear her slowly clump her way downstairs to the litter tray in the kitchen, and it wrenches my heart to hear her hobbling down, sounding like Blind Pew. Pat had said to me, however, that she needs to build up those muscle tissues, and this form of exercise is what is required to strengthen them, so I let her be. So, for the first time in six weeks, Michael and I enjoy a night's sleep without the accompaniment of the sound and smells of a bored and pissed-off cat on auto-pilot apparently, burying, interminably, something the size of a haunch of venison in a tray of cat litter.

Since the ominous warning in late January from my sister, Judy, in America, things have gone from bad to worse and she is currently intensively nursing Rod at home, but it is clear that his cancer is terminal, and nothing can be done to save him. The courage of that family is considerable though.

Rod remains cheerful and sparkly, and from time to time I talk to him on the phone and am astonished at his strength of character, although it shouldn't surprise me. He was always doughty and the same applies to his three children, Mark, Claire and Emma, the last of whom is herself expecting a baby, which is especially tough at this time; but it is Judy, in a different way, to whom I doff my cap. There is nothing that she will not do for her man, however gruesome or arduous, and it is this that makes it possible for him to remain at home and experience as full and as rewarding a quality of life as the circumstances will allow him. She too is full of optimism and shows the most amazing fortitude. I admire them all more than I can say.

Here on this side of the Atlantic, the baby-making is going apace. Jo and I meet up for a girlie lunch on Friday, and by this time she is ten days' overdue and has been told by her midwife at the hospital that if she does not go into labour naturally over the weekend, they will induce labour on the Monday – which she is desperate to avoid, wanting the birth to be as natural as possible. She is now beginning to feel very uncomfortable and very tense, and who wouldn't be? As we are driving down the road just chatting about this and that, she says to me in a low voice, so low I can hardly hear her:

'Marilyn, I think you should know that I am having contractions closer together now.' I squawk back in a very uncool sort of way:

'Jo, how long have you been having these contractions?'

'Oh, a little while.'

'Jo, I think we should go to the hospital, what do you say?'

'Do you really think so?'

'Yessssssssssssss.'

So we go to the hospital where she is booked in to give birth, and the problem with being a mother-out-of-law is that it gets difficult to throw your weight around, so I become a mother-in-law for convenience's sake. And the upshot is that she is contracting, but the baby is way off and she is only in the first stage, so, at her firm request, I take her back home and wait with her until Damian, who has been playing golf all day, finally gets home and fusses around her and is clearly set to take the best possible care of her when I take my leave of them while they brace themselves for the very last stage of their old life together before the staggering first stage of their brand-new life, when they will be three, stretching out ahead of them.

Her contractions continue in a mild way for the remainder of Friday, but on Saturday morning she wakes up at 4 a.m. and they are coming five minutes apart. By 5 a.m. she is strapped into a borrowed Land Rover and Damian starts the drive into Watford to the hospital. As they are en route her waters break, but they keep going (although I suspect that Damian is busy having proverbial kittens by this time) and arrive safely at the hospital and then, brave girl that she is, Jo delivers her baby in a stoically squatting position, taking a chunk out of Damian's shoulder in her last push to expel him (the baby that is, not Damian, she assures me!), and at 9.10 a.m. on the Saturday morning a little boy is born, called Oskar William Herbert, weighing in at 9 lbs 6 oz. I will never, for as long as I live, forget the expression of pleasure on Michael's face when he first holds Oskar. I have to say the expression of pride on Damian's face was pretty cool too!

Four days later, Emma in America gives birth to her son, Alex, who has decided to enter the world a staggering four weeks early, unlike the laidback Oskar, and he weighs in at 6 lbs and 9 oz. With considerably more difficulty than Jo, Emma too finally gets to introduce her son to his paternal grandfather.

Suddenly, on the house-buying front, there is an

unexpected complication. Our solicitor's conveyancing clerk (the solicitor himself is on holiday for almost the full period of the conveyancing, as is Richard, our buying agent, so we totally lack advisers) tells us that if we are to exchange and complete by the end of April, which is the date required by Pamela to meet her French move, we will all have to vacate Moon Cottage, because our mortgage agreement is on a buy-to-let basis and these are the rules, but not only that, we must also be resident at the new house in Hutton Roof at the point of exchange; and if we are not in residence (we had intended to be on holiday in France) he tells us, it will constitute mortgage fraud.

It had not originally been our intention to move to Hutton Roof immediately, as Michael is still in full-time work, but rather we planned to move once he leaves at the end of May. This decree demoralises us beyond words because it will be impossible for us to move our furniture in the time left, so we will move up to Hutton Roof without furniture, with cats who will hate it, without anything, not even a bed, and Michael will be commuting to London without a home, and will have to find accommodation elsewhere.

Oliver and his girlfriend Lisa come up from Wales to stay with us as we all wake up to the fact that life is about to change in a radical way, and the next time we see Ollie we will be living in the North and everything will be different. Oliver is working towards his finals, and also he has now taken the major decision to sell up the business that was his mother's and that he has been running since her sudden death last autumn; and once that is sorted, he has decided that he would love to travel the world.

As soon as Oliver and Lisa have returned to Wales I set about trying to find removal companies with the earliest possible date for our furniture to be taken up and, having phoned five companies, the best I can achieve is three weeks away but, to satisfy our conveyancing clerk, what is important is that we three residents are physically no longer domiciled in Moon Cottage and that, of course, must include the cats.

The French trip was to have involved a week's holiday for Michael and me, together with his brother John, visiting our friends Geoff and Pat in their house in Poitiers. The return flight has been booked for months and as soon as the conveyancing clerk tells us to pull the plug on it we try to get a refund from the airline, but of course that proves impossible. Cancelling our trip like this also means that Geoff and Pat, who could have rented out our accommodation to someone else, have lost that opportunity too. John, because he is an incredibly kind and generous-spirited person, offers to come up to Hutton Roof instead with us, as he had booked the holiday anyway, to help us do whatever needs to be done there.

This last week before we leave for Hutton Roof the action around the cottage is pretty intense, in every possible way, and I become very aware that the cats are anxious, even alarmed, as everything is other than it normally would be, so now, of course, I feel guilty as I have not been able to think about them, or properly spend time with them in the way that I should.

In spite of the chaos reigning within Moon Cottage I manage to secure the longed-for post-operative appointment with Titus's surgeon, Rob, who intently watches her walking. He is pleased with the results of the operation on her right leg and feels that it should hold for her lifetime, but I am fearful that he will say that the time has come to look at her left leg again. Before allowing him to speak, I fulsomely express my reservations about the cruelty to my mind of the necessarily severe confinement a further operation on Titus would entail and how, unless it is a matter of life and death, I really don't want to do this to Titus; it would utterly mess with her quality of life, and so what does he think? I know as I make my lengthy and impassioned statement that I am probably forcing him into a difficult situation, and he pauses a long time before he does reply. The essence of his reply is that the correction to her right leg may be enough to keep her left leg in place, but I am going to need to watch it like a hawk, because if it does spontaneously pop out again, as it did under manipulation, then it will need addressing, but for the moment Titus can go free. I want to hug him, but due to his extreme youth I control myself, and skip out of his consulting room with Titus jiggling around in the cat cage, eyes large and mildly concerned.

CHAPTER 13

Our enforced moving day encroaches upon us and for several days now the cats have been noticeably tense. Titus is on heat and now Fannie has joined her, and they are both squawking raucously, but Pushkin is the one who is surprising me. He has a rather disarming, quite girly alto squeak, and for two days he has been talking away all over the house, to me and to himself, at repeated intervals; as he is normally a quiet cat, it is significant. This morning, from first thing, he goes into hiding and although I know I am going to have to find him ultimately, for the moment at least it seems better just to leave him. Michael goes early to the office in London to do most of a day's work, but around mid-afternoon – it being a Friday – he will drive straight up to Cumbria from London in his own car and collect his brother, John, from the local station of Oxenholme. Michael's son Johnny, meanwhile, packs his suitcase and departs for his office in his car, and at the end of his working day he will then drive down to the West Country to stay with friends, and on his return his plan is to stay in Watford with another friend.

After they have both left, the house is suddenly very quiet and I feel sick because we have somehow been bullied out of Moon Cottage and this is not the way I had wanted to move

93

into our new home. Slowly I start to pack up my own car for the long trek north, with the cats being the last addition. They are all prone to carsickness, but Fannie and Pushkin especially, and I have not yet found any medication that a vet will sanction for feline travel-sickness; it exists for dogs, but sadly not for cats. With my three on longer excursions – I cage them on short journeys, for ease and safety – I find that if they are left free in the back of the car (with a grill separating them from the driver) they travel better. This also means I can leave out a cat litter tray and a bowl of water, and all three of them make use of both. I think the freedom of movement allows the balance in their inner ear to adjust itself more easily. On long car journeys, Fannie watches out of the window, certainly in daylight hours, and I am sure that helps her. Pushkin tends to bury himself low down in the car under blankets and newspapers and that almost certainly *doesn't* help him. Titus is the least problematical traveller and usually sits quite still, letting it all happen.

The house at Hutton Roof has no furniture in it at all, so I cram the car with as many artefacts to keep us going as I can think of, including the all-important self-inflating mattresses. It is now raining hard and I discover I have left no room for the cat-carrying cage. I start to look for the cats and I find Pushkin head down under a pile of clothes in our wardrobe, not a very good hiding place, as it was bound to be where I would look first, but that's Pushkin for you, so I grab him in my arms and manage to push him through a tiny opening in the car door and shut it again. I repeat the same exercise with Titus, but Fannie proves to be more difficult. A few days earlier I had fallen down the steps of the estate agent's office and I am still recovering from a severely sprained left ankle and swollen right shoulder, and I simply cannot manhandle her into the car on my own, as my immobile shoulder is becoming a major hindrance; so I take her back into the cottage, but I'm close to tears of frustration. Stephen from next door suddenly appears and nobly helps me, so between us we manage to force the unwilling Fannie into the car, narrowly avoiding her wriggling free to run out into the now heavy traffic; but just as we get the car door closed, a small van shoots past us through a massive puddle, comprehensively soaking us both. The three cats inside the car start up a miaowing and a mewling, and at that point my mobile goes and it is Pamela from Hutton Roof, sounding worried and impatient, because she hasn't had the confirmation from her solicitor that the exchange and completion has gone through. I know that it has because I have had the confirmation from our conveyancing clerk, but I eventually discover that the reason Pamela doesn't know this is because her phone has been disconnected pending its reconnection in our name; but as I listen to her agitation, my own stress levels rise up into the red zone.

As I set off, the rain gets heavier and my mobile goes again; it is Michael, who suddenly wants us to reconsider whether we should accept a revised offer from the couple on Moon Cottage. Distraught with all that lies ahead of me, I just keep repeating that I don't know, I don't know, but I thought we, that is to say he, I and the agent had all agreed that the offer was way too low. He vacillates a little, and then he disconsolately agrees that is right and rings off. In truth, I don't pay much attention to this call, as I don't believe he is serious and there is so much else on my mind.

The journey is long and tedious, but for the main part – the motorway part of it – the cats, although unhappy, are not ill. But then close to Lancaster, because of a flagged-up accident higher up the motorway and warnings of queues and stationary traffic, we leave the motorway two junctions earlier than I had intended and do a tortuous cross-country route, at which point we get the full feline performance of vomiting and diarrhoea from all three of them, preceded and followed by the most plaintive mewling. I daren't stop because I am scared of opening the back doors and letting them out, and I cannot access them through the grill from the front, so in spite of the severe assault on two of our five senses I keep going, singing songs very loudly to take all our minds off everything.

The delays at the beginning and then the travail of the journey itself now means that Michael is further ahead of schedule than I am, and by the time I roll up to the village of Hutton Roof he and John have already found the hidden key, unlocked the door and opened up. I stop and wearily get out and open up the stinking car. With John and Michael's help, the three of us manage to shepherd the cats into the empty house. Fannie and Titus hang around near us, clearly frightened. Although there are carpets in most of the rooms, without furniture the house is very echoey and noisy and there are almost no high surfaces for the cats to climb up on to. The second we get the cats inside, however, Pushkin just takes off and none of us sees where he goes.

'It's fine, Mo, there are no open windows, there is nowhere he can go other than inside the house, so he'll be fine. Let's get that car unpacked. Come on, we'll come and help you.' And so the three of us begin the wearisome task of transferring the goods and chattels from the car into the house. Each of the stairways consists of uncarpeted, highly varnished honey-coloured Paraná pinewood, and it is our intention to leave them exactly as they are. But every time any one of us goes up or down the stairs, either flight, the clumping noise is deafening and it is visibly worrying the two female cats; Pushkin, of course, is nowhere to be seen. I sort out fresh cat litter for the tray, and then put out some dried food and water. I know that soon I must go and find Pushkin.

Michael has had the foresight to bring up and unpack a couple of bottles of wine and even a corkscrew, and so we pull up the chairs around the little card table, open the wine with a flourish, and make a solemn toast to the house, and then, visibly relaxing, we each contentedly slurp away at the contents of our glass. The day has consisted of a series of heavy rainstorms for the greater part of the journey, and since our arrival up here it has been overcast. Now it is officially past sunset, but at the very last minute, before the sun finally sinks behind the limestone crag above the western side of the house, it makes a brave, last-ditch attempt at a watery welcome, and suddenly, as we are looking out through the east-facing windows of the conservatory, the dying rays of the sun from behind us throw out a blood-red reflection across the clouds, across the sky, and across the hills of Yorkshire. Everything as far as the eye can see is ablaze in its glow, and most spectacular of all is the highlighting of the great peak of Ingleborough, which is exactly due east of where we are by about twelve miles as the crow flies; and as we watch, every nook and cranny etched into that ancient hillside is clearly discernible and then, just as suddenly, the sun behind us drops below the horizon, the light changes, it darkens, and the moment has gone.

Sighing happily, Michael leans forward and touches my knee.

'Come on, Mo, time to go and find the boy.'

'OK. I'll go to the south wing and you look in the north wing.'

John goes off with Michael and I rootle around in what will be Michael's study and our bedroom, but I cannot find Pushkin anywhere. I can hear them calling him from the other side of the house, but as long as their voices can still be heard, they clearly haven't found him. Eventually I go back to join them, and John says:

'I think, I just think, that I might know where he is.'

'Where, for goodness sake?'

'I don't know how he got in there, but behind the sink.'

And, sure enough, Pushkin has found a hole that looks far smaller than would accommodate him, through which he has wiggled and, having crawled in there, he has followed the pipes right along the kitchen wall under the sink, behind the newly fitted kitchen units that were Pamela's pride and joy. For all we know, as we cannot see him properly, he could be stuck. The best we have managed so far is to shine a torch down at an oblique angle and we can just see his eyes glowing back.

'You are assuming it's Pushkin. It might not be,' I offer, possibly less than helpfully.

'Blimey, Marilyn, if it's not Pushkin, it's the biggest rat in creation!'

'The only solution is to pull out the fridge,' John, the peacemaker, suggests more helpfully. And so, with much effort and rather destroying the whole ethos of a fitted unit, the three of us haul out the fridge and, with the aid of a long broom handle, poke and pull and eventually grab, partly by his tail I am ashamed to say, the cat Pushkin. He emerges, terrified, covered from head to tail in cobwebs as if he had just surfaced from Miss Havisham's fossilised wedding feast.

'Block that hole up now,' Michael shouts assertively and we jump to it. (Rather sadly, we have never been able to reinstate the fridge as it should be, and the unit now is definitely a couple of inches proud of being fitted, and rocky to boot.)

I nurse Pushkin and gently try to coerce him to eat a little, which eventually he does, but he looks over his shoulder the whole time and crouches low and defensively on the ground. I then place him in the cat litter tray just in case after we have gone to bed he is too scared to try, and by dint of blocking his exit out of it (it is a covered one), after a few minutes I hear him make use of it. I then release him and off he runs.

'Let him go, he has to find somewhere he will be comfortable.'

After one more glass of wine and having, noisily, blown up the air beds with their built-in electronic pumps, which sound as if we are vacuuming a wooden floor with the loudest Hoover in the world, and which sets the cats off running for cover, we retire to our separate wings for our first night's sleep in Hutton Roof.

CHAPTER 14

I have brought up with me the big squashy duvet bed that Titus used while she was recovering from her operation, which I am fairly confident that the two girls will share, and I also brought a little circular cat bed that Pushkin sometimes sleeps on in Moon Cottage. During the night I am woken repeatedly by loud clunking noises which, it turns out, are the two girls walking up and down the stairs; cats can sound surprisingly heavy on wooden stairs I now realise. However, for most of the night Fannie and Titus sleep in the sitting room, but Pushkin's whereabouts remain a mystery. In the morning, as Michael starts the breakfast, of which in our household he is undisputed 'king', John and I go on a further Pushkin-hunt.

Eventually we find him jammed into the acute angle under the stairs behind a wall in Michael's study, on a tiny scrap of folded-up carpet. His chosen corner is very cobwebby, a bit damp and slightly musty smelling, which means that when I haul Pushkin out he too possesses these qualities. I hold him down by a bowl of cat food and he eats quickly, but he is clearly terrified, as he was yesterday. I then encourage him into the cat tray and again he uses it, but only under duress, and although I try to get him to lie on his bed, as soon as I take my hand off him he runs straight under the stairs again. In fact, he tries to get back to the pipes under the sink, but we have effectively blocked them off, so he is forced by default into the below-stairs position.

Because of our enforced move here the three of us are staying in the house with very little tackle between us. We have few changes of clothes and no tools of any kind, but as we rattle around the empty house we realise that as we are prisoners here, we might as well start doing useful things. We quickly discover that there is a big DIY store on the outskirts of Kendal and we take it in turns to do the run for various bits and pieces. I feel guilty while all this is going on, because I have to return the proofs of my book to my publisher and have a tight deadline, so while John and Michael work incredibly hard on the house, I try to shut myself away in one of the empty rooms to work on the proofs. That, in itself, is quite a challenge as we have so little furniture, and my table is an upended wooden crate.

Gerard, a younger brother to Michael and John, drives over to see us all, with his wife Sandra and sons Ryan and Benjamin. They very kindly bring over with them a large stripper-steamer which John and Michael are itching to get their hands on so they can start to strip off the various layers of wallpaper that festoon every room. On the very first morning I managed to break the shower fitment which controls the temperature of the water in our bathroom, and ever since then water has been pouring out of the wall – so poor Gerard finds that he is also required to mend that, and, being the excellent plumbing engineer that he is, he does – but I fear he is going to be wary of any further invitations to the Coach House!

Michael and John set to work with the stripper and the noise and the steam and the mess is indescribable, and it goes on for days. Needless to say, the sound of the stripper truly petrifies the cats, but I feel I cannot ask the boys to stop because it makes them feel better that they are actually doing something useful, and anyway it desperately needs doing. Whichever room I take myself off to, I find that Titus and Fannie come and join me, but I am completely unable to persuade Pushkin to leave his bolt hole under the stairs; it is, however, one of the few places where the steamer won't be used. When he does come out, he does it crawling on his belly.

The one thing that makes him change his behaviour, just slightly, is if Titus or Fannie, but especially Titus, is near him. Then his actions alter, subtly, but discernibly. His body movements start as those of a cat crawling on his belly in fear, but as he sees Titus he raises himself fractionally and instead assumes the air of one stalking low and slinking along. He wants to crawl, his instinct is making him crawl, but he doesn't want to lose his standing in her eyes. I am enchanted to discover this particular strain of feline prevarication, although I am unhappy for his distress. I hide my smile from him.

On our second night in Hutton Roof we receive a kind-hearted invitation to have drinks with Annabel and Richard who live in the 'big' house next door, The Old Vicarage, of which our house was its original Coach House, so effectively we live in their garage!

I am mildly disconcerted when I answer the door to Richard, who is issuing the invitation, by his helpful codicil of 'don't dress up', knowing that we only have the clothes we are standing up in at that moment or, at best, an identical alternative. And seconds later, I am even more disconcerted when he spies Fannie trotting across the hallway and adds:

'Oh what a splendid pair of gloves that one would make!' She pauses and stares at him levelly, and trots off again waving her wild tail.

Their house is a typical small Victorian mansion with an

attractive wooded garden full of flowering shrubs, plants and tall trees and, of course, the same breathtaking view as ours over the Barbon fells and the peaks of Yorkshire, including the great Ingleborough. Annabel and Richard are animated hosts and the wine and whisky flow freely and we talk of many things. One of the subjects that interests me greatly, however, is the problem of the wind farms, which are peppering Cumbria outside the national park, and there is a strong lobby afoot to build yet more. I had assumed until this evening that wind farms were an ecologically 'good thing'. As we talk more seriously about them, I begin properly to understand that the issue is truly complicated, but that one of the major stumbling blocks is that onshore wind farming costs more than twice as much per kilowatt-hour as most fossil fuels and also that payback time on the cost of construction takes six to seven years. They are clunky and ugly and noisy, they damage and interfere with wildlife, and while the landowner himself receives generous payment for playing host to a wind farm, his neighbours who suffer the horrors of it receive nothing at all. There is also the additional question of fair dispersal. Cumbria, this most beautiful of English counties, is already the site of much nuclear technology for the purposes of supplying and disposing of the resultant waste of Britain's energy, and many locals feel they have done more than enough in providing electricity for the rest of the UK. Although Cumbria is a county of high unemployment, more wind farms would not generate more employment in the county as they are operated remotely and maintained sparingly. Although I have very mixed feelings about nuclear power, I do begin, slowly, to see that this might be the better way forward until perhaps the scientists can crack the problem of energy from fusion. Additionally, money could be invested in offshore wind farming, which does not seem to arouse so many objections.

But wind farming is not all that we talk of and, only slightly comforted by Annabel's tinkling laughter, I rise to Richard's bait as he announces:

'You know about the rule that cats in this village are only allowed a maximum of 300 yards from their house for hunting?'

'Blimey, no, I don't! Whose rule is that?'

'My rule. I'm a serious songbird lover,' he replies crisply, with no outward show of merriment. I look across at Annabel for some sign of reassurance. She beams happily at me and shrugs. Richard then sets my mind at rest that really he is all right – well all right-ish at any rate – about cats as he tells me about a cat that adopted him in a tented camp in Nicosia when on National Service in 1956. The cat, a pure black moggy, slept in his tent and spent the day in and around the officers' mess tent. The cat was quickly adopted by the regiment as its mascot and named Maiwand after a regimental battle honour gained in Afghanistan in 1880. Maiwand, the cat, quickly learned to use cat initiative to lead a very feather-bedded existence in the camp, living off begged scraps, and every night, as soon as she heard the tinkle of coffee cups after dinner, she advanced down the mess miaowing plaintively to force the Colonel of the regiment, who traditionally always had first pull at the coffee tray, to pour her a saucer of milk. Richard describes how one evening he found her in the process of despatching a three-foot snake, which took more than half-an-hour with the cat jumping backwards and cuffing the snake each time it struck. Behaving, in fact, just like a mongoose. Eventually one cuff struck home and Maiwand had a particularly good dinner that night. This story of Maiwand leads Richard on, inexorably, to a story about a dog called Bobbie. I hold up my hands laughing, protesting enough, but he explains that in order to understand his cat Maiwand, I need to understand about Bobbie too. So here it is!

Bobbie, a small white mongrel with red ears and red eye patches, was a pet dog belonging to one Sergeant Kelly, but was also the pet of the entire Second Battalion of the Royal Berkshire Regiment (formerly the Sixty-sixth Regiment), which was severely beaten in the ill-fated battle of Maiwand in the Second Afghan War in 1880. There were many fatal casualties but the dog, although wounded, survived and then became lost on the battlefield during the retreat. He reappeared several days later to rejoin his regiment at Kandahar, over fifty miles away. In June 1881 Bobbie, along with many men and officers and one horse, was presented to Queen Victoria at the royal residence, Osborne House, where she placed the Afghan Medal around his neck. In spite of surviving all of this, just eighteen months later Bobbie suffered the ignominy of being run over and killed by a hansom cab in Gosport, at which point the regiment had the dog stuffed and put in a glass case. And I am now, courtesy of Richard, the proud possessor of a copy of that postcard in which Bobbie is, for all eternity, sporting his Afghan Medal.

Soon after that we meet several other neighbours, including Iain and his wife, Judy, who live at a farm a couple of miles away and who run a bed and breakfast. As well as helping Judy in the running of their guesthouse business, Iain works as a carpenter and loves nothing better than challenging commissions in wood. Michael has asked him to measure up his study in order to line it, floor to ceiling, with unusually deep bookshelves so that he may double stack his myriad signed first editions, the collecting and exchanging of which is now going to become his full-time hobby. He is desperate for Iain to be able to complete the job before we actually move all the books up from Moon Cottage, so the pressure of time is on. We also need some gates for the driveway and, to Iain's much greater pleasure, a long narrow refectory table to fit into our long narrow conservatory, which will double up as our dining area.

When Iain arrives this morning for his final measuring-up trip I bemoan the chaos and mess that is being generated by the three of us gutting the house, which day by day is getting worse.

'Oh I know, it all looks terrible now, but think of the end result when the pain stops!' and I know he is right. I worry, however, when he adds that the long wet dark winters of Westmorland can be quite demoralising and the sixty inches of rainfall a year are pretty spectacular. I think, until that moment, Michael has not realised quite how high the incidence of rainfall in Cumbria actually is. It is, after all, the *lake* district.

We persuade Geoffrey to drive over to see the Coach House from his home in Hawes, which, we have now measured, is twenty-five miles by road. I am on tenterhooks prior to this meeting as it somehow matters inordinately that he approves of our choice. He arrives and takes one look out across the valley and up towards the hills whence he has just emerged and says quietly:

'Oh yes, oh yes. Look at that!' and I am utterly thrilled. Later on he says that he actually feels mildly jealous, as although he is in the heart of the Dales his view does not compare with ours, and my cup flows over!

Michael and John and I each spend hours just gawping

out of the conservatory window at those breathtaking distant views of Ingleborough and the Howgills and the Barbon fells. The truth is that even in the rain they are magnificent, and when the cloud is down, they are still enchanting, as the mist gives an air of mystery to everything. Michael quickly develops a theory that when it rains 'the hills walk away' as they hide behind the cloud cover. But in this first week we are lucky, and although there is rain, there is also sun aplenty; watching the changing light scudding across the hills and the ever-changing colour is mesmerising. As I look out, I feel so happy that we are here now, but when I turn in and look at the house that we seem to be wrecking evermore, day by day, with a group of three very unhappy cats in attendance, then I wonder what on earth are we doing?

CHAPTER 15

Every day that we stay at the Coach House it continues to be uncomfortable for the two queens, but it is tantamount to a nightmare for the poor little tom. Although I thought it was going to be bad for them all, in the event it is so much worse, for Pushkin in particular, that I am filled with remorse. Three times a day I go into the alcove under the stairs in Michael's study and haul out my protesting boy and take him first to the food and water bowls and then to the cat litter tray. He suffers all these indignities and then runs back to his hidey-hole. Fannie tries to find the height she craves but, with lack of furniture other than banisters and door tops, she is hard-pressed in her quest; she does, however, manage to climb the stepladder quite efficiently. Both she and Titus spring up and down off every windowsill continually, Titus more creakily, but they are a height she can just manage, and Fannie, to my complete horror, repeatedly walks the banister rail around the top of our stairwell – and I sense that she actually enjoys my fear. Otherwise, the two girls just clump the stairs.

While we are here I am able to access the internet from my computer, balanced on the upturned crate, and I email Margot about the plight of the cats. She replies to me, forwarding an old email she had from a close friend of hers in France, Jacqueline, who, when she wrote this email, had just moved house from Paris to Ouistreham, complete with her two neutered toms – magnificently named Brigadoon and Sir Mortimer. Her move created some pretty big issues for her boys too it would seem!

From:	Jacqueline
To:	Margot
Sent:	Tuesday, 23 September, 17:25
Subject:	Speaking of all-out war

Dear Margot

Let me tell you how awful and terrifying it was here Sunday evening when Brigadoon and Sir Mortimer got into an all-out war, looking like a fight to the death. And I was in the middle, trembling, bombarding the warriors with pans of cold water, or trying that old Roman arena thing – you know, throwing the net, but using blankets and quilts instead. Finally, Sir M got out from under a blanket, Brigadoon pounced on it, and I was in the midst of dragging the blanket along, with Brigadoon on board, to the nearby closet when Sir M clawed at my left hand. Nonetheless, I continued pulling the blanket to the closet door, shoved Brigadoon in with my foot, closed the door, and then grabbed a dishtowel in the kitchen to wrap around my combat wounds dripping on the tile floor. Sir Mortimer wandered about a bit and then went out of the open backdoor to the garden. I immediately locked it, let Brigadoon out of the closet, and commenced putting compresses of disinfectant on my left hand and arm. At 1.30 a.m. I went to bed, and woke up an hour later. The two cats were again howling and grumbling and I could hear them banging into the glass door (storm windows luckily) that opens on to the garden. They were still trying to fight through the glass panes, terrifying...

Early the next morning I let Sir M into the garage under the house, gave him food, water, a blanket and a makeshift litterbox and shut and locked the adjoining door... Brigadoon was meanwhile shut inside in the rest of the house...

I then went to a nearby vet clinic that was recommended to me and told them what had happened. They didn't seem surprised and explained that it was caused by a territorial issue and stress because of moving, and with the help of two happy-pheromone distributors that plug into electrical sockets all should be well. It takes twenty-four hours for them to work. So I plugged them in, and by yesterday evening Brigadoon was purring or lying around tummy up, which means relaxed. Sir M was still in the garage while the house filled up with pheromones.

We are now living in this feline equiv-alent of an opium den, all doors and windows closed so we do not lose any of the precious divine atmosphere. The heart of the matter seems to be who owns the left corner of the living room couch, perceived as the prime piece of napping real estate by both parties. Today I moved the couch to a different wall. Now the boys are sprawled around the house napping here and there, not seeming to have a care in the world, no

doubt meditating lazily on the changing
geometry of couches.
   Lots of love,
   Tiger Mum Jacqueline

Margot sends this to me with the suggestion that I acquire
some of this magical plug-in pheromone. I then email my
friend Elspeth as I remember she said she had a terrible time
with her two cats, the young neutered tom, Arthur, and his
mother, Freya, when she moved earlier this year, and ask her
to remind me exactly what happened:

From:	Elspeth
To:	Marilyn
Sent:	Thursday, 6 May, 11:17
Subject:	Arthur

Hi
   Basically, on the morning of the move I
put their food down to get them in the open
and then grabbed Arthur, tried to get him in
the cage you lent me and, as you warned, the
door fell off and he just jumped out and ran
into the bedroom and hid under the bed.
   I got Freya in the other cage, and then
went into the bedroom and shut the door. I
took the mattress off the bed, and could see
him under the slats of the bed, at which
point he started howling. I leant the bed
frame against the wall, and the only place
left for him to hide (which was rubbish, but
he is quite thick) was behind the curtain on
the window sill, so that's where he went,
still yowling. I got him into the cage, and
took them both to the vet who was looking

112

after them while the move happened, and Arthur didn't stop crying at all.

I picked them up in the afternoon, took them to the new flat (which is a very light first-floor flat as opposed to a dark basement, which the other one was), and let them out on the bed. They both ran straight underneath it, and I put food and water in the room with them and left the door open. In about half an hour Freya came out and started looking round; if I got up she'd run back under the bed, but as long as I was still, she'd explore. She then lay in the sun in the living room, and started stretching and cleaning herself. I got down at the side of the bed and Arthur came and sniffed my hand, and I saw he was shaking. Basically he stayed either under the bed or under the duvet for the next four days, only on one or two occasions going under the duvet – I think he felt more secure in the dark. I put down poached fish, cooked liver and cooked steak for him, but he would not eat anything. After four days, my knees were in agony from spending so much time kneeling on the wooden floor with him. So I brought him into the sitting room, put cushions under the sofa and chairs so he couldn't hide, and shut the door and stayed in there with him for a couple of hours. As soon as I opened the door he ran back under the bed, but that night he went back into the sitting room, and from then on he gradually started exploring. It took almost two weeks before I came home and he behaved 'normally'.

The other problem during this time is that Freya kept hissing at him, maybe she could smell the vet on him still, or maybe she

just knew he was vulnerable. Anyway, it made
me really cross with her, but there wasn't a
lot I could do.

   It was hard getting him eating properly
again, and it's weird, but in the mornings
when I'm getting ready to go to work, he
still won't come anywhere near me, he hides
under the coffee table in the sitting room.

   Hope it gets better with yours soon – it's
really worrying when they are so upset.

   Elspeth xx

Not content with pestering my sister and also Elspeth, I then
moan on to my long-suffering agent Kate, saying never was
there a disappearing cat who was so perplexing as Pushkin,
and she then sends me this wonderful account from her
husband Charles Carroll about the introduction of a new
Siamese whom they name Catastrophe into their household
– which at this time consists of themselves, their three-year-
old daughter, and a Tonkinese called Calamity. It is great
therapy for me to read this:

> Generally [when introducing new cats to the
> household] we put the box on the floor, open the
> door, and wait for the newcomer to emerge inquisitive
> and eager to explore his new surroundings. And so we
> waited. And waited. Then we lost patience and gave
> him a little encouragement . . . His exit from the box
> would be familiar to anyone who has seen pictures of
> a Pershing missile launching from a nuclear silo. He
> shot across the kitchen floor, rose several feet in the
> air, bounced off the microwave and landed on a work
> surface before realising he was in a corner with
> nowhere to hide. In a textbook display of what *not* to

do, I lunged after him – a gesture he clearly misunderstood – and ten seconds later he was behind the oven. I turned to Kate: 'Are they meant to do that?' . . . The following morning we looked behind the cooker and – horrors – he'd disappeared.

Most of day two was spent with mounting panic searching for the new hiding place. Needless to say, underneath the bathroom floor was not the first place we thought of looking . . . In fact, it was only as I threw my socks in the laundry basket at the end of the day that I saw the small gap where one floorboard fails to meet the wall. I put my socks back on and went to find a torch. There is no dignity involved in searching for a missing cat. I grovelled on the floor with the torch in one hand and a mirror in the other, trying to reflect light round a corner . . . Just out of arm's reach a pair of red eyes stared back. It would be going too far to say that they looked smug, but something about the situation told me that the cat had the upper paw. I might have had control of the food and water supplies, but the eyes said, 'I've only got to do one poo down here and you'll have to take up the whole floor.'

I tried to tempt him out with food, I tried to drag him out by force, I even thought about trying to starve him out, but in the end I went to bed. Twenty minutes later I was asleep and he popped out for a snack.

This went on for the next three weeks. Every night he would wait until he was sure everyone was asleep, and then he'd creep out for a bite to eat before crawling back under the floorboards at first light. Eventually in desperation I pretended to be asleep and . . . while he was downstairs I whipped out a screwdriver and closed the hole. His new home was under the bed. This was an enormous step forward. Now we could see our new cat without lying on the bathroom floor with a mirror . . . But he became adept at staying hidden . . . Christmas came and went, and then one morning in January we were woken by a yowl from under the bed. After four months, two weeks and three days, our cat had spoken to us!

We jumped out of bed. He hid.

Catastrophe's reluctance to join the household continues, but all's well in the end, even if, in the course of his burgeoning self-confidence, he does, among other things, teach Calamity how to rip up the stair carpet.

'And finally,' Charles concludes 'if you do happen to find yourself with a Siamese trapped under the bathroom floor, try reading it *The Three Little Pigs* – they seem to like it.'

And the final word from friends on the subject of moving

house and cats comes in these extracts from Karin Slaughter, who rather spectacularly decided on impulse, just driving round after shopping one day, that the house in front of her was the one she wanted; she fell in love with it and went for it and, hey presto, the big move was on!

From:	Karin
To:	Marilyn and Michael
Subject:	Hey, y'all!

```
The cats are getting settled into the new
house, though Pete has been hiding in the
master bedroom closet a lot. Workers have
still been in and out and he's a scaredy
cat, as you know. Sophie has been the real
problem. We have a motion detector switch on
one of the downstairs lights by the garage
entrance and she keeps walking back and
forth, swishing her tail, running down the
batteries. I swear she is doing it on
purpose, and it was so scary the first night
when she did it because I thought someone
had turned on the light so they could come
up the stairs and rape us!
   Love K xx
```

So I conclude from all of this that moving cats is definitely not a good thing in the short term, however good it may turn out to be in the long term. And I have learned – oh, *how* I have learned – never, for whatever reason, attempt to move with your cats into an empty house and then continue to live in it, with them, while it remains empty. No, Sir!

CHAPTER 16

We have served our sentence, and for all manner of reasons the time has come to return to the South. John has now returned to his parish in Scotland following his hard-earned and, in the event, hard-working holiday, but, remarkably, because he still has a little holiday in hand, he offers to come back to toil some more when next we are in residence at the Coach House.

A couple of days after John's departure, Michael and I both drive off south in our separate cars and yet again I take the cats in mine. Pushkin buries himself deep in the car and I am unable to see or hear him, but sadly I can smell him, as he is quite ill on this return journey. Fannie complains loudly on and off at different points in the journey, and walks up and down the back of the car like a caged tiger. Titus just groans a bit and tries to sleep. On our entry into Moon Cottage, however, something astonishing happens. I lift Pushkin, shivering and shaking, out of the car, from deep under the blankets and a towel where he has been hiding, partially encrusted in his own excretions because he was too scared to move when he was ill, and I gently place him on the sitting room floor just inside the front door.

To begin with he just sits down and does some frantic grooming, but as I watch him, having addressed his

immediate needs, he turns his head around and sniffs the air. He stands up and stretches – tall and proud – and then trots, with unmistakable delight, through to the dining room, into the kitchen, and even out into the yard. I hold the door open and he races back inside and, as I follow with bags from the car, he bounds upstairs leaping joyfully two stairs at a time, straight into our bedroom and up on to the bed. He sniffs around and then off he hurtles downstairs again. He is holding his head high, and whacking his tail forcefully back and forth, which is what he does when all's right with the world. Titus, who is standing in the kitchen waiting impatiently for food to appear and who is travel worn and on edge, looks aghast as she is knocked sideways by a full jubilant head butt from Pushkin. I am taken aback. I didn't expect such an extraordinary transformation. Of course, I hoped he would be happier now in familiar territory with all the furniture and the hiding places and the things he loves around him, but I didn't expect his gratification to be *instant*. It somehow makes me feel even more remorseful. Titus and Fannie too, as soon as they have refuelled, are clearly happy and at ease to be back in the house where they were in fact born, but their apparent appreciation of it seems more modulated, but then I reckon that they *didn't* hate the Coach House; they were just slightly on edge there.

We have come back to pack up everything for the big move, the real thing, for our future life in Cumbria, and to make sure that everything is in order for the rent or sale of the cottage, as it is on the market for both, but before we embark on that there is a great treat in store for me.

I am accompanying my friend Sue to collect a long-awaited Devon Rex girl from her breeder Heather Boucher* in Swanley. We arrive at Heather's place and I cannot believe the kitten feast that greets us inside the house. There are, it seems to me, Devon Rex kittens everywhere we look; they are lying in heaps, in piles, stretched out, curled up, suckling, purring, playing and rampaging. When I ask Heather about them she laughs and says one of her friends comes round regularly just for a breath of what she calls 'Devon Heaven'. The girl, Georgie, whom Sue is about to whisk off home, is in colour not unlike Pushkin, a light smoky blue, but in looks she is her own creature completely. She has enormous bat-like ears and startling green eyes which seem to hold the eyes of whichever human is in front of her with unusual intensity – as with all Devon Rexes, she has a slightly other-worldly look to her and I fall completely and totally in love with her darling triangular face; the top of her head is the broadest wedge in the world, honing down to a tiny delicate pointed chin. She is rather dauntingly posh, I then discover, as her mother, who everybody calls Molly, is in reality Grand Champion Grizabella Ohbladi Ohblada. Molly is a beautiful black smoke colour with a jet-black triangular face. Georgie's dad is also a champ called Xenomorph Stuart Little, who, from his picture, I

---

* http://www.jonscottdevonrex.co.uk

judge to be a creamy apricot, but to my inexpert eyes Georgie takes after her mother.

Heather says that there are usually two batches of Devon Rex kittens a year 'available for sale to people with nerves of steel and no valuable antiques'. Sue has long tried to convert me to the heaven of 'Devon', but I have resisted because they are so alert and hyperactive and I am simply not sure I am up to the challenge of it, but today, just today, I waver. Eventually we tear ourselves away and make the journey home to deliver Georgie to her new quarters where she is to meet for the first time her new live-in companions.

The first she meets as she enters the door is young Max, a handsome neutered tom Si-Rex, cream in colour with darker points, who is now coming up to five years old. He takes one look at her and runs. And then her next introduction is to the two venerable old ladies, Siamese siblings, called Chatto and Johnny, who are now twenty years old.

Sue deliciously calls all her cats after the names of publishers who have always had a certain literary brio, so she has had in her stable Spotti* (Eyre & Spottiswoode), Norah (Smallwood and, in a feline context, the mother of Chatto and Johnny, but not in the world of publishing!), Chatto (& Windus), Jonathan (Cape), Max (Reinhardt), and now Georgie (George Weidenfeld). As one who calls my best ginger girl Titus, I can only applaud Sue's complete disregard for the niceties of gender. While I am there, the two 'maiden aunts' initially seem to accept Georgie with a philosophical resignation that I recognise as the way of the older cat. After watching the adorable Georgie settle in quite happily, I quietly sneak off back to Moon Cottage to let Sue have that all-important bonding session with her feline family.

---

* And before I knew her, a cat called Eyre too.

The following are edited updates on Georgie:

From:	Sue
To:	Marilyn
Sent:	Monday, 10 May, 17:31
Subject:	Re: Hello and Sunday

Marilyn

Well, day two, and at the moment she is conked out, rolled up in my T-shirt fast asleep. There have been some hefty play sessions today, none of the expensive cat toys of course, but a drinking straw and the perennial favourite, plastic packing tape. A favourite of Max as well, so he sort of joined in for a rather formal game. As she's dashing about, he keeps track and has done a fair amount of walloping, but equally, brave thing that she is, has biffed him back, they look like David and Goliath together, I must say. I think they are going to be friends, poor old Max misses all the fuss as the previous baby of the house, so I have been praising him like mad when he's been playing with her.

There was a bit of awkwardness going to bed. I left the hall light on to avoid any collisions in the dark, Johnny and Chatto had possession of the bed, and were hissing fit to bust as she gamely tried to climb up too, but they gave up in disgust and she spent the night under the duvet.

Otherwise it has got less fraught, they are not arguing among themselves much at all, and haven't turned their collective backs on me either, which is a good sign.

That she has settled in so quickly is extraordinary, she seems little fazed by all the spitting and swearing and, at one time, when Johnny was sitting on the arm of the chair, hissing like a steam engine, she just fell asleep. As you saw, she is such a loving little thing, with a lovely vocabulary of chirrups and tiny mews, hisses and growlings. Quite gorgeous and I waste endless amounts of time just watching and playing with her and trying to get her to stop tap-dancing on the keyboard.

Anyway, gone on too long altogether!
See you soon.
Love Sue

And then I receive this further update from Sue in the form of a letter, enclosing wonderful photos of Georgie.

Tunbridge Wells, 24 June

Dear Marilyn

Georgie is on my lap at the moment, on her back, playing with the telephone wire. She is rather damp round the nether regions, having fallen in the bath earlier, but my presence in the bath spared her full immersion. Her appetite continues unabated, she is so like that lamb on *Wallace and Gromit*. I am able to feed her all the varieties that make the others turn their noses up. This morning she had Swordfish in Mediterranean Sauce!

She is much brighter than the others. If you throw one of the paper balls down the back of the armchair, Max goes to the top of the chair and looks down mournfully, whereas Georgie takes a look, jumps down, and goes round the side and under the chair and gets it; quite a lot of brain processing for such a tiny creature. She is still an excellent retriever, and if in the middle of a game I get up and move around, there she is following behind with her piece of paper ready for it to be thrown again. This has had an effect on Max. He has started fetching things, which he rarely did before, other than his piece of string. But he doesn't follow through. Georgie's other favourite thing is bendy drinking straws, and again Max has started playing with those too. They are still playing around – having enormous play fights, which I pray won't turn nasty when she gets bigger. Even now he still seems to come off worse, his poor neck has grazes where she has biffed him.

Chatto [who has chronic kidney disease] has been back to the vet again. We tried another type of kidney food preparation and she won't eat that either, so, as agreed, I am feeding her tuna every day – she eats that and has put on weight again. It also seems to stimulate her interest in food and she eats more chicken and so on as well now, so a respite, hopefully. She's due for another test in two months' time, so we will see then, but it's a case of keeping as well as possible for as long as possible now.

And then a little later, after a small gap, I get the following emails:

Marilyn

We're all fine here, Chatto is carrying on, I am feeding her with whatever she wants; she has terrible poo problems, but with the aid of buckets of air freshener I put up with it; poor lamb, nothing can be done about that either apparently. Still her weight keeps on an even keel for now. As for Georgie, I am scarred all over, she is a leaper, up me, up the curtains, up anything really, but for me, having flesh, it is particularly painful and of course looks awful – as if I have been lashing myself with barbed wire; but she's so quick, the words 'George, don't do that', which should of course be intoned in the right Grenfellian manner, come too late. We play umpteen games of fetch the paper ball a day, and it is very cross-making (poor Georgie) when I am in the middle of work to see her come gambolling up with her paper ball in her mouth ready for a game or three. She is very loving at around 4 a.m., just when you don't want your chin and arms kneaded and drooled over, and my chest comes in useful as a perch when I am sitting reading. She's very smart and I love watching her work things out and learn from her mistakes. Poor Max still gets the worst of it, and he is becoming a bit of an Eeyore, very fatalistic and he is scratched as well! At the moment she is amusing herself playing with a ball in a great swathe of brown-paper packing material courtesy of Bloomsbury. And how she's grown, still fine boned and delicate, but her legs have ratcheted up, still too small to leap on the kitchen counter alas (which is where I, the human ladder, come in).

God damn it, Georgie just leapt on the keyboard and I've lost paragraphs...I can't remember what I wrote now, but I know I would love to see you and should be able to squeeze out some holiday soon. I am very envious [hearing from you about] the bird life surrounding your new house, I got excited yesterday just because I saw a sparrow and a butterfly and today a lapwing ... much love from the town!
  Sue

From:	Sue
To:	Marilyn
Sent:	Monday, 9 August, 20:12
Subject:	Re: Moon Cottage and the transition to the Coach House

Marilyn
  Am now less blood-stained as Georgie is just big enough to get on the kitchen counter unaided. First it was the fridge, then the sink, then the extra inch for the counter...I am healing nicely. Her fur is just getting long enough to start curling; she is so gorgeous to look at. I doubt if Rexes are any cleverer than other cats, I think they are just more curious and this leads them into more learning (and trouble). You can't do anything without her getting involved. I shall have to get her a clipboard ... so she can oversee things properly.

Hope you and Michael are well?
Love
Sue

And then, much later on, because both Sue and I have been submerged in work, so she never did make her holiday, I receive the following message:

From:	Sue
To:	Marilyn
Sent:	Tuesday, 19 October, 17:06
Subject:	Calamity

Marilyn
   Big turning point on Thursday, Georgie goes for her op [neutering] – will warn vet to put her first on the list or he will be driven to distraction by her wails at being ignored for more than two minutes. Like you, I was having fantasies about gorgeous little grey kittens but, as have promised not to and it is entirely unpractical, will trudge down the vets come Thursday. What a quiet day that's going to be, no typing three words and throwing a piece of paper, no trooping across the keyboard, no dive bombing, able to answer the telephone without interference, no spillages, no excavations of bin, no collapse of piles of manuscripts, I shall be down the vet's well before pick-up time suffering from withdrawal symptoms.
   All my love
   Sue

Georgie is fine, just had a chicken supper and is now chilling out on top of the computer, has left her stitches well alone and all is healing nicely; one or two spats with Max when I have feared for her wound, but no need for Casualty yet. We did have a drama on Sunday when, as per usual, she helped herself to some salad [she likes mayonnaise] and shortly afterwards starting wheezing like a grampus and gulping and snorting. Just as we were getting to the stage of having to get the vet out [late on a Sunday night] it all went away, so am presuming it was watercress or black pepper that set her off.

On Monday, however, Georgie and Johnny were stretched out on the mantelpiece (my having obligingly moved the clock, candlesticks, etc. up one end, so symmetry not to be found here), and Johnny stretched and by accident kicked Georgie, who was fast asleep, sending her crashing down on to the coffee table, where there was an ashtray, full glass of water, etc. Less worried about the mess than the cat with only three lives left, but she seemed fine and was soon as perky as ever and no glass broken, thank heavens. Am also now having to forsake wicker waste bins for horrid plastic ones with lids due to the activities of the bin raider, and as for artistic piles of loo-rolls – all disembowelled; loo looked like I had had an internal blizzard this morning.

Can only hope your cat population is

better behaved, and as for breeds, still can't tempt you with a Rex?
    Love Sue

CHAPTER 17

We start the preparations in earnest for the move, and we have asked the removal company to pack us up as we lack both time and space and also, truth to tell, I just can't face it! The plan of action is that Michael starts sorting out at the Moon Cottage end, while I return to Hutton Roof to get as much painting and decorating done as possible before the furniture comes in; Michael will commute back and forth, but this time we will leave the cats in Moon Cottage. Johnny has now moved back into Moon Cottage in order to get his things organised for his own move into his little cottage down the road, which is to happen at the same time as our move, so he has offered to do any requisite cat-sitting in the meantime.

Stephen is coming up to Hutton Roof to help us do all that we need to do, and it is agreed that he will be in charge of operations – any of us who are around will be his 'go-fers'. The big idea is that we finish stripping the paper off all the walls, make good the surfaces, and get the rooms painted before the carpets go down. Now, without the cats here, we are free to do any amount of hammering, sawing and other destructive manoeuvres that cats loathe, as well as being able to leave doors and windows wide open. So as Stephen comes up from the South, and John approaches down from the

North, the Coach House prepares to rock.

The reason we have embarked on the major redecoration is that as we strip off the initial wallpaper, Stephen, our decorating mentor, explains to us that we mustn't just slap paint over the old paper underneath, as it will simply peel off again within a year. This will almost certainly be why every room has been papered over and over again by successive owners (because the painting option was too problematic) and now the stripping-down becomes almost archaeological as the papers get older and stranger in colour and texture. The house slowly begins to reveal to us a small hint of its history as we delve into its many skins. To begin with, the house, in all its parts, had an elegant, feminine feel to it. But, as we strip back the walls in the older part of it – the original coach house – the combination of dark colours that emerge in those rooms suggests that successive masculine hands have been at work. As we labour in our separate rooms, on our allotted projects, we each get to know the house and its character more intimately.

For the first few nights John is with us, but when his 'holiday' runs out he has to return to Scotland. Each weekend Michael comes up, and in between times it is just Stephen and me. Stephen, in a uniquely tactful way, is a hard taskmaster, and he himself works astoundingly long hours, so there are many nights when he doesn't knock off until midnight. Each night, around 10 p.m., we 'open the bar' – which means uncorking a bottle of wine or opening up a bottle of beer – and that is when we wind down and talk.

One evening Stephen, who is a smoker, goes out into the garden for his ciggie and when he comes back inside he observes casually:

'That's a really lovely cat that was sitting up on the wall, and he looks really big.'

'What cat, Stephen? I never saw him.'

'Come on, you'll see.' Michael and I go rushing out, but he has run off. But later on that night, Michael sees him too.

'What does he look like?' I plead.

'He is mainly black in the body, but he has a white face and white front and white paws. He's a stunner.'

'Why do you keep saying "he"? Could be "she" just as easily.'

'No, not that large, definitely "he"!' Michael insists. I keep looking out for 'their' cat, but I fail to see him.

My role develops, by default, as that of chief cook and bottle washer, acquirer of paint, brushes, sandpaper, sealant, tiles, trim, turpentine, dustsheets, ladders, etc., and part-time scraper, sander and painter. The clock, of course, is ticking against us, as the time approaches for the great move. Stephen, in particular, works longer and longer hours and, by dint of sheer graft, the 'to do' list is showing an encouraging array of ticks. On the very last night, Stephen and I carry on painting, almost frenziedly, in order to get as much done as possible and it is well past midnight when I finally persuade him to put down his brush and eat some food. In the spirit of a job well done, we open another bottle after that first bottle, and start to put the world to rights – leaving only the smallest pebbles unturned. I go out into the conservatory to use the lavatory, and as I glance through the window I see a violet streak of light arcing across the sky, which momentarily puzzles me, but as I open the door I hear a couple of tentative trills of birdsong and I leap back inside and call Stephen out.

As he joins me outside, the two or three bird voices have now increased to at least five or six, and then suddenly they have multiplied tenfold into the full-blooded glorious but (if you have not yet gone to bed) terrifying sound of the *dawn* chorus. As we walk across the garden to the hedge on the far side and look out over the dark majestic hills of Yorkshire still enfolded in the shadow of night, the violet streak grows in front of our eyes into a broad pink glow which dramatically silhouettes the hills and, as we watch, transfixed, the sun climbs slowly up the sky, turning everything it touches into pure gold. It is a perfect sunrise. My eyes fill with tears and I feel a pleasure so intense that it makes my chest tighten in pain, but fortunately just at that moment Stephen starts to tell me something really important in a worryingly loud voice, and my doubtless misplaced fear that we will awaken our newly acquired neighbours (their house is, after all, several hundred feet away) at this antisocial hour obliterates all else as I try to shut him up. He misunderstands what is concerning me and I don't want to speak loudly, so instead, attempting to muffle our by now hysterical laughter, I hastily shepherd us back into the house where, exhausted, we retire to our beds to get what sleep we might.

The following day Stephen kindly volunteers to finish clearing up and closing down the house behind me while I drive off to Michael's farewell-from-the-office party in London – and what a send-off that is. People from the whole of his working life, some of whom he has not seen for many a year, come to that party. He will be much missed, and I am proud for him that he now truly begins to know just how much. Michael and I get back to Moon Cottage late that night, and from then on we find ourselves running on yet another 'to do' treadmill that is moving ever faster. The move is to take place over five days – two packing, one loading, one driving, and one unloading at the other end.

Although I try to keep the cats contained and out of the way as much as possible, it is quite evident to all three of them that *bad things are happening*. Strange men with large boxes and endless wrapping paper keep coming and going and it does not bode well, and of course I feel guilty because I can't explain what's going on. In the end the packing takes three days, and on our last day all three of us go into the garden and say our farewells, but in a rather rushed way, and because the cottage is not yet sold, we know that we, if not the cats, will be back again.

On the third day, Moon Cottage is finally completely empty but for a small sofabed that no one wanted in the sitting room, and Johnny and his friend, Al, who is lodging with him and therefore helping to pay off some of the mortgage on his cottage, lie on it like replete Roman emperors in a mock debauched farewell to see us off. They have already moved themselves into their cottage and are smugly grinning as they know what lies ahead of us on a more epic scale. Michael, who is one big softie, gets tearful and we all have to be very jolly indeed to stop him having a big old blub. (We had had an emotional farewell dinner with Johnny earlier in the week, at which we had all repeatedly reassured ourselves that all three boys, Johnny, Ollie and Damian, would be making regular visits to Cumbria and that we were not going to a remote inaccessible island that no one had ever heard of, and all of them would be coming up and down like yo-yos.)

Right in the middle of our huge 'joviality', the doorbell goes and it is a man from the depot opposite with a bottle of champagne scrunched up in a Tesco's bag to say they will all miss us; emotionally, this really is the terminal straw on the poor old camel's back as it is so completely unexpected. Shirley and Stephen and Karen and Mark had all come round and wished us a proper farewell a couple of nights earlier and that was painfully sad, as it was when we said goodbye to Eve and John from nearby Stocker's Lock, which is where Beetle, the brother of Fannie and Titus, lives too. It was pretty terrible saying goodbye to Father Jim, the priest who received me into the Catholic Church and who, together with John, Michael's brother, solemnised the marriage between Michael and me, and whom I adore (although he never lets you tell him that), and also the community within the church who have been so welcoming. The combination of all of these things makes us wonder why we are doing it all, and then suddenly it is all over and we are off; we pile the cats into the back of my car (of course!), and all the luggage and heavy stuff into Michael's car, and off we set.

When we arrive at the Coach House I reckon that the one room that is likely to remain off limits to the removal men will be the bathroom with the Juliet balcony, and so I collect together all the cat bedding and the food and water and cat litter trays, together with the three cats, and shut them all in there and pray. There is a small wardrobe in the bathroom and instantly Pushkin wriggles himself under the blanket on the floor of the wardrobe and doesn't budge, but as it is dry and clean and warm – unlike his hole under the stairs or, worse still, the pipes behind the sink – I leave him be. Fannie, predictably, jumps up on to the top of the wardrobe, so I find a small duvet and fold it up as bedding for her, and from here she surveys her small tiled empire. Titus looks around resignedly and, sighing, flops down on to her duvet cushion on the floor. And for the moment that is where they rest.

After the removal men finally clang shut the rear ramps of their two huge wagons and depart, Michael and I look at each other and groan. It is wonderful that they pack you up, but of course they can't unpack you; and when they have packed you, even though they write 'kitchen' on the box, it isn't necessarily certain that you would want all your bathroom gear in the kitchen, so opening each box is something of a lottery. The whole house, with the exception of the bathroom with the cats in it, is a wall-to-wall mountain of boxes and bags and cases.

'Remind me *never, ever* to move house again!' Michael says as he stoically sets about unpacking. He is tireless and shames me as I give up too easily, but between us the house begins to take shape and look like home surprisingly quickly, although in truth it is weeks before we get the final packing case open. I leave the cats in the bathroom overnight, but Michael and I, who are at this stage sleeping on a mattress on the floor of the adjoining bedroom, are well within earshot and they stay still and calm, surprisingly, the whole night through. In the morning we open the bathroom door and let them free. Fannie and Titus come out and are overjoyed to find the familiar furniture with all their smells on it, but Pushkin will not budge. For the next few hours I keep hearing Fannie and Titus scratching every single bit of furniture they can find as they do their territorial marking, and they jump up and down off every sofa, every packing case; we have mattresses propped up at weird angles, and if they can find a nook and cranny to hide within and spring out at each other, then they do. Fannie in particular, even though a fully adult matron now, is a liability. She loves getting into things. Plastic bags with duvets rolled up are her favourite, but anything resembling them will do. Both the girls are nervous and jumpy, and if either of us drops anything in the epic unpacking they instantly run for cover, but they are also curious and the presence of familiar furniture makes such a difference.

For five days now I haven't been able to get Pushkin to move out of the bathroom; I carry him out, but he simply slinks on his stomach straight back in again. I had talked to Margot earlier about the pheromone that Jacqueline had mentioned in her email, and Margot now tells me that she used a dog pheromone for Snowy, her Westie, when they moved into their new house. It had helped, and she urges me to get some. I am not yet registered with a local vet, so she kindly offers to get some from her own vet.

Seven days after we have moved, the cat pheromone arrives in the post. The magical elixir is called Feliway and it arrives complete with an electric diffuser. In other words, it comes with a plug-in contraption, rather like one of those mosquito repellents or air fresheners, and the significant ingredient within it appears to be 'a synthetic analogue of the F3 fraction of feline facial pheromone', which apparently has a calming effect on stressed cats. But the extraordinary thing is – it does! It works. I cannot believe it, but it really does work. I plug it into the bathroom and two days later Pushkin decides he is feeling brave enough to venture downstairs. He comes down, blinking a little, and looks around him. He climbs on a few things and then jumps down again and rubs his cheeks against everything in sight, repeatedly and as high as possible. It is as if he has been in a deep sleep and now he has at last awoken. For several days past I have been letting Titus and Fannie out into the garden, and Michael, by gently throwing fir cones at them when he wants them to come back inside, has 'trained' them to come in on the shout of a bellowed couple of 'In, In'.

When Pushkin comes down, the front door is open and he can see that the girls are outside, and to my delight he tiptoes out and nervously joins them. He sits down and looks all around him, in wonder. Just then a tractor comes up the hill; he panics at the noise and runs back inside, but it is a wonderful start all the same. I leave the Feliway plugged into the bathroom for several more weeks, but eventually I feel it has done its job and unplug it. Pushkin has now properly joined the rest of the household and our new life can begin.

CHAPTER 18

While all this has been going on my brother-in-law, Rod, in America, has been dying, and my sister, Judy, has bravely and stoically nursed him at home for the entire span of his illness, with only the briefest interludes of hospitalisation. It is now evident, though, that he will not live for very much longer. Their children, Mark, Claire and Emma, are at home with Judy and Rod, as it is Rod's wish that home is where he would prefer to die. Margot, my other sister, has flown out to be with them, and although I long to go, Judy feels she has more than enough on her plate with all that is going on without another body filling up the place.

Very soon after Margot has left, however, I get the expected news that Rod has died; so I fly out to Texas for the funeral, leaving Michael at home to cat-sit. One of the hardest things in the world is watching loved family members suffering grief. There is something so wretched about the sight of broken hearts, and there is so little that can be done to mend them; and time, most cruelly, takes its *time*. None of them has a cat either, and I believe cats help so much when you are hurting.

Meanwhile, the news from Moon Cottage – or, more to the point, the absence of news from Moon Cottage – begins to ring alarm bells. In May, the Governor of the Bank of

England had issued a statement urging people not to invest their money in property and it had an immediate effect on the house market, slowing it right down. Now, in June, the Bank of England has raised interest rates, which of course has a knock-on effect on mortgage rates, and the market in the south of England just goes static. We have not had any more viewings, so we change agents. When we are *still* without viewings, I begin to fear exactly what this might mean long term.

One morning, soon after I get back from America, Michael and I sit down at the Coach House and have a conversation that even two weeks ago I would not have believed possible.

'If this goes on, you do realise that we will have to try and sell up here and go back down.'

'Michael, you cannot mean this. Not after all that we have done up here!'

'I don't want this any more than you, but we simply don't have the money to go on, and we must rent or sell one or the other.' We both look out of the window at paradise, then at each other, and the overwhelming sense of sorrow is terrible. Shortly after this, Geoffrey comes to visit us and his response is: 'Listen, in a crisis keep your eye on the big picture; this house is the big picture, believe me.' Michael and I hold on to his words like a life raft.

Midsummer's day has just passed and it is raining fit to bust. Tonight we have lit a fire, although Michael complains it is far too warm for fires – which it probably is. The time is eight minutes past eleven and it is still glowing light in the garden; there is a raucous blackbird on the telephone wire outside with a long worm in its beak, tail flicking and wings flapping, going 'chink . . . chink . . . chink . . .' on and on and on. And soon that noisy pair of tawny owls will start. All night long they make their hunting calls, not so much the hoo-oo-oo-oo that everyone associates with them, but more raucously 'kee-wick, kee-wick, kee-wick' as persistently as the male blackbird has just been making his chink-chink sound. Annabel tells me that they are teaching their young to hunt, and in fact I now remember that owlets leave the nest long before they can fly and the parents spend long hours at night time feeding them up; and from the sound of it, they are about five yards outside our bedroom window.

This place is astonishingly rich in the variety of its birdlife; it is like nowhere I have ever lived. It is bird paradise right here with our tiny private forest of seven Scots pines and then the big woodland behind going up to the crags. It is as if we have landed on a desert island where no predator has ever been experienced. The birds come so close to us, they seem truly fearless. They group round the numerous feeders in the garden and come right up to the windowsills and peck at the windows with astounding bravura. Today in response to a new seed that I have just put out, there were numerous visits from several chaffinches, one crossbill showed himself, but not at the seed, up in the Scots pines, two greenfinches, four goldfinches, one chiffchaff or willow warbler (cannot tell the difference), and for the first time in my life knowingly I saw a yellowhammer. He came right up to my window and apparently winked at me. Earlier today I had had my first close-up of a great spotted woodpecker, and the richness of the colouring of the white and the scarlet was truly stunning. He banked at the feeding table, seemed to grab a beak full of seed, and shot off like a Red Arrow.

Although the cats were in the study with me, the two girls were asleep on the armchair behind me and missed it all, and Pushkin was in his posh bed under the chair, which is where he now seems to live. A permanent birdlife feature is the gathering around the hanging nuts and the giant fat balls, which regularly includes great tits, bluetits, coal tits and, wonderfully – as I have never seen them before – long-tailed tits, which is quite a turn-out. We have a pair of collared doves who sit on the wires outside my study window, day after day, and recently Michael found a fledgling, not obviously wounded, but certainly grounded, under a bush in our garden. We carefully moved it to a field across the road, so that none of the cats would find it, but today Michael made me follow him up the road.

'Look down there!' he points at the road.

'What? I can't see anything.'

'Yes you can – look closer.' And as I bend down I suddenly realise that horribly, almost like an X-ray, there is etched in the tarmac a perfect profile of a flat miniature-collared dove, so the little fledgling clearly got tractored.

Titus has started to be sick on a fairly regular basis and today she was sick several times. Michael and I have a mild spat about how many sicks ago each of us cleaned up, which results in the immortal assertion from Michael:

'The last time you cleaned it up, it was at least six sicks ago, I know it was!' So, quite rightly, I set to. I think it is pure greed on Titus's part rather than an illness, but, just in case, I take her down to our local vet, where I see Gerard, who is very charming and helpful. In fact, I take all three cats as they are due their injections. Gerard examines them all and I tell him about Titus's history with her dislocating knees. He thinks I probably should have her neutered, and I agree, although he understands that I would still like to have one litter from Fannie; he is surprised that no local toms have come a-calling. He is, as are all the other vets with whom I have discussed it, surprised that Pushkin has not performed, but presumes it is the multi-cat environment that is putting him off. He now thoroughly examines Titus and reckons she is not ailing, but suggests I use a special food for sensitive stomachs. When I try feeding it to her, though, she won't eat it; so we carry on with her usual food, Hill's, and with her being intermittently sick. Is feline bulimia a possibility, I wonder to myself, not entirely seriously?

Titus and Fannie both go out into the garden more regularly and stay out for longer. Titus goes into the field behind and spends hours eating grass, which no doubt adds to the likelihood of her being sick, and Fannie climbs the garden shed and sits on the roof, although she is nervous if left out in the garden for too long. Pushkin, although he goes out, never stays out long and the moment he hears any vehicle coming up the road he leaps inside again. He is now sleeping regularly on the chair in my study, which has hitherto been the terrain of the girls, so there is a bit of a territorial battle going on here. Cats and their chosen resting places are a mystery. One place will remain a favourite for a long time and then suddenly, for no apparent reason, it goes out of favour and an alternative snoozing place is found. And because another cat might take the place that has been vacated, the explanation cannot simply be that now it is, say, suddenly draughty.

As each day goes by, all three cats are more visibly relaxed, and are moving further afield as they go out, so I live in permanent fear of the road. The gate, which is now hung properly, does seem to be doing its job of deterrence, this in spite of Titus, who looks longingly through the bottom of it when she first comes out of the front door. Pushkin has, three times, jumped up and sat on top of it, in a frenzy of indecision as to whether to jump down into the road or not. Fannie's greatest area of vulnerability is the tall garden wall that is the shared boundary between us and the Old Vicarage next door, as that has twice been her chosen way of exit.

Having watched Titus, they have all started to go into the field at the back where they chew grass and then panic when they hear a dog either being walked by a nearby neighbour or playing with one of the campers. Fannie, as well as climbing the shed, also sometimes climbs up the trunk of the nearest of the seven Scots pines, but they are so very tall that she gives up at around twenty feet and backs down. Today she is very quietly and studiedly looking into the pond, and because none of the cats has yet made an attempt to kill either the fish or the frogs neither Michael nor I are paying it proper attention. There is suddenly a loud splash and I hear gales of laughter from Michael.

'So how was your first swim, Fannie? Good, eh?' I see Fannie streak wetly into the hallway and round into her favourite chair in the conservatory where she licks and licks until she is dry. Soon, within half an hour, Pushkin does the identical thing. Titus alone resists the temptation.

Thomas and Doreen, our Dales friends, come over for supper one evening, and although when we were house hunting they were lobbying for us to live nearer Wensleydale, they are very gracious about how utterly lovely it is in this long summer twilight on the Cumbrian side of the hills. Rather magnificently while they are here, the tawny owls sit obligingly on the telephone wires, making the odd swoop into the field opposite our window, and Doreen reckons that the owls make it the perfect evening. I subsequently discover, however, that an owlet was wounded and grounded down in the field opposite and it was rescued

by some local children. Ian, who owns the field, had to get the local wildfowl trust to take it away to their clinic where they hope to mend its broken wing. If it survives, then it will be brought back and released. Meanwhile, for two nights the parent owls make the most terrible fuss, as they 'grieve' for their little one and try to find it.

Oliver comes to stay for a few days and it is wonderful to see him. He is fit and well and I am struck at how handsome a young man he has become; although he was always an angelic-looking boy, he is now a blond athletic-looking six-footer. Michael, Ollie and I go for a walk up the crags behind us, which is quite a haul, but the view from up there is breathtaking. It is possible on a clear day to see way over into Yorkshire looking east, the mountains of the Lake District proper looking north, and Morecambe Bay looking west. The great Wainwright* says:

> All roads to Hutton Roof lead uphill and the village is well named, lying along an elevated slope with far-reaching panoramas across the valley of the Lune . . . the summit provides an outstanding distant prospect of range after range of mountain and fell to every point of the compass: a superb viewpoint.

---

* *Westmorland Heritage* by A. Wainwright (Frances Lincoln).

We walk and talk, but eventually decide that we should return home. Michael claims he wants to go the 'direct' route home but, because I know the crag consists of treacherous limestone pavements with steep hidden edges and the bracken is way taller than any man so it is impossible once you leave a path to see where you are going, I declare that I'm descending via a footpath. Ollie is torn, as he has to decide which one of us he should accompany on the return journey. On balance, he decides that Michael is the one who is being the most irresponsible so therefore he is the one who needs accompanying, so we part company and I duly find the footpath and climb back down to the village and up to the Coach House. When I get there I have no house key as Michael has it, so I sit down in the garden and wait. And wait. And wait. I can see the cats through the window, but have no way of getting in. Also, I am frantically thirsty.

Eventually, after a further three-quarters of an hour, I hear Michael's and Ollie's voices, so I hide behind a bush by the hedge. When they get to the front door Michael is concerned that there is no sign of me and I continue hiding for as long as I can spin it out although, rather disgracefully, I am childishly pleased that he sounds so worried. In the end, though, my own thirst and a wish to put him out of his distress make me reveal myself. They had had to retrace their steps back to the summit as Michael had indeed led them to a sheer precipice and there was no getting down it, it turned out.

Shortly after this, Stephen returns to finish the one outstanding decorating job, the kitchen. One of the things that happens this time, as Stephen works his way around the kitchen, is that he starts to fall in love. All his life he has been a dog man, and he and Shirley adore Dante, their huge black labrador, who is virtually the size of a small Shetland

pony; but Stephen has now become enraptured by the delicate girlie flirtatious charm of Fannie. Because Fannie has just that effect on me, I know full well how he feels. He becomes as keen as I am that she should have kittens to keep the line going and says he would love one. Sadly, he is allergic to cats, and when around them has to live on daily doses of antihistamines, so I am not sure it would work for him.

One evening as Michael, Stephen and I are all sitting in the garden quietly chatting, looking across at the awe-inspiring view, Stephen suddenly grips my arm:

'Look, look. Over there, there is the answer for Fannie.' As I look across I see a beautiful black and white cat perched on the top of the wall, watching us. He has penetrating green eyes and a jet-black crown and ears, a dramatic black eye mask, a white nose and muzzle, and a white bib and legs. He is lovely. He would be a wonderful father for Fannie's kittens.

'Do you really think he is a tom?'

'Well, one way to find out is to leave Fannie out all night?'

'Ah, now I couldn't do that.' I get up to go and stroke the black and white cat and to try to see if he is a full tom, but as I approach him he jumps off the gate and runs off down the road towards the village centre. We see this beautiful cat just once more before Stephen leaves.

For the remainder of his stay Stephen works away like a Trojan. This time it is tougher and takes longer, as he has no helpers – on this occasion I am frantically writing and Michael is busy selling books. When Stephen finally leaves the Coach House I have the distinct feeling that, if not before, then certainly now it contains some part of his essence, just as Moon Cottage does too.

Shortly after Stephen returns south, I notice that the pair of collared doves is no longer a pair but now only one. One of them had in fact gone lame and the one that remains is not at all lame, so I conclude it was the lame one that finally met its end. I am sure that this one is the parent of the flattened chick we found in June, and although I do not think doves are monogamous, as are swans, I reckon they are pretty loyal to each other. This solitary one sits on the electric wire that runs parallel to my window and its singular condition depresses me.

Shirley, Stephen's mother, widowed out of the blue less than two years ago, and still acutely missing her soul mate John, comes up to see us and it is wonderful to have her here and show her all that Stephen has done, and also for her to get a real break from school – where she works – and a change of scenery. As she and I are sitting out in the conservatory, the solitary collared dove lands on the wire opposite and I tell her what has happened. I can feel the power of her empathy for it.

Shirley is one of the most generous bighearted people I

have ever met, and it is wonderful to see her again and, as with Judy too, and many others, I ask that eternal question 'Why do bad things happen to good people?' While she is here she quickly develops a rapport with the three cats, even though I had hitherto got her down as a 'dog woman'. I often hear her calling Titus and Fannie and Pushkin with a real yearning. And Fannie and Titus both respond to her with warmth. (Pushkin remains wary, but he's Pushkin.) Every night that she is here, when she opens her door to go to the bathroom Fannie enters with her little whiney miaow in greeting.

Down at their cottage in Watford, Johnny and Alan suddenly find themselves looking after two kittens, who seem to have been abandoned. (This is an irony for Johnny as he has always claimed that he is a 'dog man', and swore that once he had his own place he would immediately get himself a dog; but he, like all Michael's sons, is truly an 'animal' lover.) The kittens are only about eight weeks old apiece when they are first adopted and are called Duggers and Hammy, after each of the boy's surnames, but Johnny, who is hopelessly biased and whose surname begins with D, texts me the following info: 'Duggers is the nice caring one, Hammy is always on the tiles, still talking cats too!' Duggers is entirely black, and Hammy has a little white pattern on his chest. They are very cute, and I reckon that they can only be good news for these two lads who are now living in what could be the perfect set-up for 'men behaving badly'; the cats may induce in them a sense of responsibility! These two small cats become significant to our cats in Hutton Roof after a quick trip I make to Moon Cottage, however, during which Johnny brings me a computer box which is a present for Michael, and I duly cart it back north with me.

One day shortly after I am back at Hutton Roof I am standing in Michael's study when I hear a quiet but

151

persistent hissing sound, like a very fine hydraulic hose, and as I turn round I see Pushkin just finishing spraying the bottom two shelves of Michael's signed first editions. I scream at him and he runs off quickly. To begin with I am mystified as he has never done this before and I cannot see any reason for it, but afterwards I realise that he was trying to hit the computer box and, being inexperienced, his aim is really bad. Michael reckons that Hammy and Duggers had each put their own marks on the box and Pushkin just felt compelled to cover it too. We both groan in fear that this is the beginning of a trend, but pray not!

CHAPTER 19

Most of July has been very wet and warm followed by an intensely hot and dry spell, which seems to have produced an unusual epidemic of wasps. It started even when Stephen was still with us and, as he hates them with a passion, his violent anti-wasp diatribes used to make me laugh. They were deliciously extreme.

Damian, Jo and baby Oskar come to stay and I am, as ever, utterly enchanted by Oskar. He is the sweetest-natured baby in the world; he almost never cries and he gurgles and laughs endlessly. Jo and Damian are both remarkably good parents and Damian has a real talent for calming Oskar and comforting him; and it is really nice to see how much he does towards the overall care of his small son. I am also moved at what a superb granddad Michael is.

I am concerned that all should be well for Oskar during his stay at the Coach House, being mindful that Damian and Jo are first-time parents and so might naturally be expected to be more apprehensive for their baby's safety than would be more seasoned baby-makers. So it's with some dismay that on the morning after their first night of this visit, I hear Damian calmly announcing:

'I just thought you should know that I have shut our bedroom window because the room was getting full of bees and Oskar is up there asleep at the moment.'

'When you say "full", do you mean just a couple?'

'No, I mean "full"; that is to say, there were lots. I didn't exactly count them – I just got rid of them and shut the window.' I look across at Michael, but he isn't paying any attention, so I go outside. To my horror, as I look up over the roof of the conservatory towards the room that Oskar is sleeping in, I see a hoard of bees flying distractedly in the air. It is hard to estimate the number, but well over fifty, probably closer to a hundred, and even to my inexpert eye they are clearly agitated. I rush inside and close all the windows and doors, but of course some have already got inside the house. Damian remains very calm and shrugs his shoulders. His view is if we simply keep everything shut, it will be fine. Michael and I go outside again and now we find that in the sloping roof vault over the downstairs lavatory, immediately under the tiles, there is a furious buzzing sound and bees are flying rapidly in and out. The number now looks greater.

'I reckon we've got a swarm, you know,' I anguish. Michael says:

'Don't worry, I'll go and get Richard.' We know that Richard and Annabel have newly taken to keeping bees and have several active hives. Richard comes and looks at the offending crack in the wall where they have been flying in and out, but there are not many to be seen now as they are all inside busy buzzing.

'They are probably all in there fanning the queen, as she will need to be kept cool,' he observes, matter-of-factly. He is uncertain that they are his bees, but I, on the other hand, am *absolutely* certain they are, because they are rather trim, pale-coloured bees and not like normal wild honey bees at all. I ask him about his bees and he says that his are partly Italian and are very hard workers, crossed with the

154

indigenous black bee. He then goes off to seek advice from an apiarist friend. Soon after he has left, Annabel comes across and has a look too; I say to her I think that they might be Richard's bees, and she laughs conspiratorially and says she is sure I could be right.

I now spend hours on the phone trying to find a pest control person to come and destroy the bees and discover, when I can get through, which isn't often, that every pest controller within a radius of fifty miles is busy destroying wasps' nests. It has indeed been a season of wasp fecundity and every supermarket within miles has sold out of wasp-killer. When I eventually speak to a man from Environmental Health I discover that it is just as well for Richard's sake that I did not find any wasp-killer as the bees, who were probably a small breakaway group with a young surplus queen from Richard's hives, might have taken the poison back to the parent hive and killed the lot. The man gives me the name of a bee specialist who promises to come out in three days' time.

'*Three days*, but we can't breathe and all the windows are shut and the doors!'

'Really sorry, but I've never known a season like it for wasps, it is phenomenal; but if you make a lot of noise inside the area where they are they may move off – they may only be resting there!' I start to use the washing machine and put on the tumble drier in the little room that is immediately below the space where the bees are nesting, and we spend the rest of the day when we are in the house behind closed doors and windows.

That evening Richard reappears wanting an update on the bees, and as he and I stand outside the little window of the lavatory we discover, to my huge relief, that they seem to have gone. The following morning there is not a bee in sight, other than the normal bumble bees going about their daily business, so either they didn't like the heat or noise of a tumble drier, or they were indeed just resting while they made up their mind where to go. We never did know where they went, though.

Meanwhile Michael and I remain totally besotted with Oskar and spend hours drooling over him. The following day Jo and Damian lay him down on a blanket on the floor in the sitting room to kick his legs and as he gurgles away I carefully watch the cats. What is touching is that each of them in turn visits him and each very delicately smells the top of his head (why do babies' heads smell so wonderful?) and then quietly walks away. It makes me think of the reverencing of the Christ child by the shepherds and the wise men, and I recall with fondness that Christmas classic by Michael Foreman* in which the slightly sceptical cat never has the heart to catch a mouse again after his encounter with the 'shepherds with their bleating sheep, the rich men with their grumpy camels, even the man and the woman with their baby'. Eventually our little family of three wend their way back south, and we know with sadness (for us) that they will ultimately go to live in Sweden, which is where Jo's family live.

This is not, however, the case with Fannie sadly – lacking the heart to kill a mouse that is, not move to Sweden. Her personal kill-toll in her new environment stands at three adult fieldmice, one baby fieldmouse with its eyes still shut, one tiny adult vole (and this is not taking into account those that Michael has rescued and released), and today all three of them did for a small adult bluetit who was foolish enough to fly into the conservatory through the bottom of the cat grill. Pushkin has now, as a result, taken up the watch and is lolling on a chair by the open window waiting for more

---

* *Cat in the Manger* by Michael Foreman (Andersen Press, 2000).

'game' to come in. I think he thinks if he sits still long enough they will just fly into his mouth. In truth, given the number of birds we have here, one bluetit is a blessedly low death toll, but I am sorry that the cats are so fast off the ground with small mammals.

People in the village have been extraordinarily friendly and generous in the way they have welcomed us, and I feel guilty that we have not returned their hospitality; but for the moment we are battening down the hatches until we know where we stand with Moon Cottage. One of the many couples who have gone out of their way to welcome us are Ian and Elizabeth, who share their house with a beautiful tabby cat called Cathy, whom they otherwise call Little Puss. The one small thing I have been able to do for them in return, while they have been away in France, is to go down to their house every other day and give Cathy a tummy rub, a few strokes and a little companionship (although their immediate neighbours, Liz and Paul, are really looking after her).

Ian and Elizabeth are wonderful on the cat life, past and present, within the village of Hutton Roof. But on the here and now, I am curious to know why Little Puss is also called Cathy. Ian explains that there was a cat called Heathcliff, who everyone in the village reckoned belonged to them, although the couple who were properly his guardians were Ian and Cynthia. But anyway the real truth of it is that Heathcliff knew the village belonged to him, and this is simply how it was. Heathcliff, sometimes known as Liffy, was a big fluffy ginger cat with a white stomach and a punishing cry – 'wail, wail, wail' – which was usually rewarded by food or milk or other attention when he utilised it. One day, Heathcliff, mature lord-of-his-domain, turns up at Ian's and Elizabeth's door with a young female cat beside him (around five months old at this time they subsequently discover, but unusually tiny). Anyway, Heathcliff demands to come in, in his time-honoured fashion and, finding the door now open, in he trots escorting this young demure little creature. Without more ado, he takes her right round the cottage, downstairs, upstairs, almost no room is overlooked by the pair. Ian, as he is telling me this tale, is laughing:

'It was like "what's mine is yours, and this is one of mine" – he really was trying to impress her and he was doing a bloody good job, so as he was called Heathcliff, she had to be called Cathy.' And Cathy, naturally, interprets the whole thing as a formal invitation to join the household, so join it she does. She has a scar with stitches, so presumably she has been neutered recently by someone, but they never do find out who.

Heathcliff was in all sorts of ways a larger than life character, but not without soul. He had a really bad relationship with Hilary's cat at that time, one Toby, and the two of them used to have serious and recurring fights. Hilary and Phil live opposite Ian and Elizabeth, and it is Hilary who tells me this part of the tale. Toby became ill and eventually died. When he died, Hilary and Phil buried him in their garden near the side of the wall. She shows me where he is. To her amazement, and also Ian's too, who corroborates this story, Heathcliff sat on the wall staring down for hours at a time for three whole days following the death of his sparring partner, Toby. Who is to say whether it was grief, or triumph, or just plain missing?

Another remarkable story is illustrated by Peter Warner at the beginning of this chapter. In 1950 an aunt of Janet Bleay, who lives at a farm just across the field from the Coach House, bred Border Terriers in Otterburn in Northumberland, for which she had won many prizes, so each litter was highly coveted. Shortly before the photo that inspired Peter's sketch was taken, the bitch who had given birth to this litter had died, reason unknown, and Christabel, one of their house cats, who had herself just had a litter, had one kitten of her own remaining and so, doubtless full of her own maternal feelings and hearing the distress of the orphaned pups, she just crawled into the whelping box and suckled the pups herself, presumably in rotation.

CHAPTER 20

We have been letting all three cats out on a more regular basis and for longer chunks of time, but I find I remain very tense while the door remains open and they are outside. For a few days I had started to relax, feeling they were all calmly self-contained within the garden, until the morning dawned that sharply reminded me of their vulnerability. Titus likes to lie on the sun-warm tiles near the pond, with her tail slightly twitching, content enough to stay for long periods in that one spot. Pushkin regularly positions himself in a place nearby where he likes to sit, back hunched, under an overhang of delicate but abundant ornamental grasses – and there he will crouch peering out at the birds, for twenty minutes on end, not quite as invisibly as he would like to think I suspect. Fannie, however, is – or can be – the problem. Much of the time if Michael or I are out in the garden she will sit near one or other of us, on or close to the bench, or stand quietly chewing grass in the field that borders the kitchen window; but if we are not out in the garden, she is unpredictable. Whenever traffic can be heard approaching, especially something large and rattly like a tractor, or lorry, Pushkin invariably runs inside in fright. Fannie, too, can panic, but she is not pathologically frightened of the road as is Pushkin.

On the morning in question, Titus and Pushkin have adopted their regular positions and Fannie is nowhere in sight, but I am presuming she is round the back in the field, when suddenly we all hear a car approaching fast down the lane. Shortly after this, I hear a scratching at the foot of our gate and I see Pushkin and Titus both going towards it. The car is getting ever closer and suddenly Fannie leaps up on to the top of the gate, having been scrabbling around at the bottom. She then hesitates and turns to drop down again on the roadside of the gate as the car is upon us. I lunge at her back and grabbing a handful of her fur pull her inside. As I do this, I register, distantly, that both of us are squawking! Michael sees the tail end of this chain of events from his study window and registers my panic as I come in clutching Fannie in my arms. He shakes his head ruefully and shrugs.

In early September, Jean and Steve come to visit us in the course of their stay in the Yorkshire Dales. They have chosen a glorious sunny day with a strong breeze to come over, and we go for a walk with their gentle collie, Meg. She is the most unpredatory of dogs it is possible to imagine, and they amuse me with their tales of how all animals

recognise this softness in Meg. Sheep and cattle in particular will gather round her in a mildly threatening way, knowing that they are completely safe to behave thus. Meg avoids all eye contact with any other animal lest it should arouse a confrontation of any kind. Jean and Steve talk of their two cats, Portia and Nerissa (now there are two superb names to conjure with, given to them by their daughter Tamara while still high from a production of *The Merchant of Venice*), who are a pair of white British Shorthair siblings and who, as kittens, had been stepfathered by another collie – Meg's predecessor, who had become so close to them that he used to carry them around in his mouth and generally take complete care of them. As a result they would both catch live mice for Meg, as they had for her predecessor, and leave them as presents for her in her bed, which completely appalled her and from whom she had to be rescued.

~

Our perception of the weather in Cumbria since we have been here is that it has been pretty damned wet, while thankfully warm, with the odd spell of glorious summer sun, although from the beginning of July until now, early September, it has rained fairly solidly. However this morning, 4 September, Michael meets local farmer Alan in the village, who bemoans the lack of rain in May and says that they have been trying to catch up ever since. Alan looks across at Michael and solemnly intones:

> Dry April,
> Drop in May,
> To fill the barns
> With corn and hay.

Unfortunately, that drop in May just did not happen this year.

In the south of England many friends have been complaining of the nearly unbearable humidity, but up here in the Lakes it has been fresher and altogether more agreeable, although as wet as any summer I can remember. September began quite as wet as its predecessor, but today dawned as perfect as any summer's day could, cloudless and calm and smelling simply wonderful, and this followed three other days just like this. The nights now have a distinct autumn tang, and on these clear cloudless days even as early as 4.30 in the afternoon the temperature drops enough for me to sneak the heating on for just a quick boost, when Michael isn't looking – for every penny counts in our dire straits with the unsold Moon Cottage.

Another unexpected expense is the wild bird food. There are so many of them and they eat so much! There are an enormous number of tits, far higher than in the South, mainly of the great and blue variety, though with the odd coal tit and, more unusually, long-tailed tits showing up for good measure. It is these very tits that Richard, our neighbour from the Vicarage, refers to as 'fodder' for other predatory birds and mammals. These birds are certainly of a suicidal nature as they constantly fly into the windows of the conservatory, even though there are frames and transfers (of flying birds, ironically) on the panes of glass, intended to warn them off. Often they recover from these head-on collisions, but from time to time we find a dead tit amid the flowers under the window. No other birds have quite this tendency, it appears.

On the feeder on the windowsill outside my study window, in which I keep pine nut kernels, I am visited by a non-stop stream of juvenile chaffinches, with the chests of the males among them just beginning to 'pink' up. At other times, when it is quieter and the tits and chaffinches are away, I will be visited by one or two juvenile goldfinches whose very smart bright yellow and black-and-white tails are somewhat belied by the almost scruffy brown stripy backs and dowdy brown faces, missing the spectacular red and white that their parents sport on their heads. The juveniles seem to relish the pine kernels, whereas their parents prefer the small black niger seeds.

Other regular visitors to the pine kernel feeder are greenfinches and siskins, the females of which have the most beautiful streaked breasts; these two species tend to visit together, but not with any of the other regular visitors. The greenfinches in particular behave quite badly with each other near the feeder. A lot of jockeying for position goes on and sneaky little stabs with the beaks at the back of the bird in front seems *de rigueur*, and they are remarkably noisy with it all. I also get three (surprisingly, as they are strongly territorial) robins, who visit sometimes singly and sometimes as a trio, and one of whom regularly patrols along the roof in a menacing manner and bows up and down a great deal.

I am missing the nuthatches that came regularly throughout July and early August, so the question is where do all the nuthatches go in the late summer? That reminds me too that I have not seen the great spotted woodpeckers for an age either. New visitors to this garden, although Richard says they are regular to his, which is deeply lawned and flowerbedded in a way that ours is not, are blackbirds and song thrushes, and the reason for their incursion into our garden is in order to raid the mass of fleshy red berries that have formed in the last few weeks and are clearly at their peak of ripeness on the deeply poisonous yew tree which stands proudly outside my study window.

Three or four days ago I was aware of one blackbird

perching 'shotgun' on the tree, chink-chink-chinking in warning as only blackbirds can, trying to ward off all comers, although the effect of this was to encourage even more birds to come to the tree as far as I can see, as today there were no fewer than four blackbirds and two thrushes. What I do not understand is how the blackbirds and thrushes are able to eat these berries in such huge quantities and suffer no ill effects. I presume they do not digest the poisonous seed, but only its fleshy surround, and that the seed simply passes straight through their gut in a propagating sort of way, and that wherever it lands, if the soil is right there is a good chance that a new yew will grow there. Although this yew stands at around thirty feet high, which is about the same height as the pitch of our roof, it is completely dwarfed by the seven massive Scots pines towering over it at a daunting ninety feet. I love those pines, and there being seven in number I have named them Bashful, Doc, Dopey, Grumpy, Happy, Sleepy and Sneezy, but dwarves, of course, is what they're not.

CHAPTER 21

Michael and I drive down together to Moon Cottage and, once there, we inevitably talk with a charged intensity about why it hasn't sold.

'I'm sure it's because we haven't said goodbye to it properly, in some way. I know we have to bid our farewells in a sensitive way. Michael, do you remember Stephen saying to me that Moon Cottage will choose who lives in it? I believe he has a special feel for these things.'

'I don't disagree. We left without having sold it and we knew we were going to keep coming back, so it was difficult to say a formal farewell, but how do you suggest we do it?'

'Each of us has to do it in our own way. You do it alone when you want to and how you want to, and so will I.' As I say this, I feel a shaft of pain at the memory of how Michael and Johnny must have felt when they said goodbye to Septi that morning before the vet came for the last time, and this solitary act of taking one's leave of this cottage is, I now realise, a terribly important ritual that we have not hitherto properly observed. We need to ask the absolution of Moon Cottage for leaving it and also to thank it for protecting us and loving us and giving us so much happiness for so long.

There is a lot going on and I never do see how Michael says his goodbye, but I know as night follows day that he

does do it in some way of his own and, as I write this, my eyes fill with tears because we sometimes are so insensitive to the glaringly obvious – *of course* we have to make this act of contrition.

I remain in Moon Cottage after Michael returns north again as I have things to do in London, and I too know that I must take my proper leave of the cottage.

On my last morning, I prepare for it for a long time with a strange sense of reluctance and then finally go out into the garden and walk round and round it. I stop in front of Septi's grave for a long moment and say my final adieu to his spirit with the hope that as he is now physically only a skeleton, leaving his bones there is no disrespect to him. I then visit Otto's grave and talk to her for a long time – she, the quintessence of life and youth and freedom who, like so many young cats, under the conviction of invincibility flew across the road into a car and never survived; Otto, the mother of my adored Titus and Fannie, who themselves were never allowed to say their farewell to their birthplace.

'Goodbye, little elf. Fare you well, forgive me for leaving you and taking your two girls with me.'

I enter the cottage and lean against the dear thick walls that have stood there for over 450 years – I enter every room and in some way acknowledge the wattle and daub of it all. I go downstairs and reach up to touch the dark oak beams, first in the dining room and then in the sitting room. I put my fingers in the carvings round the huge antique fireplace and I make my act of emotional and verbal supplication to the cottage, and all that it is and all that it has been and all that it will be; to the many people who have made up its past and to the many people who are yet to live here – I hope so much that they will be as happy as we have been here.

Shortly after this, something happens that makes me feel my contrition has been acknowledged. I am bending over the lavatory bowl involved in a vigorous cleaning exercise, with potential vendors in mind, when I suddenly become aware, really strongly, of scented pipe smoke. As I inhale the fragrance of it, I stand up and remember the 'man who smokes a pipe on the landing' in Shirley's house. She and John always used to laugh at it; he was a benign 'visitor' whom they smelt, but who never physically manifested himself. I am ashamed to say I feel a brief frisson of apprehension as I stand up, still facing the wall.

'Please God, let me not see him. I love him being here, but I just don't want to lay eyes on him.'

With a supreme effort I turn my head around. There is nothing behind me. I walk slowly through the cottage and know that I must go upstairs. I ascend the steep staircase and, although fearful at first, as I climb I am uplifted by an extraordinary sense of well-being and my heart feels lightened. I go into all the bedrooms and I feel sheer happiness. Sunlight is streaming in through the bedroom windows and I notice, with a complete lack of concern, that the windowpanes could do with a clean.

'Ah well, next time, little cottage, next time,' I murmur, and this time, as I get into my car and drive away from the cottage towards the M40 and the northwest, I know that I am properly being allowed to drive to my new home and that I leave behind me Moon Cottage, intact and loved, holding safe all its memories. The cottage has at last said its farewell to us.

I get back to the Coach House to find that their ladyships are making much of what is possibly their last oestrus of the year – but blimey, what a kerfuffle. The house is resounding to both the incessant groans from Titus, who can keep it up for what seems like hours at a low rumbling persistent pitch, and the apparently involuntary but strident wails from Fannie, which are more spasmodic but quite deafening in their force. I confess that it really now is altogether too much and it is not only Pushkin who has a headache, but his human companions also. Both the female cats lie in wait for Pushkin, and in the case of Fannie this is the first time she has persistently presented herself to him; but although he kisses their noses with what seems like genuine affection, he continues to tiptoe round them and find places to rest where they will leave him in peace. Our sleep and the sleep of our guests is now regularly being interrupted. Indeed, last night it was so tremendous that I finally resorted to shutting Fannie, Titus and Pushkin in our bathroom, having added a cat litter tray and water. Finally I relented and got up and let Pushkin out, leaving the girls in where they stayed quiet until morning.

Fannie's calling is more ardent than I ever remember it. It usually starts at 1 a.m. and recurs in bursts throughout the hours of darkness, sometimes at the bottom of the stairwell leading up to our open-plan bedroom (oh for a door to just be able to shut her the other side), and sometimes at the bottom of the other stairwell leading up to the guest wing and my study (so when friends are staying overnight, I lie in bed listening to the distant sounds, rigid with guilt). I presume these positions are chosen for their acoustic virility. Michael swears that these strange guttural noises Fannie emits are beyond her control – it is true that if you look at her face and her body language when she is doing it, she appears to be quite unaware of it. The sound seems to come from deep within her and emerges as a harsh strident bass cry. It is quite different in tone from the plaintive high cry when she has been shut out and wants to come in, which becomes even shriller if it is raining. This call is primeval and dark and compelling, and why no neighbouring cats come to call can only be because, as everyone in the village assures me, there are no full toms around.

Pushkin is beginning to have a very hang-cat look about him as a result of Fannie's remorseless pursuit of him. She lies in wait for him at every opportunity and calls to him; she rolls on the floor in front of him and in every possible way tries to encourage him. This morning as I am putting down dried food for them I see him very mildly (almost experimentally?) grab Titus, who is busy eating and doing no one any harm, by the scruff of her neck; she immediately lets out a squawk of protest and drops the food in her mouth and strides off in high dudgeon, waving her tail crossly.

'Oh Pushkin, I despair of you. Wrong cat, wrong moment, wrong everything!' He looks up at me and then down again and eats another couple of mouthfuls of dried chicken. The expression on his face remains enigmatic.

'Michael, I am going to have to take them all to the vet. It's simply not fair on them all, this constant unending frustration. The girls are horny as hell and Pushkin is being harassed out of his existence and no one is gaining from this.'

'Hold your horses a moment, Mo. I'm going to talk to Anne at the post office, she'll know if there's anyone around. You know we would both love Fannie to have kittens.'

I duly hold my horses for this day at least and Michael

returns later on to tell me that although there are definitely no full tomcats in the village, there is a farm some distance away with the usual assortment of farm cats – which is likely to include at least one tom. The farm is in a village called Lupton and is owned by Alan and Margaret.

'Michael, you can't just ring them up and say "Oi, do you have a stud, please?"'

''Course I can,' he winks as he always does when he's on a roll, and I catch myself apprehensively running my hands through my hair. 'Anyway, there's nothing to stop you doing it if you prefer.'

'I'm doing no such thing.'

'In that case, there's nothing for it, I'll do it. It's now or never.'

'Oh Michael, we have to be so careful. He must be healthy and mustn't have any hateful diseases like feline leukaemia or one of those.'

'The important thing to establish at this stage is whether they have a tom at all, so let's cross that hurdle first.'

He walks across the room and picks up the phone and presses the buttons. I hear only his side of the conversation.

'Yes, that's right. I'm looking for a full tom. Oh good. How old is he. Ah . . . I see. Just a few weeks. No, that wouldn't do the trick. Yes, quite.'

I move across the room and, after more murmurings, I hear Michael begin to make goodbye noises laced with sentiments of gratitude. He pulls a face as he puts the phone down.

'They were really nice and he wanted to be as helpful as possible, but no can do. Not an adult full tom to be had, so now it's back to Plan B then.'

'What's Plan B?'

'The vet and neutering.'

This next night, for the first night in ages, Fannie hardly

calls at all, so at last her terrible torture of frustration is at an end.

This morning I received a rather moving letter from Marion Elliott, a reader of both my previous books. She had numerous cats, most of whom adopted her – in fact, all of whom did. Some of these cats were on the wild side, and some had wonderful protective natures and herded their fellow cats to safety – as Septi tried, but gave up, with the wayward Otto. However, Marion says of the death of Cosmic, her beloved and beautiful grey and white kitten with a loving nature who developed feline leukaemia:

> I have never been affected by the death of a cat so much. How my husband drove to the vet's with tears dripping down his face I will never know. We missed Cosmic so much that both Paul and I thought we 'saw' her several times after her death.

This happens. This happened to me and to Michael following the death of Otto. It might have happened to Michael after the death of Septi; certainly the kittens kept jumping around from corners and behaving most strangely immediately after he died, quite as if his spirit was in the cottage and coming to them in some way. And very soon after this, another reader of my books, Doreen Jackson, writes to me of one of her cats from long ago, called Timmy:

> Timmy was a bit of a stop-out at night and wouldn't come in however much we tried, but he knew if he stretched up and lifted the knocker with his paw and let it fall back hard enough my parents or I would get out of bed and go downstairs to let him in. No one taught him to do it, so it proves that cats use their brains.

CHAPTER 22

Peter Warner, the gifted artist who illustrates these books and who understands so well the idiosyncrasies of our three cats over the time he has worked with them, pays us his first visit to our Cumbrian eyrie. He is surprised to discover how ascendant Titus now is, manifesting full matriarchy within the pecking order of the cats, as the last time he met her she was about to have her leg operation and was in pain and unsteady, which must in turn have contributed to her lack of self-esteem. Fannie, at that time and indeed since the birth of all three kittens, had been the undisputed pack leader. These shifts of power are inscrutable and subtle, but the end results are very clear. I fear for Fannie, who within the new social structure seems to be unsure of how much she may come to me.

Titus spends much of the day on the chair behind me in my study and at regular intervals climbs on to my knee as I type. She is also newly proficient at leaping from a standing start near the door right up on to the desk, often crashing down on to the computer keyboard, a form of invasive behaviour she has learnt from Pushkin and something she could never have done pre-op. Fannie, who spent almost all day in my study/bedroom in the Moon Cottage days and who in the early weeks at our new house also spent much of the day in my study, will now visit me as little as twice a day. If during these visits Titus is at all assertive as Fannie is considering jumping up on to my lap, Fannie backs right off and immediately leaves the room. She spends much of the time on the bed in the next-door spare room or in an armchair in the conservatory. I feel a pang of guilt towards the other two cats as I recognise the sharp intensity of my own sense of loss within Fannie's affections for me, but equally I remain unsure whether her aloofness is her own uncertainty of what she 'may' do rather than a cooling-off.

For the record, as a rule Pushkin visits my study once a day, usually late in the afternoon, exactly as he did at Moon Cottage, so no change there. He too leaps up on to the desk from the doorway, but he is less clumsy than Titus, so he rarely scatters things around. His foible is that if his visit coincides with my absence from the study he will elegantly sprawl out across the keyboard; but in the course of turning round several times to make sure he finds the warmest and most comfortable position a key-board can offer, he regularly reprogrammes my computer, and I have learned the hard way to always refuse changes to my 'normal dot'!

I am in awe at the care that Peter Warner takes to make his fluid sketches of the cats. He is able to capture on paper the essence of cat in the most remarkable way. He is astonishingly self-disciplined and will never allow me to gather up and corral the cats in any way to make it easier for him to draw them. He always sketches them where they choose to lie and I have only ever heard him curse under his breath once, when yet again they decide that being stared at with quite this intensity is frankly just too much and they have suddenly thought of a darker, more private place to lie; or, more often than not, the thought of a quick snack crosses their minds, and they shake, turn, stretch and hop down for a quick 'pit-stop'. I conclude that cats like to watch, but do not like the process to be reversed.

One night, after work for that day has stopped, Peter enraptures me with an account of a cat of his called Pelé. Peter, being the all-rounder that he is, can number among his accomplishments the art of music-making, as well as that of writer and artist. Peter is a jazzman as much as he is a classicist, and many of his cats have been named after jazz musicians. His cat Django (Reinhardt) stood in as a model when he was illustrating the first book* and he needed an older feline statesman to represent Michael's ancient cat, Septi. Django died just days after the book was published, having posed for numerous press photos, and even his first (and last) television appearance around the time of the publication of that book.

So this tale from Peter starts with a cat called Bix (Beiderbecke). Well, actually it really starts with a Great Dane called Nora, who has been used, unscrupulously for five years, as a breeding machine. The rescue is complex and involves Nora disappearing into the large garden where she hides in the middle of a patch of stinging nettles. Here she remains resisting all entreaties to come out. Finally, she is

---

* *The Cats of Moon Cottage* by Marilyn Edwards (Hodder & Stoughton, 2003).

tempted out by a bowl of milk a few days later, and persuaded to come into the house. Peter's household at this time consists of Bunny (Berigan), a tabby Shorthair, Benny (Goodman), a black Shorthair, Bix (Beiderbecke), a seal point Siamese, and now Nora, a black Great Dane. Bix becomes pregnant and gives birth to a litter of three kittens. She has two Siamese kittens, and a totally black kitten with similarly foreign type. This last kitten is apparently born dead. Well, this is what Peter thinks at the time, and Bix rejects it immediately as is often the way of cats when they know one of their litter is ailing or already dead. So the kitten is left in a kitchen cupboard, where it is found, still warm, by a friend, Martha. They try hot and cold water on its heart, and massage it, and in a magical moment it shows signs of life and squeaks. Nora, the Great Dane, hears this and takes the 'dead' kitten and licks it and licks it. As he is telling me the tale, Peter adds:

It was extraordinary to watch it. She believed in that kitten and its possibility of life. She licked it back into being. And slowly, slowly, he recovered, for he it was. I named him Pelé for his speed and turning ability, thus breaking the jazz name mould, but appropriate to his new canine identity. His mother never did accept him or feed him and we had to feed him with a dropper. As the kitten grew up, he would often play right inside Nora's mouth, and submit to bathtime by tongue. There was an astonishing trust and bond between them. She would even shut her mouth with him inside, but he remained calm and unharmed.

Pelé grows up to be a handsome black cat, and walks often with Peter, Nora and Lorraine (who was the one who made Peter rescue Nora) to a local pub, and he learns to hide

inside Peter's coat when crossing the road, and while in the pub.

When Pelé is about six years old, Peter has been on a day trip to see his father in Burgess Hill, some thirty miles distant from his own house. He returns that night to find that Pelé is missing. Two days later, his father phones him to say:

'Peter, I could swear that today I saw the spitting image of Pelé just across the road from me. But just at that moment a lorry drove past and after it had gone there was no sign of any cat.'

Peter becomes increasingly concerned about his little black cat and alerts all his neighbours to keep their eyes open for him. Four days after Peter's trip to Burgess Hill, Pelé turns up on the doorstep, dusty, dirty and hungry. Having eaten and drunk, he sleeps for hours and hours.

'So, unbelievable though it may sound,' Peter continues the tale, 'I believe that Pelé took it into his head to come and find me in Burgess Hill. He was altogether a remarkable cat – he used to play with a pen when you were writing, and it could really be quite difficult to continue. But the extraordinary thing was that he never, ever interfered with pencil or a brush. He would just watch the business end of it with absolute concentration.' As he says this, Peter does a wonderful imitation of Pelé, shaking his head from side to side in the most catlike manner. As I laugh I wonder to myself if Peter is himself a reincarnated cat. He *can* draw cats as no other, and I see now that he moves as a cat does too!

Peter then adds sadly:

That summer I went on holiday to Somerset. The night before leaving, Pelé came on to the bed as I read, and fixed me with that all knowing and infinite gaze cats have, and in that moment I knew he was William Blake. I've no idea where that thought came from, just an absolute conviction. It explained Pelé's distinction between pen and pencil, and his absorption in the creative process. I also knew I wouldn't see him again, and woke Monika to tell her. 'Don't be silly,' she said, 'you are worrying too much.' But afterwards it was she who asked the neighbour who was to mind the cats to be especially alert. And, true to form, he went missing a few days into the holiday, and we never saw him again. Did he attempt to follow us?

Shortly after Peter returns to the South, Halloween draws ever closer and I am more aware of this day than I ever normally would be because it is the first anniversary of the death of my friend and once literary agent Giles Gordon, and I am filled with a deep sense of my own loss for this remarkable man. I find that I am thinking a lot about his family and all those who love him. In spite of my awareness of this, however, I am caught completely off guard when, up to my ears in grouting some tiles around the shower, I hear the doorbell ring. I race downstairs complete with spatula and a fist-full of drying grout to discover two attractive girls in their early teens dressed respectively as an angel and a devil. I open the door, flapping my encumbered hands feebly, and am afterwards told by the she-devil that I say:

'Oh shit!' which I learn is the first time she has been greeted in quite this welcoming way. I continue, marginally more graciously:

'Sorry, sorry, what I mean is, I'm up to my ears in grouting and it's drying really fast and I know that Michael took all my change and I don't have any sweets in the house, oh dear, oh dear. Forgive me.'

Both girls laugh, indeed in a forgiving way, and the she-devil says: 'Don't worry, it's all right. It's just trick or treat night.' I swallow hard and smile back at them both, really gratefully. Trick or treat night in the Dales used to get quite 'heavy', as it did around Moon Cottage, with serious reprisals if no treat was forthcoming.

Two days later I receive a phone call from Hilary, asking me if I have a cat carrier. (Hilary, whom I mentioned earlier in the context of Heathcliff and Toby, made us feel very welcome early on by inviting us to a riotous birthday party, and who, I have been told by several people, is one of the most significant bonding elements within the village because loving people with a passion, she adores any excuse for getting everyone together to celebrate and raise a glass.) I say yes, of course, would she like to borrow it? And she then says:

'A small black kitten has been found and we don't know who owns him and he needs some veterinary treatment and I'm really not sure that I can keep him.' My mind races as she says all this, as I'm not sure whether she wants to find him a home, and I know that another small tom into the mix of cats within the confines of the Coach House is not going to be the answer for my venerable crew of felines. She continues:

'He has lice and also he seems to be incontinent.' As she adds this, I feel my enthusiasm for this tiny creature of the night waning and I feel completely guilt-ridden. But at this point she adds, philosophically:

'I know it's hopeless and I'll end up keeping him anyway, because we've already given him a name. He is black and shiny, exactly like a little olive, so he's called Oliver, but he's already become Ollie. I'll pop up now and get your cage.' And shortly afterwards she lands on the doorstep and I duly hand over the cage, wishing her all luck.

Michael and I have to go away and have coerced Elspeth and Clive to stay in our house with the small request that could they just look after the little menagerie for us? As the time arrives, however, I leave the house feeling completely guilt-ridden. On the night before our departure, Fannie is so frantic with her writhing and calling on our bed that I hold her by the neck and bring Pushkin to her. She makes the pre-nuptial screaming sound that is peculiar to queens in oestrus, but exceptionally loudly at which point Titus comes clumping up the stairs and runs into the room. Pushkin, who jumps down on to the floor the second I let him go, is sitting the other side of the room. He and I look at each other with probably identical expressions of surprise on our faces. Fannie is still making her screaming noises even though I am no longer holding her and nor have been for some time. At this point Titus jumps up on to the bed, walks purposefully towards Fannie, and hits her across her face with her left paw, hard enough for a 'thwack' sound to be audible to the human ear. Fannie immediately falls silent and then turns over on her back into the full submissive position with her front paws bowed over and her head tipped towards her sister. Titus stays on the bed, crouched, and watches her but makes no further move. On reflection, it is almost as if Titus was trying to shut her up rather than be aggressive, but I'm simply not sure. But I do know now that I must have Fannie and Titus neutered. This is simply not fair to either of them, as it seems to me that they may even be suffering to some extent, added to which it is now becoming unending and enough is definitely enough.

The following day, before I can change my mind, I phone up the surgery and make an appointment for Gerard to neuter the two girls and castrate Pushkin. The appointment is made for December, well after we return from France.

Elspeth and Clive arrive at the Coach House late on the night of the day we have already left, so I am unable to speak to Elspeth until the following day. When we do catch up with each other on the phone, she is very relaxed and forgiving, which is far more than I deserve.

'They are being very good and Titus is schmoozing up to Clive. She's been sitting on his knee. But today Fannie climbed on my shoulders and stayed up there and I was able to walk around with her, and she regularly comes across and talks to me. Pushkin just seems to wander about and he comes in and out of the rooms where we are sitting, but mainly he does his own thing. Fannie is being a bit frantic though!'

I am enormously reassured that the cats are OK and also that Elspeth is being so understanding about Fannie. But I am ashamed for my pang of envy that Fannie is responding so positively to Elspeth, who is a real cat person, and who I knew would win her over, but I so miss the closeness I had always had with her in the past, and even at this distance wonder how I might recapture it. But I do know how lucky we are to have such wonderful friends who are prepared to come and look after the cats in this way.

CHAPTER 23

We return home to find the Coach House and its cats in
apple pie order. As I follow Michael into the house, having
heard his calls to all the cats while I have been unpacking
the car, I echo the reparation that he has already performed.
The rite I speak of is that of attempting to stroke the cats,
while each of them exacts their own need to respond with
complete avoidance of any human contact. Fannie winds
herself between the legs of the piano stool, holding her tail
erect and shivering, and then tentatively greets me first
fondly by a small forward advance, and then distantly, by
jumping up on to the top of the piano, which is just inside
the front door, in order to take stock of all that is going on,
as is always her way when we return from a trip involving a
number of nights' absences. I bend down to stroke Titus
and she shuns every kind of caress with overt disdain. She
actively shakes off the touch of a stroking hand with a
wriggle and a shimmy and a tail waving crossly from side to
side. This is her way of dealing with our betrayal. And
Pushkin is nowhere to be seen, which is emphatically his
way at all times regardless of whether we have been away for
days or merely hours. As we finish hauling in our suitcases
and other artefacts from the car, Pushkin finally emerges,
yawning, and head butts us each in turn. At least this time

he seems to know who we are. Now Titus, too, is prepared to speak, and in her manner greets us with an open mouth and a rusty-sounding miaow.

We do the chores we need to and then start to get ready for bed. The cats perform their time-honoured ritual of all coming up to witness the-entering-of-the-bed-routine. And each must be stroked in turn. (On reflection, that latter is our ritual, my ritual even, rather than theirs!) Pushkin usually sits on the stairs and watches, apart from the other two, while Fannie and Titus both lie on the bed until all the lights are put out, when they thumpily jump down and go to their sleeping places elsewhere in the house.

The following day is what the gently spoken Irish captain of our plane had announced as being a 'soft' one – that is, faintly misty but with a low autumnal sun breaking through it, sending long shafts of gold to the far edges of all the fields and making the drops of water on the long grasses and the leaves in the hedgerows sparkle. I bounce down to the kitchen to start the coffee percolating and as I look out of the kitchen window I see an amazing sight. Cows, thirteen large Friesians (except, under scrutiny, they turn out to be three-quarter grown heifers who, from time to time and with no apparent provocation other than for the sheer hell of it, stop their gentle rhythmic grazing and instead boisterously mount each other), are gently pottering around the three interlinked fields that come right up to our kitchen window. Fields that in the summer months serve as a small campsite and separate us from the thick woodland behind that climbs up to the top of the crags. I love having those beautiful beasts close to me. They exude a calm and gentleness behind their great size that is profoundly comforting, and the sweet clean breath of cattle is one of my favourite smells in the whole world. (It is strange, and to me most sad, that the synonyms for bovine in most thesauruses are untrue negatives such as dense, dozy, dull, slow, sluggish, stolid, stupid, thick – they are not these things.)

I rush back up to our bathroom whose back window overlooks the field, with a higher and therefore longer view, and I find Fannie reared up on top of the towel rail with her back legs on the towels and her front feet up on the windowsill, her whiskers thrust forward, quivering. As I stand next to her she turns to look at me with her eyes large in fear. She jumps down. She jumps up again, laboriously clambering up on to the side of the bath, and from there higher still on to the washbasin, then up to the towel rail, and so on, to the windowsill. She presses her nose to the window and makes a low growling noise. As we both watch through the window, one of the nearest heifers moves a couple of yards further forward to reach a new clump of grass and Fannie gasps in fright and jumps straight down on to the floor, groaning slightly as the breath is knocked out of her as she hits the deck and races off to look through other windows. For the next half-hour or so Fannie intermittently stares out of every window in the house. Sheep routinely surround us, although not usually in the field that now contains the heifers, and even when we first moved here I never remember the cats responding to the sheep in this way. They did watch them, slightly warily, but not with the fear that the heifers are engendering now. The size of these beasts is of course considerably greater, and yet for the moment Fannie has only seen them through a window, which is not the same as being a tiny cat at the hoof of a Friesian cow when the differential in size would be truly awesome.

As soon as I am able I phone up Elspeth and establish that she and Clive were perfectly happy during their stay.

'Tell me, tell me, though – when did the cows first come in?'

'What cows? We never saw any cows.'

I explain, and Elspeth reckons that they must have been put into the field on the Monday that we got back, so in fact when I saw Fannie freaking out in the bathroom, it most probably was the first time she had set eyes on them.

We wake up this morning and there has been the first ground frost of the autumn, not severe, but it feels astonishingly chilly in our unheated bedroom with its three windows. Following a grisly day yesterday in which both Michael and I had sunk into the pits of despair about Moon Cottage and its lack of sale, I instinctively know this one will not be so shabby. We now have the heating on for a burst of an hour in the morning, which brings the house up to a bearable temperature. Michael is sounding cheery and bouncy and his normal noisy self, and I hear him drive off to Kirkby Lonsdale for the Saturday newspapers, and shortly after he returns he shouts up to the bathroom that he has done a fry-up, bless him. I come running down, and not only is there beautiful bacon and egg, there is piping-hot coffee and hot toast and marmalade. So wonderful, what indulgence! As we sit down together and look out through those windows across the valley, and to the hills and over to Ingleborough on the other side, I have never seen it all look more beautiful, on any day, than it does today and I feel tears come to my eyes.

'I know exactly what you are thinking and so am I,' Michael says as he picks up my hand. 'We cannot leave here, we mustn't leave here. *We mustn't!*'

'Yup, that's it in one,' I whisper back squeezing his hand. He hits the table with the heel of his free hand more triumphantly than despairingly I choose to think.

I clear up the late breakfast things and walk into the kitchen with my arms full of crocks, and as my eye is drawn towards the light I realise that I am looking through a glass dimly as the large plate glass kitchen window is streaked with a curious opaque film. I have to conclude that this is the legacy of the teenage giants in our field outside who have been spending a few idle moments licking the window in that way that they do, and artistically cross-hatching it with blades of grass. I go outside and clean the window, knowing full well that in a few minutes, or possibly a few hours, it will no doubt be opaque again, but I can live with that!

Tonight we go off to the village hall where we, along with all other villagers, have been invited to join in the French Night, the rules for admission being that you must wear something recognisably French, you must speak with a French accent, and you must take one course, either a

starter, main or pudding (and which must also be French, *naturellement*), enough to feed the number of you attending. Michael and I both don French berets, which we wear normally anyway, so this is a bit of a cop-out. For the food, I rather unimaginatively open a tin of two dozen snails, the French edible kind of course. When we arrive, with the mandatory French stick apiece clamped under our arms and clutching a couple of bottles of Bordeaux, we rather embarrassingly find that everyone else is already seated, that the hall is full of folk, that there is a French stick mountain, and that loads of other people have taken snails too – so in the end we find ourselves eating snails and more snails, and also someone else's frogs legs, which have in fact been cooked to perfection.

We find a couple of free seats at a table near us and sit down to find that we are on the same table as Hilary and her husband, Phil, so I hungrily ask for news of what is happening with the 'Halloween' kitten. The last report I had from a mutual friend was that he was still incontinently not performing in his cat litter tray, and I am well aware that Hilary is really concerned about how long she will be able to put up with that state of affairs.

'Marilyn, he is just the most gorgeous cat in the world. He is still tiny and adorable and there is no way I would give him up now. Please promise me you will come down and see him as soon as you can.'

The evening becomes more animated as large quantities of French wine are consumed, and in between the last two courses various couples are asked to change tables. Michael and I nominate ourselves, as we are the new kids on the block, and we move across to a neighbouring table. Shortly after we have joined our new table we are all issued with a quiz sheet consisting of questions to do with people, subjects and things French, and we make a reasonable fist of our collective answers – although we only come third or fourth in the final score. The couple who are filling in our quiz sheet are called Jeff and Karen. In a lull in the proceedings, someone mentions cats and I gaily shout across the table at Jeff and Karen:

'Do you have a cat?' Karen looks across the table at me and her face twists sadly. She replies:

'We did until two weeks ago.' I feel terrible and ask them what happened. Tinkerbell, their beautiful long-bodied, long-haired black and white cat, who was a real character (and all the people on our table enthusiastically vouch for what a sweetie he was), had gone missing one very windy day when Jeff was working on the village hall. When Jeff got home at lunchtime and found that Tinks was nowhere to be seen, he already knew something was amiss because Tinks never missed coming back to greet him at lunch time; so, with a heavy heart, that afternoon he went off hunting for him. Eventually he found him in an unused sewage drainpipe lying alongside the wall of a field. He had been wounded, probably by a vehicle, and his instinct must have led him to crawl inside the pipe so that he might die undisturbed. By the time Jeff found him, rigor mortis had set in.

'I think that the wind was responsible. He must've been so

deafened by the noise that he simply failed to hear a vehicle approaching him.'

Even though I have several times experienced the pain and sense of loss that the death of a beloved animal causes you, it is supremely hard to find any words that might give proper comfort to a family so recently bereaved, and I think I probably resort to all clichés known to man and woman, and probably the only cliché I consciously avoid is the unhelpful one of 'life must go on'.

As it turns out, this day does end less buoyantly than it began because when we finally return home after the ten yards' walk from the village hall to the Coach House at the end of this splendid French Evening, our boiler, which heats not just the radiators but is also the only source of hot water, is flashing its emergency 'lock-out' light, indicating it is no longer functioning; although we have learnt to live without heating, living without hot water is, for me, just too awful to bear. The following morning we ask our serenely accommodating neighbour, Annabel, who rescues us uncomplainingly from all our domestic plights, who might help us this time and when, yet again, she flicks through her little black book to give Michael the appropriate telephone number, Michael realises happily that the Jeff whose number she is proffering is the very same Jeff who was our table companion on the previous evening.

He comes, even though it is Sunday, like a knight in shining armour and by Monday, with the appropriate spare part in his hand, Jeff has got our boiler in full working order again. After he has finished working on the boiler I urge him to talk some more about Tinkerbell, but not without experiencing a little guilt as I sense the pain I am stirring up. As he gently talks about their much-loved cat, I slowly grasp, with overwhelming sadness, that the beautiful cat who had come calling late at night in the summer when Stephen was with us must have been Tinks and that I had often seen him as I had driven through the village, hunting in the hedges near the dry stone walls at the far end. In fact, his full name was Tinkerbell, although once his masculinity was established he was always known in the family as either Tinks or Bella. (I'm not the only one to sex kittens wrongly!) Tinks was one of a litter of four kittens, two tortie and two black and white, born two and a half years ago to a neighbouring friend of theirs called Catherine. Their oldest daughter, Lesley, worked on Jeff to persuade him that, having vaguely spoken to some vet somewhere, it would not cost more than £15 to give the kitten all the injections it needed and, she continued, he would be great company for her, her brother Neil and, especially, for their much younger sister, Alex. Jeff laughs wryly:

'Load of rubbish of course, it costs far more than her £15, but by then we were hooked and he was part of our family. He was such a patient cat as well as loving, and would let himself be picked up and dragged around like a little doll without complaining. He loved to lie on his back and have his tummy tickled. I had had a cat of my own when I was in primary school, which I had swapped for two dinky toys, so I did know how she felt. But Tinks was a really special cat and the kids chose him themselves out of all the litter. They had the chance to work out which one it was to be as when the kittens were very young we looked after them all for a spell, and Tinks was the one for them. He loved people.'

'I always think,' I offer, 'and many of the cat manuals say this, that cats that have been socialised from a very early age, and handled by a large number of people when they are very young, prove to be the friendliest of cats when they mature.' Jeff nods quietly.

'He had been brought up with a cat litter tray, and for a long time he would never go outside, but always come back inside to use his litter tray. Sometimes at night he would stop out until late. Although he had been neutered he was still interested in the ladies, I reckon, and if I woke up in the night and knew he was still out and went down to let him in, he would shoot past me just as if he had missed the last bus, and race over to the food bowl to eat whatever might still be in it.'

I ask Jeff if they will look for another kitten or cat, but he delays answering and when I pursue it further, he shrugs in a sad way and says out of respect for Tinks's memory he would rather not just yet. But cats always seem to present themselves when you are least expecting them, and anyway it isn't just down to him of course, but the whole family who are missing him, so they may get one sooner rather than later.

Shortly after this conversation, Karen and Jeff, when out walking with their two girls, Lesley and Alex, call on us to see all the cats and I tease Lesley about her scam on the price of injections, but she reckons it was well worth it. She and Alex between them tell me that shortly before Tinks was killed they had taken him to see Gerard, the vet, because Tinks alone out of the four kittens had been born with a heart murmur, and Gerard always liked to check he was in good health. Tinkerbell's purr was always so consistently loud that Gerard would unfailingly have to put his fingers over Tinkerbell's nose to stop the purring, so he could hear his heartbeat through his stethoscope. Lesley and Alex both say to me sadly that their family has had bad luck with animals as Lesley's horse had to be put down, Neil had problems with his dogs and they had to be rehomed, and now Tinkerbell has died. I try to reassure them that it is not bad luck, and there will bound to be more animals in their lives soon.

Animals often die before what we feel should be their due

time, but I do reckon it should never put us off loving another animal again, because that limitless flow of love to be given and received between people and the animals they live with, if they are lucky enough to be able to do this, is truly life enhancing. I know, tetchy thing that I am, that I am better by far with animals in my life than without them, and that is in spite of the love of Michael.

The following week an irresistible desire to go and see young Ollie takes me down to Hilary's house. (I have always suffered badly from kitten-lust, but truth to tell I also want my cat carrier back as I feel slightly uneasy without it in case of emergency.) Sure enough, this fluff-bundle of what seems to me pure black heaven is flying round Hilary's hall, batting a wine cork about with his two front feet, alternately equal to the skill of that shown only by the greatest of the ball masters. This is definitely a Georgie or a Becks if ever I saw one. (Could it even be a reincarnation of Peter's Pelé I wonder to myself?) Hilary tells me that Catherine, her youngest daughter, first wanted to call him Pepper because of the tiny traces of silver hairs in his otherwise immaculate 'pure' black coat, and after that she wanted to call him Charlie because he clearly must have fallen off a witch's broomstick, appearing as he did from nowhere, a completely black cat, on the day after Halloween.

'But anyway, Ollie he is and he is definitely staying.' On gentle enquiry I learn that the adorable black kitten in front of me, who lies on his back and waves his paws in the air and stares up at me with the greenest of green eyes and who the vet reckons is about three months old, has now mastered the use of the litter tray and also goes outside. All the health problems that he had on arrival have sorted themselves out and he is shaping up to be a much-loved and very loving small cat. Ollie, too, has now properly befriended Thomas, Hilary's and Phil's beautiful thick-pelted grey tabby aged seven, and lord of his domain until this moment. Hilary laughs as she says:

'Thomas was so good with him under the circumstances. He hissed a couple of times. He belted him once and then, with only the smallest sigh, he accepted him into his world.' Just as I am about to take my reluctant leave of Ollie, Peter and Catherine both return from school and we talk for a little; and it is then that I discover, to my intense embarrassment, that the she-devil I so inelegantly greeted on All Hallows Eve was none other than young Catherine, accompanied by her close friend, the angel Hayley!

CHAPTER 24

A tiny paragraph appears in the gossip column of the *London Evening Standard* about Moon Cottage being up for sale, but it is so obscure that I cannot believe it will actually generate a sale; but, who knows, perhaps the longed-for miracle will happen. Michael and I have another serious conversation in which he makes me understand exactly how much money we are losing and he warns me that we may yet have to sell up here and move back down to Moon Cottage. We seem unable either to rent or sell and the tension for us both is painful.

We are not sleeping well, and this sleeplessness is being made even more unremitting for us both by Fannie's strident guttural calling, which she does every two hours right through the night. She seems to trot up and down the corridor that runs from the bottom of our stairs to the sitting room door, pausing at each of the conservatory windows in turn, and then shrieks her lustful cry to the world, but no tom comes a-calling. Sometimes I lie in bed and I hear her voice very distantly and far off, then I realise she must be up in the spare room calling out of that window, and then the cycle starts all over again.

One day I am sitting at my computer and she starts; it is worse at night, but she does call during the daytime too –

and for the umpteenth time I go into a website called www.studcat.co.uk. My eye is suddenly caught by a cat stud in Lancashire under the heading of SKYBLUE PINKSIAMESE & ORIENTALS, in which the breeder has used the phrase:

> Storm is a much-loved Stud cat, lovely temperament, super blue eyes, but not very typy bodywise. He sires wonderful kittens and is most kind and gentle to his girls, especially maiden queens. Inspection welcome any time.

I am much taken with the compassion in tone for her stud, the honesty of the absence of 'typy', and moved by the thought that gentleness with a first-time queen is a consideration. Lancashire is a big county, but the stud might just be close to the Cumbrian border. There is an email address and so, feeling I have nothing to lose, I nervously send off an exploratory email. Herewith is an extract of the reply:

From:	Marje and Ian
To:	Marilyn
Sent:	Wednesday, 17 November, 18:54
Subject:	Re: Siamese/Oriental Stud and your help please

```
Dear Marilyn
    Yes, I can help . . .
    My cat Storm is not very well but he has
a son by the name of Skybluepink Zimmy who
is an experienced virgin woo-er. He is an
Oriental Apricot. As he is an Apricot and
belongs to the red family he would go
brilliantly with your tortie colourwise.
```

Regarding the rest I cannot say.

Zimmy has very, very, very, very naughty clever kittens, very bright and very beautiful.

I do require that your cat has a blood test, but I can get this done here. Zimmy of course is done and up to date with inoculations. He lives in a heated pen outside my patio window, is a pain in the bum, and is very noisy and very nosy. He has creature comforts, fur beds, heated oil-filled radiator, evening lights and a radio, plus of course passing leaves floating down, birdies in trees and me.

I like to keep the cats about a week. He is free now if you can get her down real soon.

Marjorie

The attached picture in the email shows a slim, elegant apricot-coloured Oriental cat, tall and handsome with a faintly arrogant look to him. He has rings on his tail and faint stripy markings (which when I see him in the flesh I discover are intermingled with superb leopard spots), and he sports the distinctive large pointed ears endemic to the Oriental breed. As I look at the picture repeatedly I find myself feeling mildly apprehensive, because this is like choosing a mate by catalogue, but at the same time I am also much taken with the idea of this striking-looking cat, named after Zimmy the lion, husbanding my little Fannie. I ask Michael what he thinks we should do. He replies simply:

'Well, it's now or never.'

That evening I talk to Marjorie on the phone and find she

is reassuring and kind, as well as business-like. So, without more ado, the following day, a Thursday, finds Michael driving a car with me in the back behind a wire fireguard separating us from the driving area, with Fannie on my knee and the cat carrier next to us heading straight down the M6 towards east Lancashire and Rossendale. It is a

bitterly cold, grey November day and Fannie is not at all happy at her enforced journeying, and intermittently wails forlornly and most unlustfully. After two hours we reach our destination and, after talking things through, we finally bid them farewell, leaving Fannie behind us. As we walk away from the house I feel a total rat. I have transported my virgin girl to a strange house a long way from home containing a male stud who has only one thought in his head. While Fannie was in Marjorie's sitting room Zimmy came into the room and immediately came up to the side of the carrier and sniffed repeatedly through the side, and then he walked all round it and yowled, oh how he yowled. Zimmy has a very big voice. Fannie stared at him with large eyes through the bars. It was a totally inscrutable expression she bore on her face.

As Michael gently manoeuvres the car out on to the main road and we head off towards the M62 motorway, large lumps of water hit the windscreen heavily.

'Michael, it's sleeting. We're going to get the first snow of this winter. Yikes!'

'Mmmmn!' he replies, non-committally.

'Whaddya mean "Mmmmn"?' I ask.

'I was just thinking, poor Fannie.'

'Don't do that,' it's now my turn to wail. 'I feel bad enough without you saying stuff like that. Whaddya mean "poor Fannie"?'

'Well I s'pose what I'm trying to say is she'll be very upset for a few hours, and she's now got to go to the vet for that blood test, and then she'll be put out into the shed and it's really cold outside now and she'll be all by herself and she'll miss Titus – I should think she might even miss Pushkin, but . . .' there's a sigh, and then a laugh '. . . but by tomorrow morning I expect she'll have a smile on her face.'

'Oh, typical man!'

'Hey, it was your idea, coming here. You found Zimmy, not me.'

As we drive homewards the sleet falls more heavily, and as we near the high hills of home we see a ring of snow on the peaks. It is very beautiful but deadly cold. As we walk inside the house, I shudder fretfully. Titus greets me in a rather dull sort of way. She is clearly looking for Fannie. Pushkin is nowhere to be seen.

I go up to my study and wonder how soon it will be acceptable for me to phone Marjorie to find out how things are. As I turn round from my desk to look at the armchair where normally I would expect to see Fannie and Titus together, rolled up in companionably adjacent balls, I am somewhat disconcerted to see Pushkin and Titus together instead, lying next to each other like two large peas in a pod.

'Didn't take you long, boy, did it?' I enquire gently of Pushkin. He just looks dolefully across at me, sighs long-sufferingly, and puts his head back down again.

It is now Thursday evening and Fannie has been with her stud for one whole day and I feel the need to get an update from Marjorie. We speak on the phone but Marjorie also does me a very funny series of emails as if from Fannie, and from these two sources I discover that Fannie has passed her blood test, she is in a pen next to Zimmy, hissing at him at regular intervals, and the plan is that tomorrow, Friday, she will be let out of her inner sanctum and put in the bigger cage with Zimmy.

The following evening Marjorie phones me with a further update and tells me that Fannie is eating well, but that she is continuing to hiss and slash out at Zimmy, who remains stoically unfazed by her hostility. The snow is heavy and the weather very cold, but Marjorie soothes my disquiet by assuring me that Fannie has a hot water bottle under her bedding and that she is next to a warm radiator. She has not let the two cats alone together yet, but only under her supervision, as Fannie is still hissing regularly.

I spend a restless night worrying about her. The following morning I go into email and find this:

From:	Marje and Ian
To:	Marilyn
Sent:	Saturday, 20 November, 10:58
Subject:	HRH Lady Fannie

```
TO WHOM IT MAY CONCERN
    This Royal notice is to confirm that
Fannie (now known as HRH Lady Fannie) was
mated by Skybluepink Zimmy after several
hundred tries at 10.15 a.m. this morning.
She is now laid out on the lounger posing
for pictures.
    Marje K

---------------
```

I email Marje, immediately asking her to congratulate Zimmy and to say what a great boy he has been, but I also tell her that at around that time on Saturday, Titus suddenly miaowed out really loudly for no reason that either of us could determine. Shortly after this I telephone her and inquire how soon I might collect the Lady Fannie, but she tells me firmly that I must leave Fannie with Zimmy for several more days yet to be certain that he has properly fertilised her, and now I find I am becoming, somewhat tardily, fiercely protective of Fannie. That night, the Saturday night, I am wide awake from 2.30 a.m. onwards. The cold spell has lessened its iron grip slightly, but I still worry about how low the temperature is at night. Now, however, I am even more concerned that Zimmy's attentions might become suffocatingly overzealous and am aware that if Fannie were out in the wild she would have the option of running away, which she cannot do in her little cage. Eventually, in the dull grey light of early morning I creep up to my study and email the long-suffering Marjorie to say that I really would like to come today.

Just as we are about to leave for church the phone rings and it is Marjorie. She is not pleased with me. As tactfully as she can, she tries to dissuade me from coming over and collecting Fannie. She really wants Zimmy and Fannie to have more time together and believes that I am going to mess things up by collecting Fannie too early. I know I am being difficult and groan with embarrassment. After a further agonised conversation I say that I will phone her later in the day. While I am in church I pray for some sign that I can interpret as guidance on what best to do. We return to the Coach House and I race up to my computer just in case Marjorie has emailed me while we have been out, and I find an email saying I can collect Fannie.

I prepare to leave the Coach House as soon as I have read

the email. The weather has now turned very wet and foggy as the cold gives way to a rapidly enveloping warm front. I remember almost nothing about that journey except the fog and the lights and the drippiness of it all and an extraordinarily heightened sense of pleasure and anticipation that I shall be seeing my girl, that she is fit and well, that she will soon be safely back home, and that she is now a-mother-to-be. Marjorie and Ian welcome me, with an air of mild surprise that I have got there so quickly. We do all the paperwork and then, with all the boring bits sorted, we go to the pen that is housing Zimmy and Fannie, and there they both are lying together on a fur-covered upright chair.

Some few moments after Marjorie and I have entered the pen with the intention of putting Fannie into her carrier, I become aware of Zimmy quietly but deliberately grabbing Fannie by the back of her neck, high up near her ears, and without further ado he mounts her and promptly mates with her. I feel extreme discomfiture at being there and try to move away, but Marjorie persuades me that I should stay and let it be. After a suitable passage of time during which Fannie is able to regain her composure, I go across to her and attempt to place her in the cat carrier, which is standing on a high table. She resists this at the beginning, but in the end I manage to reverse her in. Just as I am closing the wire-fronted door, Zimmy stands up on his rear legs to his full height and puts his paw through the door to touch Fannie. He then stretches his head right up and touches her nose with his. As their noses touch she gives him a tiny lick. Marjorie is really moved by the affection that her stud boy is showing towards my wayward little queen – and the whole episode makes me feel I need to take Fannie away as quickly as possible before we become hopelessly emotional. Just as we are about to leave, Marjorie nearly does make me cry by very shyly giving me a wonderful curly cottony wool blanket for 'Lady Fannie' to lie on, as a memento of her mating with Zimmy.

As I drive off into the murky grey November day, Fannie, whose cat carrier is strapped on to the front passenger seat with the door facing me, presses her face against the wire grill and mewls long and sadly. I cannot gainsay whether it be for the loss of Zimmy or for the horror of yet another car journey, or simply for the whole bang shoot of it. I talk to her and gently stroke her through the bars and I feel the rough warm pull of her tongue on my fingers as she licks me in greeting. She and I have missed each other and we have a lot to say to each other, whatever else might have been happening.

At our journey's end I unload the car and remove anything that might have the smell of Zimmy on it, lest it disrupt the status quo. Marjorie has suggested I cover all three Coach House cats with a small sprinkling of talcum powder, which I do, the intention being to confuse them all, but the smell of Zimmy on Fannie is clearly very strong and overrides all other scents. Titus, whom I had expected to welcome Fannie as if she were the prodigal daughter, is clearly very ill at ease and behaves most strangely the second that I release Fannie into the house. She stares at Fannie with big eyes and with what looks like hostility or fear showing in them. Fannie quickly sidesteps Titus and rushes into the kitchen where she eats rapidly. As soon as she has taken the first edge off her hunger she runs upstairs to my study. She climbs on the chair. She jumps down again, and runs the length of the house and up into our bedroom.

I find Pushkin in the spare room unaware at this moment that Fannie is back in the house. I put him in the same room together with Fannie to see what, if anything, might happen. He is fascinated by her smell but again, as with Titus, she sidesteps him and trots off, tail up, pursuing her own business and checking, checking, checking, and then I hear her clattering around the food bowls again. While she is distracted with eating, Titus keeps making dives at her rear end to sniff for the story of what has been happening and at one point I see Titus round the back of the sofa pushing her whiskers into Pushkin's ear.

'Michael, I just saw Titus whispering to Pushkin round the back of the sofa!'

'You are really losing it, Marilyn. Call yourself an animal behaviourist. Cats don't talk, OK?'

It looked like whispering to me, whatever anyone says!

That night Marjorie phones me to check that we have got home in one piece and I assure her that all is well and we talk about when I may see the first signs of whether Fannie is pregnant, and also at what point she will have passed the danger of aborting. Marjorie reckons that certainty of a pregnancy will only be ascertained at five weeks from the mating, as by that time Fannie will start to show, or, if there are any problems, she will have naturally aborted by that time. That takes us to early January, and until then I will just have to be very patient. What will be will be.

So slowly, gently, everything subsides into its normal, or near normal rhythm, although that first evening when Fannie tries to lie next to Titus, Titus hisses long and loudly and eventually Fannie gets down. Pushkin, who has taken to lying in that chair, only lies in it now when the other two cats are away, and Fannie is even climbing back up on to the top of her wardrobe, which Titus briefly took over as her domain. In other words, it seems to me that the status quo has reverted to how it was before the recent power struggle when Titus became the ascendant cat.

This weekend my sister Margot, her husband David, and their son Laurence come to stay with us. Laurence's sister, Victoria, is in the last week of her absolutely frantic first term at Cambridge and understandably cannot be distracted from it at any price. It is the very first time any member of my family has come to see the new house since we moved here in April and I am longing for it more than I can say. They arrive more quickly than I had estimated their journey would take them and I am out shopping for food, so when I get back Michael has had the pleasure of showing them the house and I am childishly disappointed, as I had so wanted to see what they thought of it. I think they like it, but I missed whatever first impression it made on them. As I walk in, however, I am confronted by the sight of Margot desperately trying to move Titus off her knee without touching her fur, which carries the allergy-inducing saliva that causes asthma in those who suffer from that beastly affliction; and with a sinking heart I realise that this, and the complication of Snowy, their dog, who is also allergic to cats as well as hating them, are likely to fuse together to keep them away in future. However, in spite of so unpromising a start, Margot, David and I climb up to the top of the crags, and in spite of the cold greyness of this November weekend, the views across the fells, in one direction towards the

Yorkshire peaks and in the other toward the Lakeland mountains, is breathtaking and awe-inspiring and I am gratified by their enthusiasms. Michael and Laurence disappear together to do some shopping, although it emerges later that this entailed going into a bar somewhere that coincidentally was showing a football match that involved Blackburn Rovers, so no greater love hath Laurence, as the Arsenal supporter that he is.

The following morning, after breakfast, Laurence also climbs the crags with his father, and as this day is a glorious clear sharp frosty day, they have the benefit of those really far-reaching dark blue and mauve views of the big distance. Shortly after this, when we are talking of breakfast-related things, they make me collapse with laughter as David recalls:

'Do you remember that morning, Laurence, which might possibly have been the happiest day of your childhood, when you opened your packet of Cocopops and out fell not just one, not just two, but a whole string of those plastic trophies you were collecting?' Laurence grins widely, but then replies somewhat lugubriously:

'Yup, they really messed up. It wasn't just a few; it was a whole plastic run of them, hundreds – hardly any Cocopops, but a whole cereal box of plastic tat! The only trouble was it did include an awful lot of duplicates, so I still had real trouble collecting a set. In fact, I never did get a complete set together.'

Geoffrey comes across for lunch too as it is a long while since he last saw Margot, David and Laurence, and in the early afternoon Michael and I wave them all goodbye. As we watch them drive down the road I say a prayer to St Joseph that this completes the proper acknowledgement of the Coach House as our new home, because now much of Michael's family has seen it and some of mine, and surely that will mean that we are allowed to stay here and start our new life with possibly even a small new feline family?

The following day we are told by our estate agent that a lady who had viewed Moon Cottage, and on whom we were counting, said she wanted to live on a quieter road. Two days later I get an email from Margot, which helps me to know, in spite of the difficulties with Moon Cottage, that we are in the right place:

From:	Margot
To:	Marilyn
Sent:	Tuesday, 30 November, 21:35
Subject:	Thank you – late, sorry!

Dear Marilyn and Michael
    Thank you for a really lovely weekend. Your house is wonderful and I do so hope that it all works out and you get a buyer for Moon Cottage.
    Love Margot

And shortly after we get this email we hear from another agent that there is someone else interested in the cottage. She saw it on Monday and loved it. So yet again everything remains up in the air, but we are well and we have each other, which is what counts. We wobble a little sometimes, oh yes, we wobble, but what's a wobble here and there?

The Coach House
Cats

MARILYN EDWARDS

ILLUSTRATED BY
PETER WARNER

CHAPTER 1

Richard's eyes crinkle up with glee and he beams at me wickedly.

'Oooh, small kittens can be drowned quite easily in watering cans, can't they?' I grab my neck, hand on hand, in mock horror and grin back at him, ruefully. Michael and I are about to take a walk in the Cumbrian hills on this brash breezy November day and we have just told our friend and neighbour the news that Fannie, my beloved tortie queen, is pregnant. Richard is well aware that my Achilles' heel is the cats and takes every opportunity presented to him to tease me about them. As we take our leave with the intention of walking up the road, he turns towards his own driveway, but as he does so he calls out over his shoulder:

'When are the kittens due, by the way?'

'Twenty-third of January,' I call back.

'Ah, that's still within the shooting season,' he laughs, disappearing behind our dividing wall before I can think of a suitable reply. As we walk away I find myself grinning broadly; Richard is at heart one big softie.

Fannie has been different since the first day that she returned from her visit to her boyfriend Zimmy, an apricot Oriental stud who lives over in East Lancashire. It is just eleven days since she was mated and she is showing small signs already that some biological change has taken place. She is sleeping far more than is her normal pattern, but when she is awake she is busy all day long, trotting round the entire house, looking, looking, looking. I have never seen her so distracted. It is as if she has lost something and she must find it, but I know, early though it is, in reality she is trying to find a nesting place. She has been sleeping in the bottom of the wardrobe in the spare bedroom for much of the time. She no longer lies next to her sister, Titus, but perhaps this is a necessary form of burgeoning independence. Titus is rampantly on heat at the moment and Pushkin, the Russian Blue whom I had hoped would father kittens with one or other of the girls, continues, fastidiously, to avoid her advances.

When I hold Fannie on my shoulder she is more clingy and purrful than normal, but that might be to compensate for her changing relationship with her sister. She seems to ignore Pushkin completely.

A date is in the diary for two hysterectomies and a castration for, respectively, Fannie, Titus and Pushkin, to be performed by our local vet, Gerard, in just over a month's time, but Fannie's longed-for pregnancy will now of necessity reduce the number of patients to two. A friend fervently advises me to consider not spaying Titus at this time, as she believes that it could cause Titus to show aggression towards Fannie, who might then miscarry. I phone the long-suffering Gerard and ask him what I should do and he reckons that spaying Titus and Pushkin is fine, although he does express some concern that Titus is on one of her semi-permanent heats, but we agree to stick with the arrangement and I quietly offer up a prayer that all will be well. I deeply regret that Titus will not be able to bear one litter, but Gerard, when last he saw her, recommended that, as a cat who has endured separate operations on each of her back legs in turn to correct luxating patellae, she should not be encouraged to reproduce.

Since moving into our little eyrie in the county of  Westmorland, it seems to me that the cats' lives are now so eventful that, were they capable of such a thought process, they would see that the move they had originally hated so much was in reality a good thing. It is probable, however, that the three cats have no perception of what life in Moon Cottage was like compared with their new life in the Coach House.

Their new life means that now, for two hours at a time, they go outside freely to roam; they have the stimuli of the smells and sounds borne to them on the country winds; they regularly experience the thrill of the chase and, more rarely, kill; all this they have, while I quietly torture myself about their newly increased vulnerability.

The strangest thing has just happened and I am filled with remorse, and yet I am uncertain what it is that I should have done to prevent it. It has been raining on and off for most of the day but the rain finally stops at around 8 p.m. and, as I look out of the window of the conservatory, through the gloom I see large dark clouds scudding across the sky heavy with more rain. It is a dark, dank night and the tang of autumn hangs in the air. I open the front door to go out to the freezer in the shed to bring in some fish for supper and, as I move forward to cross the threshold, I see Titus speeding across the tiles of the conservatory floor towards me and as she reaches me, in spite of my best endeavours to stop her, she shoots through the door and out into the garden. Although I am now letting the cats out more and more during daylight hours, I draw the line once it is dark for the dangers that lie in wait in such deep countryside as this for so unworldly a crew as these three cats frighten me too much. I shout out harshly: 'Come here, Titus, at once!' She ignores me completely. Well, not completely, in truth, she runs away as fast as she can so that as I try to stop her, I end up chasing her. She comes to a halt at the bench under the seven giant Scots pines and as I reach her I grab her by the scruff of her neck. She wrenches herself away from me and as she does so she makes the most extraordinary howling, screeching sort of noise, the like of which I have never heard her utter in her entire life. Although I feel sure I can barely have hurt her, she hisses at me with either fear or loathing or both – I stand helplessly by as she runs into the furthest corner of the garden, amid bushes and trees and where there is not the earthly possibility of my catching her if she doesn't wish it. I walk dejectedly back into the house and shut the door. Fannie is there waiting, presumably having heard her sister's ear-shattering protests, and miaows several times to be let out which I resist. I tell Michael what has happened but I try to persuade him to leave her to get over whatever it is that upset her, believing that she will come back on her own in due time. Michael, however, insists on trying to comfort her himself. I hear him calling her but she remains hidden in the dark. He lets out Fannie, who disappears briefly but quite quickly reappears on her own with no sign of her sister in tow. Fannie comes back into the house with me and I shut the door again. I start to cook the supper and try to persuade myself that all will be well and Titus will be fine and will get over it, but I am completely perplexed at whatever it was that upset her so much. Yes, she was cross that I was attempting to curtail her dash for freedom but the screech was so strong that it was as if she thought I was strangling her. I finally can't bear it a second longer and go out into the garden and then the field at the back and whistle repeatedly. If she is within a quarter of a mile of the house she must be able to hear me, but there is still no sign of her. She has now been out about an hour. I turn to come back into the house and as I do so I hear a scuffling noise from the bushes by the ashbin and Titus slightly shiftily appears out of the gloom. I call her and pick her up. She stiffens in my arms and there is no purring, but she doesn't scratch or wriggle to get free, so in some sense a truce is established.

Later on that night Michael makes an observation with a note of sad questioning in his voice:

'I have been thinking, and you know, you must agree, Titus is the most balanced of the three cats. She is the least neurotic, she shows affection the most easily of all of them – if you think about it she is always the most responsive, and she really is the least nervous.' He pauses for a little while,

and then he adds, 'It makes her being so odd with you even stranger!'

'Well yes, but she *was* odd and we'll just have to live with it,' I retort between gritted teeth. But, of course, I am tormented with guilt about Titus whom I never love enough, although I do spend time with her, consciously loving her, to compensate. You can't manufacture love, you can only try to give as much as you can, and to be nice if all else fails.

CHAPTER 2

Right through the long hot summer and now the damp blustery autumn of this first year of our new life in Cumbria every move we have made, every penny we have spent, has been overshadowed by our fears that if we are not able to sell Moon Cottage soon we will no longer be able to afford the two mortgages and the day will shortly dawn when we must put our new home, the Coach House, back on the market, on the grounds that in a tourist beauty spot we stand a better chance of a quick sale than in the commuter lands of the Home Counties.

However, the cats remain untouched by this for the moment and Fannie continues to flourish and occupies herself incessantly around the house hunting for her ideal nest. I am amazed at how much food she is eating and the variety of what she eats. She is now prepared to eat food she would not formerly have touched and I have started to feed her kitten food when the others aren't around, as it is higher in nutrients and good for a pregnant queen. As I watch the cats I mull over the complication of the bond that humans feel for the animals who share their lives. I am still haunted by the hurt I feel I cause to Titus because I do not love her enough in *her* mind, or is that in truth in *my* mind? I find this diary entry, which I submit unedited, guilty as charged:

Fannie jumps into one of the big boxes on the bedroom floor and looks out over the high side of it, with just her eyes showing, which has the effect on me of melting my inner core, not just my emotions but it feels to me, as I write, my whole being.

When Fannie peeks at me over the top of the box I think the reason I dissolve is that all I can see of her are her two pert ears and her adorable, large, liquid eyes. I can't see her nose or her whiskers or her mouth and indeed when I do reach over to look at her whole face, the bottom half is comparatively expressionless, the intensity of her expression is conveyed solely through her eyes in the manner of a veiled woman and it's utterly beguiling.

Throughout all of this anguishing somehow Pushkin does not generate any of these anxieties within me. He and I know and understand each other well and it is very straightforward. He comes to me when he needs love (and sometimes he will go to Michael, although Pushkin is more of a one-person cat than the others) and otherwise he sleeps. He remains nervous when he is outside although he does love going out, but at the slightest sound of a vehicle or even a strong wind he comes racing inside. Pushkin is a very beautiful wuss-puss. Of all the cats it is Pushkin who most shares my fear of road traffic and its possible effect on the cats.

My heart was broken when Otto, the mother of Fannie and Titus, was killed on the road outside our house. When I started to write the book about her life and was talking about the grief I felt at her death, my bookseller friend

David told me the sad story of his beloved moggy, Jack, who one day went missing from his terrace house in Lancaster. David says that he will never forget the anguish that he went through on the days following that first night that Jack didn't come home.

'You imagine the worst, and you almost want to know the worst so that there is nothing terrible left to discover.'

After phoning the vet and speaking to other folk in the street he establishes that on the night of Jack's disappearance a cat is discovered at the end of his long street, dead, having been run over in the main road. The vet tries to reassure David that the cat is not Jack, but eventually – Jack never reappears – David convinces himself that it is too much of a coincidence that a cat with exactly Jack's colouration has died the same night that David first misses his little cat. In his reluctance to contemplate the death of Jack, it is two days before David finally drags himself to the vet's, intending to inspect the corpse, but by then the cat has been cremated and so, with a heavy heart, he returns home none the wiser. I so empathise with him and all those other bereaved cat owners who will never know for certain what has happened to their loved feline companion. And now, three years later, having returned North at last, I decide to seek out David on his home turf. When I arrive he has to introduce me to no less than *three* significant-other male companions. One, his human partner Peter, is a warm and gracious man who is just enchanting, and the other two, by whom I am no less captivated, are a pair of feline brothers named Merlin and Gizmo. Merlin is long and lean and muscular and reminds me, exactly, of Pushkin in his build, his shape, his sleekness and the conformation of his ears. He must surely have been fathered by a cat with some Russian Blue in him, I quietly ponder. He is a beautiful dark grey, almost black, and his eyes are the striking amber of

Titus's. He has a strong otherworldly look to him. Gizmo is altogether different. He's a white-bibbed, white-stockinged tabby with an adorable pink nose and he is a hopeless flirt. He is also indubitably fat. As this patently applies to me as well, it is with some hypocrisy that I cry out:

'Good heavens, Gizmo! How on earth did you get to be that shape?' I hear Peter laugh, but David rather defensively says:

'It's not his fault. He's an indoors cat, and simply can't get enough exercise.' David is too much of a gentleman to ask me if that is also my problem. On full investigation of the whats and wherefores of the domestic arrangements of this very male household I discover that Merlin is the shy, heat-loving, purring fave of Dave and that Gizmo is the wayward, engaging passion of Peter's life whose day starts with a big cuddle with his precious Gizmo. Mine with Fannie begins the same way.

'Ah,' I find myself murmuring indulgently, 'the morning cuddle, I understand, I understand.' But I quickly discover that the ritual in this household is significantly more complex than mine. There are two fish tanks – one upstairs and one downstairs. The fish tank upstairs 'belongs' to Gizmo and the one downstairs to Merlin. Peter diffidently reveals to me that Gizmo has to be allowed to smell the fish-food, which has to be first shaken up and down in its little cardboard carton before the fish upstairs can be fed and that this procedure must be strictly observed however tight the human time schedule might be. After Gizmo has sanctioned that the food is good and the fish may be fed, he then has to be taken to the tank so that he might watch the feeding from its beginning until the last morsel can be seen no more. I am so awestruck at this snippet of intelligence and its being an unwavering rite of passage that I forget to ask Dave if Merlin gets the same treatment downstairs, but rather assume not on the grounds of horses for courses, or rather cats for fish tanks. Dave, later on in the evening, makes an astute observation of their boys, which on reflection is something I have often unconsciously seen in my three resident cats.

'Have you noticed that when one of them starts to lick himself, the other one immediately seems to go, "Oh yes, good idea, I think I'll have a bit of a lick and polish too"?' The act of imitation is endemic to companion and especially sibling cats it would seem. Dave later embarks on his concerns about Gizmo's recurring attacks on Merlin, almost always that way round, which will start with passionate allogrooming[1] and quickly descend into a full throatal attack on Merlin.

'I shout at him to stop it immediately, I really yell at him. He always pauses and looks up at me with an expression of "don't know why you're shouting at me, I'm not doing anything, really I'm not" and stops and turns away and then the second he thinks I'm no longer watching he just goes straight back into attack mode, straight for poor Merlin's jugular.'

As I drive home I relive the pleasure of a splendid evening spent in the happy exchanges of cat lore, the imbibing of a very decent bottle of dry Chardonnay, the company of two charming men and two magnificent boy cats. Peter and David are waiting to move house and have gone through all the agonies that Michael and I did when looking for the house in Hutton Roof, which is the name of the village we now live in. What will be cat-friendly, what will be cat-safe? I greatly look forward to their next chapter.

On 17 November a tiny six-line piece appears in the *Evening Standard* Homes-Gossip page about the cottage, but

---

[1] Allogrooming is the grooming of each other to mutual advantage.

there is no accompanying photograph as they have run out of space. The description is so low key that I realise reading it that it would be a miracle if any potential buyer responded and, predictably, no buyer does. Michael and I sink into gloom, although we knew that once October had passed the possibility of selling before the end of the year would become ever more elusive, but we are unable to rent it either, and life in the Coach House noticeably tenses up.

CHAPTER 3

I find myself worrying about Fannie and her 'condition', and although I watch her carefully it is hard to tell what her state of mind is. Spasmodically she will suddenly call out, as if she is still on heat, but certainly not for any length of time, nor with the raucous, distracted-but-somehow-driven intensity of her earlier calls. Yesterday she was lying on the sofa next to Titus – the only source of heat in the Coach House at this time being from the wood-burning stove – when I witnessed a new piece of behaviour. She started to groom Titus, which she often does, but as she started the process it became noticeably more intense than her normal spit and polish. She did a thorough going over of both eyes – corners, lids, lashes – and then started a most earnest excavation within Titus's ears, pushing her tongue right down inside them, at which point Titus started to object. Fannie immediately clamped her front leg over Titus and pinioned her to the sofa, so that she was unable to move. Titus dropped her ears down unhappily into the Yoda position, but surprisingly sat still and let it happen to her. Fannie had a completely mesmerised expression on her face, as if she were barely aware of what she was doing and I felt most strongly that I was witnessing a rehearsal on autopilot of things that she will need to do in the future. She continues to look for new places to climb into and is constantly hiding inside the spare room wardrobe. On the other hand her weight does not seem to have changed very much. It might have increased slightly but it is hard to be sure. I should weigh her, of course, but already it is too late for that.

Today is Saturday and I hear our ship's bell outside the door clanging loudly and, as I run downstairs, I can see our village friends, Jeff and Karen, with their two daughters, Lesley and Alex, smiling in a group outside.

'We've come to look at Fannie,' Alex beams up at me.

'Well, come in and have a good look. She will let you hold her.' As I push Fannie forward towards Alex and she gently strokes her, she looks up at me.

'Can we definitely have one of her kittens, please?' she asks me beguilingly. She knows that I have already said they should have one since their lovely cat Tinkerbell died only a few weeks ago. I watch Alex longingly stroking Fannie, and her yearning for animals and gentleness with them reminds me of how passionately I cared for animals at her age too. Some people never grow out of it!

'Alex, you may have first choice. Oh, well, I have promised a female kitten to Peter Warner, the illustrator of the books, but as long as he can have a female you can choose which one you want. I have also said that Janice, my agent, can have one too if there are enough to go round, but I do want one for Fannie to keep as well, but yes, Alex, you shall have one, I promise.' When Alex smiles it is like the sun coming out.

It is now the Sunday preceding the Monday morning of the operation to neuter Titus and Pushkin and with its dawning comes an overwhelming sense of guilt on my part. In the past we have all lived out our lives, the cats and me, without my invasive interference and now I am interfering every which way in their lives. First I consciously take Fannie to a stud – however, in my defence I have waited five years before doing it and this is the very last chance she has of mating and she was calling this last time fit to break my heart – but nevertheless it was my decision not hers and now I am taking Titus and Pushkin to be neutered, again my resolution. And yet, is that true? The truth is that my interference has been there all their lives. I have consciously contained them within the garden, for example, rather than giving them complete freedom as I have deemed it safer for them. I have kept up their inoculations for their own protection. I have allowed Titus to be operated on, twice, most painfully, for her greater good even though through the period of recovery it undoubtedly felt to her for her greater suffering, so to take these decisions now is no more than I have done throughout their lives. And yet, and yet . . .

In some ways my guilt is made worse by the fact that tonight Titus and Pushkin must starve, while it is essential that Fannie eats at regular intervals throughout the night. Because of the open-plan nature of the Coach House I decide that I should sleep in the spare room, which does have a door that can be closed, and have Fannie shut in there with me with her high-protein cat food, leaving the two other cats free to roam in a house with no accessible cat food. As luck would have it I too have to starve, as I am due for a cholesterol test first thing just before I take Tites and Pushie down for their two ops; the difference being, of course, that I know why I am starving and so it makes sense to me, whereas they don't and are really upset about it. Titus in particular sits squarely in front of me and looks up at me with serious, large eyes and makes her strangulated squawky miaow more demandingly every minute. Eventually Michael and I say strangely formal goodnights to each other and he goes off to his wing and I to mine. I take Fannie into the room with me and after a lot of tossing and turning I get to sleep. At 2.30 a.m. I am woken by a snuffling, scuffling noise outside the door, which is then greeted by an equally noisy set of sniffings my side of the door. I turn the light on and see that Fannie is trying to dig her way out to meet the other two and, of course, when I open the door there is a reception committee made up of one ginger and one grey[2] cat, both of whom manage mysteriously to exude an air on the one hand of feeling betrayed and on the other of being really hungry. What will not have helped the cause is that Fannie will certainly smell of the food that she has been eating through the night, even if she has not communicated the fact to them. I quickly grab the food that was down for her and shove it into a drawer. Fannie is not happy at being separated from them so I decide to leave the food hidden and the door open. For the remainder of the night I get up at hourly intervals and shut Fannie in by herself to allow her to feed and then open up again. By 7 a.m. I am actually pleased that this night is over and the dreaded day has begun. It is a strange fact but, yet again, once I have actually left them in the tender hands of the vet nurse Liz, having waved cheerfully across the lobby at Gerard and then rather embarrassingly nearly bursting into tears while I ask Liz in a wobbly voice to be sure to phone me as soon as she has news, I feel absurdly cheerful. I have renounced my responsibility. I no longer have any decision left to take. It is out of my hands and what will be, will be. At 12.30 the gentle Gerard phones me to say that they have come round and they are fine, but he would like to see me about Titus when I come down to collect them. I go down and he tells me that Titus had possibly the largest uterus of any cat he

---

[2] technically speaking red and blue!

has ever operated on and that the likelihood of her becoming pregnant with so much build-up in it was remote and that it really did need to be removed. His biggest concern is, however, that he thinks she is experiencing pain in her back legs from her earlier operations – a pain akin to arthritis – and he suggests that I put her back on Metacam which she had been on when she last had her patellar operated on. I have to take her back again in a couple of days' time anyway. I take my wounded burdens home and now dread the effect it will have on Fannie. I let them out and they both move quickly towards the feeding station. Titus sits down and starts to eat. Pushkin falls over, picks himself up, and tries to run upstairs but falls over again and then runs away and hunches himself up in a corner. Fannie comes down and sees them both and hisses mildly. Every time she smells the antiseptic on Titus she hisses again, but her hissing is quiet and seems almost involuntary and she clearly recognises Titus as her sister. Cats are so bad to other cats when they return home with vet smells on them. Later on I find Pushkin dragging his bottom across the carpet leaving small streaks of blood behind him. Poor little castrato, what have I done? Titus takes herself up to our bathroom instead of lying with Fannie on the chair in my study, which is where she would normally lie. Later on Pushkin swells up so badly that the following day I take him back to the vet. Liz the vet nurse is wonderfully reassuring and gets another vet, Ben, to come and inject him with antibiotics and give him painkillers. Meanwhile Titus receives an all clear on her condition; she is one brave girl as always, but I am anxious to get her Metacam painkillers into her when we get home.

One weekend Karen and Alex pop in while they are walking so that Alex can stroke Fannie and check up on her unborn kittens. During their visit Alex tells me that Lesley has managed to acquire a young kitten from a pet shop in Manchester who is called Joey and he is currently at home with them. Will I come down and look at him? As ever, with my weakness for kittens, I bound off to meet young Joey. He has darling white socks, a white chest and prominent tabby stripes. When Peter Warner saw him much later he loved his looks and called him a 'classic tabby'. He is so tiny and I reckon that he was no more than six weeks old, if that, when Lesley first saw him. It always distresses me when pet shops sell kittens as they often sell them dangerously under-age, and they need that time with their mother. Lesley adores him, as does the whole family, but she is having problems with his feeding. He is flea ridden and he needs worming. Each night when they put him to bed in his basket they lie him near a warm hot-water bottle because he is so shivery and cold. Lesley says to me:

'Well, he cost £70 and then we've spent nearly that again in vet's fees.'

'That's awful for you and I'm so sorry but at least he has come to a good home, so it could be worse and he is a safe boy now.'

'We did try cat shelters but they didn't have any kittens, this isn't a good time of year. And then when we saw him in the shop he was the last remaining kitten.'

He doesn't seem to be drinking and I remember Susan Hill, whose cat Tallulah was the grandmother of Fannie and

Titus, saying to me that kittens that were in need of cat milk would often benefit from doses of carnation milk, so I suggest that they try that, and it seems to get Joey through this initial problem.

CHAPTER 4

In spite of the anxiety we both feel because of the lack of the sale of Moon Cottage I find myself beginning to look forward to our first Christmas in Hutton Roof. Money is a bit tight, but if you are able to stay warm and there is enough to eat and on top of that you look out over 'paradise' and you are surrounded by animals that hold your heart and you have the love of a good man or woman, then life is not all bad. On the good man or woman front, Michael and I are snapping at each other from time to time, sometimes quite fiercely, but we both know that this is a direct result of our financial situation, which cannot go on forever and things will surely get better. Just before Christmas a piece about Moon Cottage appears in *Country Living Magazine* and we get very excited. We then receive two calls, which come to nothing. Two days later, we are phoned by our agent who thinks they have found a renter, but they are still awaiting confirmation. This will give us some leeway if it comes off and psychologically it will help.

One day, in a splendid and I might say successful endeavour to cheer me up, my chum Jane tells me on the phone that her late mother had been very fond of a dear farmer in Suffolk who, some time during the sixties, had been the proud guardian of three cats who were fabulously named Magnificat, Terrificat and Gloria-in-excelsis-Deo. I would love to feel that their feline namesakes might walk the land again. While on the subject of Gloria in excelsis Deo, around this time Michael volunteers to join the Christmas carollers on their rounds and on a cold dark evening shortly thereafter he is summoned to a rendezvous in the village, where he meets up with a group of twenty or so grown-ups and children. Hours later he returns, full of good cheer and mince pies and tales of mock horror at the way people have 'paid us off'.

'What do you mean, people paid you off?'

'Well, if anyone had given us a tenner, say, before we actually set out, all the carollers took that as a sign that they would rather we didn't call on them, so although we walked the full length of the village street, at certain houses someone would say, "No, not that one, we've been paid off", but it made it easier because we still stopped at about fifteen houses and we would never have got round them all, so it was a good thing.'

'Did you get invited in by anyone?'

'Oh yes, the Armisteads invited us into their kitchen at the big farm in the village and also Bernard did down at Gale Triangle. He offered us mince pies and wine. That was our last port of call, but if we had started there we would never have got round.' He smiles seraphically. 'It was really nice,' he murmurs happily.

Shortly after the house-to-house carols there is the annual Carol Service accompanied by the Kirkby Lonsdale Brass Band at our little church of St John's, immediately next to the Coach House, and although I have been to many carol services in my life this one is simply the most lovely, for its simplicity and the feeling of love and warmth that seems to radiate from everyone there. The church is lit up enchantingly and looks quite beautiful with its splendid decorations of flowers and holly and ivy and it is packed. As we stand jammed into our little pew singing 'God Rest Ye Merry Gentlemen, Let Nothing Ye Dismay', I am overwhelmed with a sense of everlastingness.

Johnny and Oliver, Michael's two youngest sons, both come up for Christmas and the celebrations start in earnest. On Christmas Day, to my childish delight, when I first look out of the window I find the entire world outside has turned white.

'Michael, wake up! Look! Look! We really do have a white Christmas!'

'Don't believe you,' he mumbles from under the warm duvet.

'Go on, go on, get up and see it!' I wallop him with a pillow. But as he lifts himself up on one elbow that wonderful eerie bluey-white can be seen round the edges of the pale cream curtains. He rushes to the window and flings the curtains apart.

'Wayhay, that's FANTASTIC!'

I run downstairs and let the cats out. As always when they tread in snow they fastidiously shake each paw as if that will sort it out once and for all and then put their feet down again and stop and shake again, perplexed at this cold white stuff. They peer nervously through the fence into the field at the back, but because it is totally unrecognisable to them, they stay in the garden and eventually all three of them sit in a line on the bench looking around them. Soon they quietly jump down and come back inside the house.

Later on in the day, just before the sun drops below the horizon, I go out for a solitary walk and climb part of the way up the crag behind us so I can look down over the village. Seeing the little houses huddled together with their bright lights twinkling out and the smoke floating up from many a chimney is strangely affecting. Being not part of it

and yet part of it is sad and beautiful at the same time. Being on the outside looking in through the windows, being a small element within this village and being made so welcome and yet knowing we may still have the entire dream snatched away is heart-rending. I sit down on a small outcrop of rock and watch the light over the Yorkshire fells until the sun starts to sink behind me. As the sun starts to set, the monochrome world in front of me changes from its stark varying shades of white broken only by the brown bracken twigs sticking up through the snow, to a glorious pink and then burgundy red as the reflection of the sun bleeds across the snow and over the ice-covered summit of Ingleborough in one majestic farewell to daylight and the end of Christmas Day.

The snow stays for another couple of days and then almost imperceptibly melts away and our green, brown and purple landscape is restored to us in its former glory.

Several days have passed since Christmas and Fannie has been sick again, this morning, twice. She has had this intermittent sickness for a couple of weeks and it does seem to be very like a feline form of morning sickness. She keeps miaowing, but I'm not sure what she wants nor, I think, is she. Pushkin is much better and now at last walking with his tail up. Titus, on the other hand, although she showed little side-effect of the hysterectomy at the beginning and is self-evidently stoic, is obviously in quite a lot of pain still and currently hates to be picked up by either of us. She is such a sweet-natured cat and so forgiving.

January is upon us and so far there has been a worrying silence from our agent, but finally on the third of January we are told at last that our renter will be taking possession of the cottage on the seventh. We celebrate this event in a low-key manner, but it is a great deal better than not having a renter.

It is now seven weeks since Fannie was mated by Zimmy with just over two weeks to go if she is indeed pregnant. 'If' must seem a slightly surprising thing to say at this stage, but although her uterus is undoubtedly swollen, there hasn't been any noticeable change in her size for the last couple of weeks. I am fearful that the litter might be very small or, worse, that the growth of the kittens has stopped altogether. Since Pushkin has been neutered and recovered, he is far more energetic than he used to be and chases both of the girls at least twice daily, quite vigorously. Fannie always hisses at him; Titus more often than not just claims 'pax' by lying on a bed somewhere to keep out of the firing line. I am feeding Fannie more highly concentrated kitten food and Pushkin is eating it too, could this be the reason? When he gets close to them he merely wants to pounce at them not mount them, but they both appear to dislike it from their responses.

Tuesday night and we have gales that it later transpires do untold damage to the whole county. For the first time since we moved into Cumbria I am really frightened. I lie in our huge bed and listen to the wind howling. We have three windows in our bedroom, one facing north, one east and one west, and as I lie there the wind buffeting every surface of the house begins to sound like hugely amplified wild beasts, chomping, whining, squeaking, and squalling around the house. I keep hearing distant bangings of doors and rattling of windows in the other part of the house and sometimes in a brief lull I just catch the rustle of one or other of the cats moving around restlessly. Michael, bless him, doesn't hear a sound because he has been working his socks off all week down at Moon Cottage, getting it ready for the renter, and arrives back in the early evening, exhausted and falls into a deep coma-like sleep. Trouble is when you are lying next to someone who is fast asleep and you are frightened, it is strangely lonelier than if you are alone when you can get up and make a cup of tea and turn the lights on. I am aware of his brother, John, too, who is on the other side of the house and I know he is a light sleeper, so I imagine he is sleeping only fitfully if at all with this fearsome racket. In between the huge sounds of the roaring wind the rain lashes at the house in a way I have never heard it before and now a new worry starts. Will the wind get under the tiles and lift the whole roof off? The wind does seem to be alive almost; it pauses as if in some way it is mustering its energy and then it comes in and hits the house apparently on three sides with a massive sound and then it goes quiet again and then another huge onslaught. This is wind at its most savagely brutal.

In the morning we go out nervously to see what the damage is. We find branches, huge branches, the size of small trees, ripped off our Scots Pines, fallen in the road outside. A farmer with the aid of his tractor has moved one of the branches which was blocking the road to the side so we now cannot get our cars out of our little yard, but we just feel such relief that they appear not to have damaged any passers-by, which they so easily might have done. We are without electricity for twenty-four hours, but I quite enjoy the challenge of cooking on top of the wood-burning stove. Not having hot water is less amusing, however. There are terrible floods in Carlisle and we realise, bad though it has been, we got off lightly compared with other parts of Cumbria. Five nights later we have more of the same. The noise from the woodland behind the house is particularly spooky, with repeated creaking and crashing sounds, and indeed afterwards we find there are many ancient trees which have been uprooted and much forest is laid low. On this second night of high winds the cats patrol the house more restlessly than the first night and are clearly very alarmed. I wonder too on such nights how high the mortality of birds, small mammals and insects might have been.

CHAPTER 5

Following the great gales I receive a phone call from Hilary, our friend in the village, who has two cats, Thomas, her long-term resident neutered tom, and Ollie, a three-quarters-grown male kitten who appeared on Halloween in need of a home. Hilary adores Ollie, who is jet-black and shiny like a little olive, hence his name, although they have had problems with him from early on. He started to wet their bed. Hilary reckons it was because he was frightened of Thomas but also because he was just entering his difficult 'teens'. She took Ollie to be neutered just before Christmas and that seemed to have resolved the problem.

Now, however, she sounds at the end of her tether. He has started 'performing' in the dining-room, downstairs, close to the window, behind the curtains, and this time it is bowels as well as bladder that he is evacuating. I can tell that if the problem is not resolved soon she is going to be forced to rehome Ollie, and she clearly doesn't want to do this. I feel slightly helpless as I would offer to take him for her, but I cannot with Fannie's brood about to be born. I take her down a copy of a brilliant book by Celia Haddon, the pet correspondent for the *Daily Telegraph*, called *Chats with Cats: How to Read Your Cat's*

Mind,[3] in which, among other feline problems, she very sensitively discusses the stress factors that might make cats go to the toilet outside their litter trays and how to resolve the impasse. Having read that chapter again I suggest to Hilary that it might be other cats trying to get in through their cat flap, or through the French windows, or even the stress of the gales that is upsetting poor little Ollie, as my own cats were clearly very disturbed by them. Hilary agrees to read the book and see if they can work out a modus vivendi. I make a promise to her, however, that if it doesn't work out I will find Ollie a home.

Today I go down to the vet's to pick up some kitten food for Fannie and see Gerard just as he is about to start operating. I shout out gaily:

'Hope I won't have to call you out on the night of the twenty-second or twenty-third, but are you around? Those are the nights that Fannie should perform.' He groans back at me in mock alarm. Earlier on when I had taken Titus and Pushkin back for their post-op check-ups I had told Gerard how worried I was about Fannie being small, but he had said if it is a small litter, cats often don't show very much beforehand. It could just be a couple of kittens.

Fannie continues to search assiduously throughout each day for a nesting place, and I am having ongoing problems with Pushkin wanting to be in every possible litterbed I provide and Fannie not liking to lie in it after Pushkin's smell is there. She continually grooms Titus vigorously in an instinctive rehearsal for what is to come and Titus is clearly not terribly amused by the unrelenting ablutions she is forced to endure.

Today is the sixty-third day from the first mating of Zimmy

[3] *Chats with Cats: How to Read Your Cat's Mind* by Celia Haddon (Little Books Ltd., 2004) £8.99 ISBN 19044 3531 9.

and Fannie, and Marje, the breeder and carer of Zimmy who phones up from time to time to check how things are going, says that if Fannie makes it until the sixty-fourth day, tomorrow in other words, there should be no problem with the survival of the kittens. Fannie seems in very good health. She is full of beans and she is eating like a horse. She is slightly more jumpy than usual, but I am sure that is normal as her instinct must be telling her she is vulnerable.

Michael and I are now sleeping in the spare bedroom as it is more likely that this is where Fannie will choose to have her kittens and from now on it could be any time, and my most experienced kitten-midwives seem to think early hours of the morning is optimum time usually. We rose this morning early, by our new standard of living that is to say, at 6.30 as Michael is going to the christening of his grand-nephew, but I am staying on kitten watch back at home and there is a breathtaking sunrise which has taken several glorious hours. There was an iron-hard frost overnight and the eastern sky in front of us is ablaze with a huge red globe of a sun and the day is promising to be gorgeous.

Later on, Karen, Alex and Lesley all come up, as they have most weekends, to see how Fannie is progressing and Alex, who is yearning for one of the kittens, strokes her gently. Alex is also scrupulous and wants to say hullo to Titus who has stayed out of the way asleep, so just before they leave I take her up to my study where we find Titus and she makes a big fuss of her. Alex is a born cat lover. Lesley's young kitten, Joey, is now doing very well and is spending more time at Hutton Roof to Alex's delight. Alex loves Joey because he will play with her, although she tells me he bites her playfully, but she missed this with Tinks a bit because 'he was always Daddy's cat, and that was it!'

Another day comes and goes and Fannie's sixty-fifth day of pregnancy dawns, which one of the feline websites says is the true average length of time for most domestic cats.

She is currently nesting in the box down to the right of my desk which is where I would love her to have them, and certainly where I would love her to nurse them, so I can keep an eye on them and the other cats too, but yesterday Titus kept sitting in there and simply wouldn't get out. Titus has left it alone so far today, but just now as I was writing this, when she tried to join Fannie in the box, Fannie very gently pushed her away, so now she is lying in front of Fannie half in and half out of it.

One of the things that made me laugh this morning is that Titus, who again insisted on sharing the box with Fannie, had her bottom very thoroughly cleaned and looked completely outraged while it was happening and eventually struck out mildly at Fannie, but clearly Fannie's instinct to 'mother' is so strong that she was unable to resist it. So at the end of that round, Titus stays put in the box and Fannie gets out and goes into the cold bedroom. But right now she has come back and is lying on my lap, purring loudly.

This morning, on the sixty-sixth day, Fannie is more urgently than before searching for a nesting place, so surely it must be closer now. Marje last night on the phone urged me to phone the vet 'by tomorrow morning' if nothing has happened. One of the things that is strange is that Titus seems to have taken on the symptoms of pregnancy along with Fannie. She is lying in the box and seems strange in the same way that Fannie is.

I am trying like mad not to get stressed out, but it is very tense-making, this waiting and not knowing what is going to happen. I have a gut feeling that it is going to be tomorrow now, but I am beginning to be really concerned.

The following day we find Titus repeatedly licking Fannie, who is cowering down allowing it to happen, looking very subdued, which is the complete reverse of Fannie's previously zealous administrations to Titus. It is as if Titus is comforting her in some way. I phone the vet's and tell them that Fannie is now overdue and I am worried and I need them to take a look at her. I take her down and Gerard agrees to scan her. He shaves her belly and puts a large animal scanner on her because his small animal scanner is not around. As I watch his face my heart sinks.

'There are no kittens in here, I am fairly certain, unless she has two tiny ones hidden up under her ribcage. Are you sure she couldn't have had some kittens and they are lying dead somewhere? Her nipples are engorged and she has all the appearance of a pregnant cat, but her belly isn't large enough for a litter I would say, so she must have lost them.'

I know there are no dead kittens and I explain to him that I have been sleeping with her every night for the last four nights with the door shut and there is nowhere she could have hidden them. He looks mystified.

I put Fannie back in the carrying cage and by the time I get her home her stomach has shrunk and there is no appearance of pregnancy of any kind. In deference to Gerard I look all round the spare bedroom for any dead kittens, but there are none as I had assumed. I get on to the internet and look up 'feline phantom pregnancy' and very quickly I realise that poor little Fannie has gone through the full term of an imagined pregnancy right up to producing milk. Cats have phantom pregnancies more rarely than dogs because they are induced ovulators so must have been mated in order to go through it, and the chances then are that they will have been impregnated, whereas with dogs a hormonal bitch could just believe she is pregnant without being anywhere near a dog. Therefore it is unusual for a vet who doesn't deal regularly with cat breeders (in these days of widespread spayed cats from an early age) to encounter feline phantom pregnancies whereas canine 'phantoms' are much more common.

Fannie herself is all right but I would say she has the air of a very depressed cat. Could that possibly have been why Titus was first imitating her and then consoling her? She already knew then that it was 'wrong' in some way? Fannie just takes herself off to the chair in my study and Titus lies curled up next to her, and I leave them to work it out with each other. She has now stopped looking in the nesting boxes and so with a heavy heart I remove them all and return the house to its previous order.

Michael and I are both utterly devastated by it and I feel completely flattened and empty. We had wanted kittens from Fannie more than I can easily explain and if this is how we feel, how much worse is it for that poor little cat? I phone Peter and break the bad news to him and he is, of course, disappointed but very understanding, and then that evening I phone Alex. Alex is heart-broken and says:

'Oh, I'll never get a kitten now, it will never happen.' I try to reassure her that somehow I will find a way and she will get a kitten.

CHAPTER 6

By coincidence on 26 January I receive two emails of note, both about Pushkin. The first is from reader Rita Lawson in Durham, who responds to something I have said in one of my books about cats and their powers of reasoning, which I strongly believe I witnessed in Pushkin when he was trying to escape from his enclosure in Moon Cottage and she too has observed how they can solve problems by thinking hard about them.

– – –

From: Rita Lawson
To: Marilyn Edwards
Sent: Wednesday, January 26, 5:51 pm
Subject: Sam and his thought processes

Dear Marilyn

I have two cats, Lucy and Sam, and in response to your story about cats thinking through problems, I have one about Sam. If Lucy tries something and it doesn't work, she forgets about it and gets on with something else. She has no patience, but Sam is a different kettle of fish.

He has a 'thing' about plastic bags (I can never leave any lying about, as he gets inside them!). He saw me one day with a plastic bag of sugar, and saw that I had put it in a top kitchen cupboard. No problem, he thought, I can open doors, but what he didn't know was that that door opened from the left side and not the right, so he was trying to open the hinge side.

He sat on the floor and stared up at that cupboard for about 20 minutes, before jumping onto the worktop, onto the extractor fan and from there onto the top of the offending cupboard. He then opened the cupboard with his paw from the top, leaned over, and delicately lifted out the bag of sugar with one claw, dropped it onto the ground and jumped down after it. Success!!!!

And then a little later I receive this addendum from Rita about something that happened to a friend of hers:

My friend told me this story that I thought was just great. If I had read about it in a magazine I would not have believed it, but this was a tale about her own dog and cat.

The animals were not allowed in the bedroom so every night the bedroom door was shut firmly. However, one morning the cat was found on the bed and the dog on the bedroom floor. Margaret told her husband, Roy, off for not shutting the door, but this happened night after night.

The mystery was solved one day when they caught the culprits in the act.

The dog was standing with his nose pressed against the bedroom door, the cat jumped onto the dog's shoulders, then proceeded to reach up and pull down the door handle with his paws and the dog then pressed on the door with his nose and opened it!

I just love it. Hoping all are well, both humans and felines!!
Rita

What is especially wonderful about this second story is that it gives weight to the concept of cross-species communication and then the question is, who thought it out? My money goes on the cat as the solution depended upon one of the animals envisaging the manipulation of the handle, and that had to be the animal that was going to be the highest up.

The second email is from Ruth, who has a cat called Pushkin, and some extraordinary instinct in her makes her ask me where I got my Pushkin. By a process of elimination via email we find that both Pushkins came from the same breeder, Mary White, and are cousins, well at any rate definitely related, and I enclose this extract from her about her Pushkin because it is very typical of a Russian Blue boy. Ruth's Pushkin is about six months younger than my lad.

– – –

From: Ruth
To: Marilyn
Sent: Wednesday, January 26, 1:58 AM
Subject: Pushkin and Pushkin!

Dear Marilyn

I have kept in touch with Mary White from time to time and sent her photos of Pushkin. They had a baby a couple of years ago and have given up breeding cats and have had them all spayed, so my Pushkin was one of the last of the line. We don't have any other animals (although I'd like more).

My Pushkin is a cat of deep thoughts and, as you say in your book: if only we could get inside the cat's mind! But I guess that's what makes them so incredibly fascinating. And those disdainful looks: when I'm singing loving songs to him, or speaking in that silly baby-talk way telling him how beautiful he is, or dancing around with him in my arms . . . *what on earth is she doing now? Put me down, I'm far too dignified for this type of behaviour. I'm Russian for goodness sake not a common type of cat!* . . .

He certainly is a one-person cat and, although he's gone through periods of not wanting to sit on me or be affectionate, he has now settled into spending time snuggling up to me, on the bed or chair and I just love it. Of course, one can't possibly move until he decides to jump off or my arm goes dead, whichever comes soonest. He also loves to head-butt everything, but he has never done that rubbing around the legs that other cats so often do. His most endearing thing is to snuggle right up in my arms and rub the back of his head hard against my face. Also, he makes lots of funny grunts and groans while he is sleeping; sometimes I do them back and can have quite a grunty/groany conversation with him!

Kindest wishes,

Ruth

In the Coach House, cat life resumes a normality of sorts. Fannie continues to be depressed, but slowly she recovers and her nipples very quickly shrink back to normal. Gerard thought she had actually lactated they were so swollen, but the very acts of taking her in the car to the vet and the trauma of shaving her for the scan seem to have speeded up the 'termination' of the imagined pregnancy, and since then I have spoken to two other cat breeders who have experienced the same sort of scenario. I ask various experts whether they think I should risk taking Fannie to the stud again, but the consensus is that as a near-maiden cat of six years of age I would be exposing her to unnecessary risks by pursuing the possibility of her breeding again. Within days she is back on heat again and with this her spirits lift and ours sink, as she is astoundingly vocal. However, I am glad that she is feeling so much better. Nature is a remarkable healer as well as trickster.

Michael and I agonise about what we should do. We had always intended to have one litter from the kittens that grew up to be Fannie and Titus, and that was why Pushkin joined our household. Having lived all this time in the belief that Fannie was going to have kittens we feel bereft now by their absence. We talk about future possibilities and throw various ideas up in the air. After a while I ponder, as with everything in life, has it happened for a purpose? I assume from her silence that Hilary is still worrying about Ollie, and so I decide I should take this as a sign and I write her a letter. This is an extract from it:

The Coach House – 9 February

Dear Hilary,
Am writing you a little letter rather than ringing you . . . to give you a chance to think this through before you phone me.

Michael and I have talked Ollie over and have decided to offer him a home with us with our cats, but it is of course risky because of Pushkin and if it turns out that Ollie still has his incontinence problems we would have to find an alternative home for him, but because Pushkin is very gentle it is just possible it will work out OK between them. (I am envisaging trouble between the males as that is how it usually is, but of course the females could be a problem too!)

However, it is just possible that in the meantime you have found a way of all living together and you would rather he stayed with you, hence the letter, because I want you to be sure either way.

I have been advised not to let Fannie get pregnant and what I would ideally like to do, therefore, is get a young female kitten and breed from her, and if we take Ollie on then I couldn't do that, because I will simply have too many cats . . . Having said all that, I would love to give him a home and would do every-thing within my power to make it work out for him.

Hilary . . . could you phone me when you have had a chance to digest all this and let me know how you feel and if you want him to go, when I can come and collect him?

All the best,

Marilyn and Michael

This produces a phone call by return from Hilary, who very positively tells me that things have improved completely at their house and that Ollie and Thomas are getting on fine and Ollie has stopped soiling the dining-room – she has been using the Feliway plug-in pheromone and that has helped, but whatever was stressing him has ceased. The whole family have discussed Ollie and his future and are appalled at the idea that I might take him away and that it is very sweet of me to offer, but they definitely do not want Ollie to leave them. I am absolutely delighted for them and also I find relieved for me too, as I so want to pursue the idea of acquiring a female kitten, and this now frees me up to do that.

Ann, a book-selling friend from the West Country, comes to us en route for a family holiday. Ann, quietly spoken, gentle and cat mad, enters the house and refuses to be coerced upstairs to her room where I want to make her feel at home, but insists instead on pursuing a long schmoozey intro-duction of herself to all three of the cats. Even the one-person-loving Pushkin, Mr-Timid-Incarnate, responds briefly to her overtures before wandering off to find a suitable spot for a nice sleep. Fannie spends some considerable time taking her on board, watching her and then lying near her, squinting sneakily at her through half-closed eyes while pretending to be asleep (in fact she does this for the whole of Ann's visit). But Titus – now there – I have never seen anything like it. Immediately, there is an exceptional rapport between them. To begin with Titus just lies down and over on her back for her tummy to be rubbed, as she does with anyone and everyone who is prepared to invest their time in this way – such a floozy – but soon it develops beyond that. Having been doing chores out in the kitchen, I return to the sitting-room to find Titus sitting upright on Ann's knee, her eyes half closed in a semi-transcendental state, her head held high and her white bib to the fore, with an expression of such supreme self-satisfaction on her face that it defies belief. She maintains this expression of extreme rapture for what seems to me like hours and I have to say I'm pretty impressed with Ann's endurance too. Later on I overhear Ann whispering to Titus about a little visit to Gloucester and Titus looks back up at her with large quiescent eyes. As Pushkin saunters across the dining-room table for a brief head-butt and Ann runs her hand along his muscled flank admiringly, I explain how frustrating it was that he never attempted to mate with either Fannie or Titus and there always seemed to have been some block there of some kind. Ann laughs and says:

'Oh, I do know what you mean. It's like when you see a really attractive man and then you discover he's gay and as a woman you just can't help feeling "what a waste!"'

I discover that Ann, who has had many cats in her life, when searching for a new companion cat who in the event became her beloved Bella, went to a cat sanctuary in Stafford where she then lived. As soon as she arrived a beautiful black cat came towards her and when she put her hand out to it, the cat climbed straight up her shoulder and wrapped itself around her. She turns to me as she is telling me this and smiles disarmingly:

'Oh, I just knew that that cat would do that to everyone and anyone; I was sure that the very next person who came in would get that treatment and find it a home. But when I saw the tortoiseshell cat that is Bella she was scrunched up in the back of the cage with body language saying, "Don't touch me – don't come near me – leave me alone" and I knew it was her that I needed to take home with me.'

Ann, having got Bella home with the full assurance from the sanctuary that the young couple who had brought the cat into them for rehoming because they had started their own human family and did not feel a cat could be kept in a household with a new baby (on which subject Ann's comment, which I share, is "rubbish") had had the cat injected and spayed, was somewhat disconcerted when Bella started to show all the signs of being on heat. She was so much in denial of this as the possible explanation of Bella's miaowings and rollings around that she looked up all manner of diseases in the belief that it might be something else that was ailing her young queen. She finally took her to her local vet who assured her that Bella was indeed on heat and offered to do the operation the next day, which he duly did.

On the day that Ann prepares to take her leave of us all I find myself actively counting feline heads, as it hasn't gone without my notice that she is the owner of a large, squashy sort of zip-up canvas holdall that could be quite useful for cat-carrying purposes. But in the end, after she has gone there are still three cats, all present and correct, so it was all talk, Titus, all talk!

CHAPTER 7

Michael and I have several conversations about how we should go about tracking down a kitten, but he is seriously distracted by the lodger in Moon Cottage, who keeps making complaint after complaint about equipment not working and other problems, and both he and the agent are beginning to be exasperated by it.

I try a local cat rescue home but there are no kittens needing homes, only spayed cats, so I try local farmers but again nothing doing. I have been studying different breeds and am attracted to the Bengal cat for two reasons: they are very beautiful, of course, but also and more importantly they have very outgoing personalities and, while I adore Pushkin, his tendency to imitate the dormouse and keep himself strictly to himself can be slightly maddening. My friend Sue always teases me, as the guardian of Siamese and Devon Rex all noted for their outspoken behaviour, with phrases like: 'Come on, Marilyn, when are you going to get a real cat?' Actually I am not sure that she has ever actually said that, but I know that is what she thinks. In fact, Sue is due to visit us in the near future, so I decide I must get the ball rolling on the kitten-acquiring front, pronto. I start to put out feelers with different breeders and finally discover that melanistic (black) Bengal cats[4] are considered less desirable to anyone who is breeding Bengal cats since their colour is not accepted by the Bengal Cat Club as suitable and as a result they are sold as pets for markedly less than the asking price of the standard Bengal.[5] There are two types of patterns in Bengals: the Spotted (Leopard) and the Marble, and many variations of colour within these patterns, but black is shunned as a breeding colour. I am astonished. Black cats are just beautiful creatures, almost always they have astonishingly shiny fur and vivid green or amber eyes; it is so strange to me that they are ostracised in this way.

Here is a wonderful poem, sent to me by Doreen Dann, which she wrote from her own experience in the cat sanctuary where she works, and it made my heart ache:

The Kitten House or Why not a Black One?

'Oh, see that pretty one fluffy and sweet,
Little white legs and four tiny grey feet'
Please look at the dark shape alone at the back,
I'm cuddly, I'm pretty, but I'm also BLACK.

'Come see the tabbies with markings so fine,
Look at that ginger one, Oh let it be mine'
We are the dark shapes – there at the back,
We're cute and adorable but, sadly, we're BLACK

If you want a pet that will love you to bits,
Come, take a look at these little BLACK kits.

---

[4] The Black Bengal, or melanistic Bengal occurs occasionally in Bengal litters. Both parents must carry the recessive gene in order for a melanistic Bengal to appear in a litter.
[5] The asking price for a standard Bengal queen to be used for breeding is considerably higher than most other breeds of cat.

Our eyes will shine just as bright as those others,
Just give us a cuddle – me, and my brothers!

Look into my eyes, what do you see?
A beautiful kitten, so playful – that's me.
You've seen all the pretty ones – now choose from the
 back,
Say 'look at that treasure, it's mine – and it's BLACK'.

© Doreen Dann 2000

Two different breeders I approach have black Bengal female kittens for sale and both agree to allow me to breed one litter on three conditions. The first condition is that I must have the cat spayed after one litter; the second condition is that any kittens from that litter may not be allowed to breed; and the third condition I volunteer, which is that I won't sell any of the kittens from the one litter I am allowed to have, but give them away only to friends whom I trust to adhere to this agreement. In the end I decide to pursue the northernmost breeder as the kitten is older and therefore likely to be ready to have kittens that much sooner, added to which I like the way they look after their cats and the way they sound. They live in a large house and the cats are free to roam around the house and it has none of the feel of a kitten factory that some cat breeders exude. So, having researched this far and, of course, after long conversations with Michael, I pick up the phone and commit!

At this point Sue comes to stay with me and teases me about my condition of 'pregnant' anticipation at the delights of the black ball of bliss that is about to enter my life. I love Sue's company and she is wise beyond words on the manners and motivations of cats, not to mention Victorian prints, counter-tenors, music in general, organic gardening, cookery, books, reading and all other manner of things. She has, however, just reached a difficult stage with her companions of many years as her cat Chatto, sister to her existing cat Johnnie, has recently died leaving her with one twenty-year-old Siamese cat, Johnnie, whom she hand-reared with a tiny bottle when she was just a wee sick scrap of a kitten and two young and energetic Devon Rexes, so we have much cat talk to catch up on.

After Sue departs, I set off on my great expedition North, where I find the house and meet the Bengal breeders, a gentle young couple who care a lot about their cats, and I am introduced to their black girl, whom they call Beauty. She sashays into the room and I am enchanted by her sleek shiny black looks and her striking gold-green eyes. She is the essence of feline femininity and from her first entrance she dramatically grabs the attention of all who watch her. This one demands centre stage. She starts a completely manic game with the man of the house who is holding out a rod with an elastic string and a feather at its end, and she jumps high and repeatedly like a true jack-in-the-box. I am next introduced to her mother, who is an elegant tawny-coloured spotted Bengal with well-defined rosettes and she is very striking; she looks exactly like a miniature leopard. They play-fight amiably with each other on the carpet in front of the fire and I feel an enormous pang of guilt at knowing that I am about to take this lively kitten away from her mother. At more than seventeen weeks she is old to be with her mother still and she has been fully weaned for some weeks, so the older cat is probably more than ready to see her go. She was born near the end of October, which makes her a Halloween kitten I suddenly realise with pleasure. I ask if I may hold her, and they warn me, laughingly, that although she has been well socialised, she is still outspoken about when and how she will be handled. As I scoop her up she makes a deep, loud, almost boorish protest, but as I turn her on her back and she continues her vocal remonstration, she also starts to purr simultaneously. Her fur is the softest, silkiest fur I have ever touched. I am new to the world of the Bengal, but now I understand their allure. Her eyes hold mine unblinkingly. They have a determined look in them, but also they are full of emotion. I find myself extraordinarily moved by her and a little awestruck; she has a beauty to her that is almost that of a wild creature, something akin to the quality of an unbroken horse. She isn't perfect, though; she has strange broken whiskers and the end of her tail is oddly lumpy. I find myself falling madly in love with this black, purring, protesting, noisy, wriggling, bouncy creature. The couple who run this business are very kind and spend a long time initiating me in the things that make Bengals different from other cats and in the problems that I might expect to encounter from early on, and I am touched at how concerned they are about what is to happen to their kittens once they start their new life. Assuring them all will be well, together we bundle her up and put her in the cat carrier and I take my leave.

On the long drive South she protests sporadically, but most especially at the beginning of the journey after which she sleeps. For the rest of the journey from time to time she wakes and squawks for a few minutes and then again falls silent. I try to suppress all thoughts of what her mother may be going through now with a greater knowledge than her offspring of this habit of kitten-kidnap; also of what she herself may be thinking of this unfriendly business of being snatched, boxed and put into a sick-making moving noisy machine or of the grief that the breeders feel at losing their beloved black kitten. To help me expunge these dire thoughts, I sing songs, loudly, and then I go on to tell her all sorts of things, although I fail to mention the big scary cats back at the Coach House and eventually she gets bored and falls asleep.

When we first get back to the Coach House
I feel a new pang of guilt as I realise
that I may not have appreciated the
degree to which the world for the
resident cats is likely to change
with the introduction of the
new kitten. I walk in, swinging
the cat carrier and its burden,
and watch Titus and Fannie
begin their reaction to it.
Fannie hisses at a few feet away, Titus just sits back and
scents the air. Pushkin emerges after half an hour and is
silently curious and just watches, and then he slinks away to
mull it over on his own. Fannie continues to hiss like a
steaming kettle on the hob. Michael takes the lid off the
carrier and lets out the little black cat, while I stroke the ever
agitated Fannie. The kitten is surprisingly brave and
immediately does the rounds of the room, apparently
completely unabashed by the adjacent hissing. The breeders
have given me the igloo on which she always slept and I have
it on the floor beside me and from time to time she returns
to base, just to check that it is still there. Michael watches
her entranced and I see him also falling for her hook, line
and sinker. We talk of her name. All the cats in the Coach
House are named after writers or characters in books, and
although Beauty[6] would fit that category, such terrible things
happened to that poor horse that I find myself resistant to
it. However, she was born close to Halloween and it was
close to Halloween a year earlier that Giles Gordon, writer,
poet, agent and dear friend died, so I decide I would like to
name her in his memory. As she is so completely feminine

---

[6] as in Black Beauty.

Michael and I agree on 'Gilly', with a hard G as in 'ghillie'[7] – Giles, being a Scot would have liked that – so Gilly it is from now on. As soon as I had got Gilly back to the Coach House I had phoned her former home and reported on her progress and that night I do the promised email update before we turn in for the night:

Things are better now. The three resident cats have all retired to different sleeping places and are leaving her alone. She is currently on her igloo by Michael (who has fallen in love with her totally as I knew he would) and she has eaten quite a lot (of your biscuits, for the moment she won't touch ours but I'm sure that will change) and she has used the cat litter tray once and she has played quite a lot and walked around. She has climbed a tall set of library steps. Climbed into the sink, got behind the dustbin in the kitchen and a couple of times she has let out the most heartbreaking squawks which I am sure are for you both and for

---

[7] or as in that old song, Gilly, Gilly, Ossenfeffer, Katzenellen Bogen by the Sea.

her mum and her feline mates, but tonight will be the worst for her and then it will get better. She is going to be fine I can tell and she can more than hold her own against my bunch of wimps – she is loved already by us both I promise you.

CHAPTER 8

On this first night I feel I need to give her full, exclusive attention, so I opt to sleep alone with her in the spare room, which has a door, and leave Michael to say the ritualistic goodnight to the three adult cats on his bed in solitary splendour. When I first walk into the room and get into bed, little Gilly is utterly miserable and walks around the room wailing, and my heart sinks – poor little mite! I call her several times, and eventually she comes to me and then, as brave as a lion, a rather small lion, she buries herself under the duvet and sleeps stretched out next to me, pretty soundly too. At some point during the night Titus tries to dig her way in under the door, which is shortly followed by Fannie making a loud protesting miaowing outside, but we stick it out à deux until Michael and I both have to leave for church in the morning. I leave Gilly shut in the spare bedroom, which is at least familiar territory and has a cat litter tray and food in it, and when we get back she seems fine and I settle down to work in my study, where she joins me. Titus, as ever, is the one who tries to make friends, but now there is a lot of hiss and spit coming from Gilly back at her. Pushkin, when he comes close to her, doesn't hiss unless he is hissed at and then he hisses back, but she doesn't like him. Sadly, however, it is Fannie who is the big problem for Gilly. And Fannie reciprocates her dislike with equal fervour. Every time the two of them are in a room together there is a lot of noise. Gilly has now consumed copious amounts of food and water, so I feel I can relax in that department at least. It was wonderful that the breeders gave me her igloo. That was such a clever and thoughtful thing to do because it clearly has very important smells of home for little Gilly. As I write this, she is lying on it completely exhausted, in the deepest cat sleep I have ever seen.

Several days have now passed and one of the things that is remarkable about little Gilly since she has been with us is her voracious appetite for real food. I remember now that Pushkin was just like this until he too became addicted to his Hill's biscuits, like the other two. At the moment Gilly is eating the last of the biscuits that the breeder gave me for her although she has flirted a bit with Hill's Rabbit, but it is sardines (with the tomato sauce rinsed off, but not in oil) and pilchards (ditto) and underdone lamb laced with garlic cut up small, but the lamb has to have been freshly cooked not reheated, that send her into a frenzy. She needs only to get a whiff of one of these on offer and she bounds into the kitchen, races up the library steps, walks along the kitchen units (clumsily, her balance is not very good still) and round the edge of the sink and yaps. Her demands are both raucous and rude, and they make me laugh. However, one of the most gorgeous things she does when her nose is well into her bowl of sardines, or whatever it is that she is currently loving, is to emit a muffled series of 'mnnn, yumnnn, yummmn' sounds of sensual bliss, the like of which I have never heard from a cat before. She is almost crying from pleasure.

One of the first of our neighbours to meet Gilly is Richard, from next door, and knowing how he loves to tease me about the cats I am braced for trouble. I am completely unnerved, therefore, when he first sets his eyes on her and says with genuine admiration in his voice:

'Now that's what I call a real cat, that one. I can see she has a *big* personality.' Then later, as he carefully studies her, he adds:

'But I *am* worried that she might be a hunter.' Finding myself reluctant to impede the flow of the conversation I merely think, rather than say, 'But so are you', and anyway I know exactly why he says this, as he is a passionate observer and lover of birds of almost all kinds, with the exception of the corvine family (crows, rooks, jays, magpies and jackdaws – the relentless stealers of other birds' eggs and chicks). I have noticed on many occasions in my life before that men and women who are really keen hunters have a profound understanding and respect for wildlife. Richard's interests range across a wide spectrum of the natural world, and he is also commendably green. We both look down at the ground at Gilly, the black huntress-in-waiting, and I reckon that he is probably right – she could be a killer, but time will tell.

Karen, Lesley and Alex come up to look at the new addition to the household when they are passing on one of their walks, and I explain to Alex that I am hoping that Gilly will be able to go back to the breeders to one of their studs to have kittens when she comes into heat, or maybe the heat after that. Alex asks me nervously how long this might all take and I rather helplessly shrug my shoulders. I try to get Alex to nurse Gilly, but she yowks her disapproval at being picked up and cuddled, although, as ever, she purrs while she is complaining.

I email pictures of our new handful to Sue and get this response from her by return:

From: Sue
To: Marilyn
Sent: Wednesday, February 16, 6:54 pm
Subject: Re: !!!

Marilyn

Isn't she gorgeous!! I long to hear how you are getting on and if she's as bumptious as you say, then she will have the others under her thumb in very short order. At least now you will know what it's like living with a kitten hell-bent on LIVING LIFE to the full. Everyone thinks I exaggerate Georgie's exploits, but now you will know . . . The kittens will be very tempting I can see. As to my lot they all seem fine, perhaps a closer group now, it's difficult to know if I am making up their emotions or they are genuine, hard to say. Max and Johnnie seem to spend a lot more time together and Johnnie seems quite oblivious to the fact her sister has gone. Perhaps if Chatto hadn't been so old and always the loner it would have been different. And as I look round the room, pictures hanging askew, bits of paper everywhere, cushion in the middle of the floor and my recycled paper bin turned upside down, then no change in Georgie either . . .

Sue

Back at the Coach House all is not completely well with the other three cats, but Michael and I are reasonably sanguine about this, as it is very early days, and Gilly is stronger meat than they have yet had to contemplate, so she is bound to take some getting used to. The bed-time ritual has become one of the tensest moments of the day, as pre-Gilly the three cats would all sit on the bed until we put the lights out and then one by one go back downstairs, although sometimes Titus would stay either on the bed or in the neighbouring bathroom on a cushion on the floor. The situation now is that Fannie and Gilly are at such daggers drawn that Gilly wins out and Fannie is beginning not even to come into the room for that last precious cuddle. Pushkin and Titus come into the room but are somewhat uneasy in Gilly's presence. Gilly sleeps on our bed all night every night and that is that.

Early one evening, just as I am starting to prepare supper, the phone goes and it is Jeff on the other end. He tells me Lesley has brought her kitten Joey back from Manchester. She and her boyfriend had been having problems with him in their tiny flat and they just felt they couldn't give him enough exercise so Lesley has, with some regret, decided that he will have a much better life having his freedom to run and play in Hutton Roof and she will at least see him at weekends. This means that they won't now be able to take a kitten from me.

'Jeff, it is great for Joey and of course I understand and Joey is a lucky boy. I imagine that Alex is thrilled, isn't she?'

'Yes, she is very happy to have him home, and it's better for him, without a doubt.'

'Well, anyway we are a long way off getting young Gilly pregnant, so it's fine with us.'

In fact, since the introduction of the little black bundle to the inner sanctum of the Coach House, a bundle who perpetually triggers the question 'Where the devil is she now?' or sometimes by Michael, who is deeply infatuated by the little madam, 'Where's Black Magic, it's too quiet?' the now seemingly enormous, adult feline residents are variously put out. As ever, Titus, the most benign and the most amiable of the three cats, is the least disrupted and, also being the most selfish, has been at some pains to maintain her sleep station in the armchair in my study, which is the only room that's guaranteed to be warm during the daytime. In spite of all manner of trials to her composure put up by the young scallywag she has resisted them all and simply turns her back on whatever provocation she is offered and continues to sleep in the armchair. Occasionally, very occasionally, she will hiss at

Gilly, or clock her one with her front leg, but mainly she just keeps her head down, literally and metaphorically.

Pushkin, on the other hand, is more seriously alarmed by the black kitten and regularly growls at her as much as she growls at him. He mainly avoids her, but at certain times during the day he will be involved in a hectic game of chase in which she, always, chases him, violently and frantically, all over the house, up and down both flights of stairs until he finally finds some high place of retreat. However, there is an early sign that this is about to change. I noticed this morning that it was Pushkin chasing Gilly and they were both clearly enjoying it, so perhaps a real friendship will develop here.

Fannie and Gilly together are more of a worriment. Gilly has a way of staring at Fannie that is quite unnerving, even to me, but the effect it has on Fannie is explosive. When Gilly decides to 'do' her stare she is usually crouching, or sitting. I have never seen her 'look the look' standing up. It is a steady unwavering look with barely a blink to be seen and is directed at Fannie and only at Fannie. When Fannie sees this she becomes visibly agitated, and will unconsciously lick her nose. She hunches down in a crouching position and to begin with she growls. She follows her growl with hissing which becomes increasingly intense and then she makes her mistake. She runs. Gilly chases. Fannie panics. If she cannot get away she will crouch low down on the floor with her head close to the ground and her ears fully back against her head, in a combination of full submission and complete aggression, hissing as if her life depends upon it. As Gilly closes in on her she will jump up and leap over Gilly and run. Often in this part of the chase Gilly will get very close to Fannie and the combined noise from both of them is terrible to hear. We keep finding lumps of Fannie's fur at the top of the stairs where Gilly has managed to catch up with her just to give her a nip out of the back of her thigh. She hasn't yet drawn blood but I live in fear of this.

Within three weeks of Gilly joining us we meet and start a friendship with a young couple called Mark and France. France is a French Canadian school-teacher who teaches French at a school in Bristol and who, as a hobby, undertakes feline portraits as commissions. She is a very talented draughtswoman, as I am to discover. They arrive with us around lunchtime one day near the end of February and are both bemused by Gilly's antics, although France expresses some concern about the reaction of Fannie to Gilly's 'bullying'. We talk of many things and I discover that she and Mark have no children but share their lives very happily with four cats, called Apollo, Spooky, Grippette and Uni, all of whom I hope to meet in the future.

In the course of our talk France admits to me that she is hoping yet again that Spooky, who remains her only entire cat, will have a litter of kittens later in the year. She never stops her or encourages her, but leaves her to find her stud as she will and when she will. I also speak of my hopes for Gilly and her kittens.

'You could have your hands full with that one,' France laughs as we watch Gilly chasing Fannie upstairs yet again.

CHAPTER 9

I have dwelt with some enthusiasm on the subject of our new scamp, Gilly, and her relationship with the resident adult felines, but still hanging over us is the spectre that the almost-realised dream of living up here may be shattered and we shall have to return South, complete with cats, to a housebound life again. Already the cold wind of financial ruin is blowing around our ankles as eleven months on we are still paying out on two mortgages. Michael is continuing to have problems with the renter and a possible sale of Moon Cottage seems to be as elusive as ever. The property market in the South remains as static as it was at the end of last year. Following a viewing in early January, some serious interest in the cottage was expressed by a couple to our neighbour Shirley, who showed them round. They remained very keen until on their next viewing they brought their very tall teenaged son from their house in Central London. As he entered the cottage, Michael who had decided he better go down for this himself afterwards told me, he ducked and visibly hated it. The beamed ceilings downstairs are very low, it must be admitted, but I also suspect that the lad may well have not wanted to leave the bright lights and the stimulation of his metropolitan friends.

As well as complaining about everything under the sun,

the woman who is renting the place, having initially agreed to allow one viewing a week by any potential purchaser, starts to be difficult about that too and as a result we fail to show the cottage to a couple from Shepherd's Bush who had sounded very interested. There have been one or two other desultory viewings too, but they have come to nothing. Michael and I hardly dare to speak to each other on the subject of the cottage – it is becoming a forbidden topic laced with mutual recrimination. One night, however, I am profoundly disturbed by the sound of Michael sobbing heavily. As I turn towards him I find that he is crying in his sleep, but when I do wake him from what I hope is just a bad dream, for dreaming he was, I discover that in waking too he is torn apart by the fear that all our savings are evaporating and without jobs and incomes we have a bleak outlook in store. I try to reassure him all will be well, but I know my reassurance has a hollow ring.

The most healing thing I know is having a cuddle with the cats, and I long for Michael to find peace in that way. He does interact with them, a great deal, but it is more through conversations than touch, although Titus sits on him often. For me it is Fannie who has that magic touch. I can feel stress leaving me with every breath when she is in my arms. I had a powerful email on just this subject from Shirani. Her mother died from a tumour and she was utterly stricken by her death. At this terrible time, although she received love and help from her husband and family, it was the silent help of the cats that seemed to be most healing:

From: Shirani Fernando-Bradford
To: Marilyn Edwards

What amazed me was the compassion that Lucky and Barnaby, my two cats, showed to me . . . If I cried, Lucky would come and sit next to me and put her tiny paw on my hand to comfort me. Barnaby would be near me but there was very little physical contact.

Until one night I had a terrible nightmare about Mum, I awoke so suddenly and I know I didn't make a sound. I didn't even sit up. Barnaby was sleeping at the bottom of the bed. Suddenly, I felt him walk the entire length of my body, and he lay on my chest . . . He put his head on my left shoulder and cuddled me purring gently till I went back to sleep. I find cats every bit as compassionate as people, and sometimes more so because of their sensitivity to emotional changes.

～

This coming Thursday Fannie is booked in for her hysterectomy. She has been intermittently on heat again since the abrupt end of her phantom pregnancy and she is becoming increasingly loud when she is calling, so we are both really glad that the date has arrived at last.

Yet again we have to go through the nil-by-mouth business with all four cats even though only Fannie is to be subjected to the horrors of surgery, and a restless and complaining sort of night is had by all. In the morning, with dark rings under my eyes, I scoop Fannie up to put her in the cat cage. Just before I do, Michael reaches across and, gently fondling her ear, says with real sadness in his voice:

'Fannie, Fannie, Fannie – I can't bear that you aren't going to have any kittens. You would have made such beautiful kittens and you would have been such a good mother.' He's right, dammit.

277

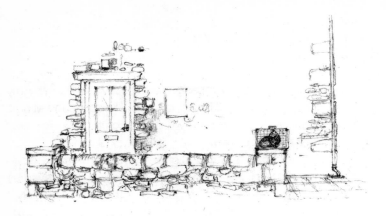

I drive off to the vet's with a heavy heart. It goes without saying that I am, as ever, terrified of the actual procedure. Gerard, always understanding, takes receipt of her and assures me that there is nothing to worry about. I don't help matters by introducing the thought that as she is a tortoiseshell and therefore more highly strung than her sister, Titus, she is more likely to panic in recovery. He smiles his beatific smile and says:

'Marilyn, just phone me around midday, and I will be able to tell you then she has had the operation and I'll be able to give you a time to collect her.' I throw back a wobbly smile at him gratefully and potter off. I mess around all morning, unable to settle down to anything, but before it is time for me to phone him, the phone goes and it's Gerard's voice. He is so good, because before I can get into a further panic he just says very calmly and precisely:

'She's had her operation and she is just coming round nicely now. She needs another hour or two down here, but you can come down at about 2 p.m. and collect her then.' I issue a silent prayer of thanks and start my first proper work of the day. After I get Fannie back home I am delighted that the other cats do not hiss and spit at her in the way that she always hisses and spits at them post-operatively. Titus gives one token hiss but very quickly accepts her completely. Fannie's recovery is immediately faster than that of Titus, but Gerard did say that he had an almighty struggle removing Titus's uterus which was not the case with the much slimmer Fannie, and what happens on the operating table is directly connected to the manner of recovery.

It is thought by some veterinary surgeons that physiologically pain in humans and their companion animals is the same but that the intellectual knowledge that pain is about to be inflicted (in the case, say, of a woman voluntarily undergoing hysterectomy) can make the perception of pain much greater for the human. It appears that animal patients recover much faster than humans enduring the same procedure. Animals seem to be back to their pre-operative activity levels within days, sometimes hours, whereas it can take weeks for humans to recover to the same degree. On the other hand, it is also surprisingly difficult to read an animal's response to pain as in the wild an animal that manifests its pain will become vulnerable to its many potential predators, so it may well post-operatively sit quietly without any observable indication that it is experiencing pain. Sometimes veterinary care staff or clinicians may mistake this as 'resting comfortably'. Instead, this is more likely an instinctive response for survival. Gerard, however, is superb at detecting pain in animals and although I thought I knew Titus well, it was he who picked up her arthritic pain in her back legs and he knew that she was uncomfortable after his hysterectomy on her. Fannie is showing little sign of discomfort. On her return home she goes upstairs with a little difficulty, but she manages it and lies down on the chair in my study and sleeps, and the following day she appears to be back to normal although I am sure she must be feeling some pain. Outwardly the only

visible sign of what she has undergone is a large neat scar on her flank surrounded by a large square of white shaven flesh, which she ignores for the main part. Gerard is a master at concealed internal stitching and none of my cats have needed to wear collars post-operatively.

For some time now there has been a cooling down of the strong bond that has existed since birth between Fannie and Titus. I'm not certain what has caused it, but from my diary entries I suspect it started around the time of Fannie's 'phantom' pregnancy and was then exacerbated by the spaying of Titus. I find I have not wanted to acknowledge this rift as their closeness was such a key part of their relationship with each other and possibly because I am fearful that this breakdown has been caused by my intervention. They still occasionally allogroom, but almost always now it ends in 'tears' with Titus getting quite cross with Fannie and biting her or putting her paws round her throat and then one or other of them flounces off. Fannie usually shuns Titus and whereas they had always previously shared the armchair in my study, only one of them now sleeps in it at any one time.

Pushkin maintains his distance from Fannie, although he gave her hindquarters a sound sniffing on her return from the vet's, but he still follows Titus around doggedly, when he is awake that is. He especially likes to follow her down to the feeding station (it is almost as if unwittingly she signals to him that that is where she is going) and probably rather irritatingly to her he will walk back and forth in front of whichever bowl she is aiming for. He watches Gilly with what seems to be increasingly keen attention, although that is hardly surprising as Gilly is, of course, a young pre-pubescent female and therefore definitely interesting to a male cat, even if neutered.

Gilly continues to chase all of them. Mainly she is trying to play, but some of it appears to be an assertion of dominance. Her stare is overpowering, even to me, and she does a lot of that. She also talks a great deal. I would even say shouts. She talks about going out. She talks about having bowel movements. She talks about her food; about having it and also about not having it. She talks about being picked up. She talks about not being picked up. She talks to closed windows and to closed doors a lot and I have had to beg Michael not to respond by opening them, as I learned a long time ago that cats will miaow remorselessly for things they want, and you will become their complete slave, once they learn that vocal demands are met. So far it has worked with Gilly too. If she sits silently by the door she gets let out, if she makes a racket she doesn't.

There are some early signs of our Northern Spring burgeoning forth, but March is a treacherous month and can change at any moment. February was very wet and mild, but recently we have had a cold spell and now, suddenly, there is warm sunshine and I have just seen an early bumblebee. A couple of nights ago I could hear frogs croaking fit to bust and I am sure it is the males beginning to come in to fertilise our females. The horse chestnut tree is in leaf and the blue tits have been nesting for some time now. The dawn chorus has been building up day by day and it is on close to full voltage now and, although I am not sure if there is a connection, the owls seem especially noisy at night too. There is a day of wonderful sunshine and Michael and I walk up the crags. Near the top we turn round and look back down and across to the two Yorkshire Peaks of Whernside and Ingleborough and the Barbon fells and then turn at an angle of 90° in a northerly direction to look across to the high hills of the Lake District. After a bit more walking and scrambling we reach the summit and look down in a south-westerly direction where we can glimpse the shimmer of water that is the distant Morecambe Bay. We have just looked over a part of the three counties of North Yorkshire, Cumbria and Lancashire – counties which Michael always refers to as 'God's own country'. Michael puts his arm round my shoulders and I squeeze his hand. We don't need to say anything, we know it is paradise. We sit down back to back for support and look out at the far horizons and we both, completely simultaneously, let out huge sad sighs, which acts of melodrama make us giggle helplessly.

CHAPTER 10

Meanwhile, life goes on at the Coach House. As spring surges forth in fits and starts both the birdlife and the vole, mouse and shrew life start to multiply too. The four cats, who through long dark wet February have been content to stay mainly indoors, are now trying to get out into the open air from early in the morning and stay out there. Fannie is the most virulent hunter and kills her prey very quickly. Since Gilly has joined the household Fannie has if anything increased her kill-rate. Small mammals, rather than birds, tend to be her chosen quarry. When they are outside Gilly watches Fannie with a controlled respect that is quite different from her behaviour with Fannie inside the house. She may be consciously learning. Her own mother would never have had the chance to teach her hunting skills in the open air with live prey as they were all contained within the house. Pushkin is probably the next most prolific hunter and, as with most cats, he has that tenacious and slightly terrifying ability to stare for many minutes at a time at some potential victim who in the end just has to move, being unable to sustain immobility any longer. Titus of the three is now the least active as a hunter, which may be because she is lazy or more likely because she finds fast movement difficult. She hunts and kills if something offers itself up to her, without her needing to move very much.

Today Fannie catches a wood mouse,[8] which she despatches quickly but, before I can stop her and to my immense surprise, she starts to eat it, very quickly and while I, and the three other cats I might say, look on with our mouths hanging open, the head and body are no more. All that remains are the feet and a tail. Fannie will barely eat wet cat food and certainly not any fresh food raw or cooked, so

what stimulus suddenly caused this behaviour, natural in a predator but not anything I have known Fannie to do earlier, I cannot properly say.

Titus, Pushkin and Gilly come forward to sniff the remains and then saunter off. Perhaps it was establishing some form of ownership or authority on Fannie's part.

When the cats are outside I am able to get the three adult ones in fairly easily, by shouting 'In! In!' loudly, or at worst by going out and catching them individually and carrying them back in my arms, but Gilly is completely impossible to corral and, at the slightest suggestion that the time has come, she will hide for long periods under the garden shed, where she is beyond reach until she and she alone chooses

---

[8] aka field mouse (Apodemus sylvaticus).

to return in. Gilly is, however, adorable, although she still hates to be picked up and one of the things she does if she is really trying to get away is to stretch herself out rigid in my arms, which is apparently a very 'Bengal' thing to do. When I nurse her on her back in my arms she makes a long low guttural complaining sort of moan, which she can keep up for a long time. It is very funny. She also emits wind when being picked up, but so pungently that you have to be strong to withstand the smell. She loves to be stroked which makes her purr really loudly. As her fur is the softest in the world and she is shiny black, she gets stroked a lot and being purred at is very rewarding. She is a very person-oriented cat and follows either Michael or me around the house doggedly and likes to lie down near to wherever each of us is. Her breeders have put me in touch with Beth, a friend of theirs, who acquired a melanistic

Bengal from them a year earlier, called Treacle. I talk to Beth and she reassures me on the wind and loose bowel movement front:

'Treacle did that too, but his tummy settled down once he was on grown-up food. He was a greedy pig and wouldn't eat his own food, thinking Teddy's[9] grown-up food was quite delicious. Thankfully, it suited him down to the ground and the farting pretty much ceased. It was disconcerting to be nasally assaulted every time that we picked him up. Enjoy your Gilly.'

Shortly after this, however, Treacle has to have an operation for the vet to try to find an undescended testicle,[10] which is causing problems and Beth writes of her fears on that day with an exquisite eloquence:

We had an early start to our day today. Treacle has gone to Thornhill, to the vet's. I feel very wobbly and it will be a long day.

I don't know how well I would take it, should Treacle be one of those cats that doesn't come out from the anaesthetic.

Treacle is anachronistic – the ever-present shadow that brings light into our lives. He is always there. Just 'there'. Just 'present'. He's not fussy; he will lap-sit sometimes, but generally just sits about six inches away on the desk (right of keyboard) – with that amazingly long and prehensile tail elegantly swathed about his front paws. Just . . . Sitting . . . and Being Black, with amber eyes watching our activities with a deep and

---

[9] As well as Treacle, Beth and Steve share their lives with Teddy, another Bengal and Lulu a half-cross Bengal together with two dogs, Suzie, a Border Collie cross, and Griff, a mongrel collie.
[10] unilateral cryptorchidism.

abiding interest. There is a hole in my life today. A piece of me is missing. I can't even begin to think about it becoming a permanent one. We had a Siamese once, who Didn't Make It. So I wobble. Until 4 p.m.

He did make it, thank goodness, but he was a sore boy, who removed most of his stitches and ended up with a collar. And then Beth tells me:

Poor Treacle – I promised him his collar was coming off today – and now because it isn't healing properly they need to investigate and he will have more stitches! He clawed the final three stitches out, by the way. He's a bad, bad cat! Treacle has discovered why he keeps Human slaves. He's constantly pushing his face up for scratching and saying, 'It's your fault, you do it!' He bites our finger ends if he doesn't get his own way. It's really charming, this collared but determined face looking up and demanding a scratch.

Beth's poignant utterance, 'There is a hole in my life today. A piece of me is missing', is hauntingly witnessed in the grief felt by Dedde for his companion Duff as expressed here by Anette Nyberg[11]

---

[11] who lives in a deeply remote part of Sweden with her two current feline companions, Lisa and Maja.

From: Anette Nyberg
To: Marilyn Edwards
Sent: 21 March 17:01
Subject: Re: The Cats of Moon Cottage

Dear Marilyn,
Strange you should say you think that Otto's death triggered Septi's cancer. My first cat Duff (a beautiful black girl with the loveliest personality you can imagine) grew up with Dedde (a tabby boy who was 'all purrs'). They were as close as two cats can be that aren't brother and sister. When Duff got ill and I had to take her to the vet one final time Dedde was heart-broken . . . didn't want to eat much (he loved food before) and nearly didn't purr . . .

For Dedde it seemed that once his companion in life, the one he 'loved', was no longer there to share his life, it was as if he didn't want to live any more . . . Before this he was fine, playing and purring as always, but that changed when Duff died. I sometimes could see the pain in his eyes and also that 'the spark' if you like was fading away . . . and indeed so was he.

I talked to the vet about it and he said he was sure that animals can grieve in just the same way that humans can. Dedde didn't have anything seriously wrong with him that a diet couldn't sort out, but when he was left alone he deteriorated fast . . . I'm sure he wanted to die, the sad thing was having to watch this lovely cat just let go of his will to live . . .

One day I found him in the kitchen by the fridge door, and there are no words to describe the look on his beautiful face as I realised that he had "wet" himself, the poor little cat. I then realised that I could no longer postpone that trip to the vet. There was no reason to make him suffer any longer, and I called the vet and a close friend who offered to go with us. It is quite a long drive to where the vet is, 90 kilometres to be precise, but this day it went so fast . . . and all the time as I drove there I was thinking that soon he will no longer be with us, but with his much-loved Duff instead.

It was such a sad goodbye, but I was sure as I held him in my arms that he was much better off without the humiliation and constant grief. There and then ended the life of a wonderful cat and I'm quite sure that a part of me died there too.

I felt as if I didn't want to go on without my 2 dearest friends for 14 years, and as soon as anyone tried to mention that perhaps a kitten would make me smile again I remembered thinking: I don't think I'll ever smile again and that I just didn't want to replace them, ever . . . But as you know yourself things can change, the pain and loss is not as bad anymore, but these two are always in my heart because they gave me so much.

I believe that much-loved cats leave an essence or impression behind them that might have to do with all the strong feelings and love, after all, is energy, isn't it?

Yours,

Anette, Lisa and Maja

$\sim$

After a long silence, on 7 March we receive the following announcement from the internet agency which is selling Moon Cottage.

– – –

From: info@halfapercent.com
To: Marilyn Edwards
Sent: Monday, March 07, 3:51 PM
Subject: Viewing Request

Dear Marilyn
I have two applicants interested in viewing your property, see below.

Appointments
Saturday 12 March 12:30
Saturday 12 March 13:30

Please let me know what days and times that you can do, if you are unable to do the above days and times.
Regards,
Viewings Department
1/2% – Halfapercent.com

We scurry around to make arrangements for the two viewings. One is to be done by a local agent and the other by our saintly neighbour, Shirley. Our renter on this occasion accommodates us by allowing these appointments. Michael and I are wary of getting too excited, we have been here so many times before, but all the same our hearts are beating faster and we spend the next few days doing some distracted nail biting. I manage to have a phone conversation with Caroline, one half of the couple wanting the second appointment who, like her partner Nathan, is a medical research scientist working in Central London and who both, it transpires, now want to live further out. I explain to her that there is a 360 degrees virtual tour of the cottage which, if she has the patience to let it download, she can view online on the Halfapercent website and she says she will try to get into it. She has already been on the website for some time studying the stills.

Saturday 12 March comes at last. The first couple are again worried by the low ceilings and decide that it is not for them, but Shirley phones us to tell us that Caroline and Nathan, the second appointment, like the cottage very much indeed. Later that weekend Nathan and Caroline phone us and tell us themselves how much they love it and then, heart-stoppingly, they make an offer. It is inevitably below our asking price and with some trepidation we negotiate a compromise and suddenly Michael and I, to our tearful near-disbelief, find we have agreed a sale.

On Monday morning I receive this email from Caroline:

– – –

From: Caroline Wallace
To: Marilyn Edwards
Sent: Monday, March 14, 10:07 AM
Subject: RE: Moon cottage

Dear Marilyn,

I haven't been able to sleep since Saturday. I just keep thinking about the cottage and how wonderful it is! I completely understand that it must have been a real wrench for you to leave such a beautiful place. If the cottage picks its owners, then it certainly worked its charms on my husband. I already knew that I would love it but Nathan had some concerns about the busy road and the lack of off-street parking. However, after about 2 minutes in the cottage he was more excited than I have ever seen him.

I have been in touch with Halfapercent . . . and they will contact you today . . . The couple who came to see our flat on Saturday seemed very keen. I will keep you fully informed of our progress with the sale of our own flat.

Thank you very much for your kindness.

I'll be in touch soon.

Best wishes,

Caroline

Dr Caroline Wallace

CHAPTER 11

In the middle of all the wonderful things that are happening around Moon Cottage, I receive this note. Letters from other cat lovers frequently bear tidings of joy or heartache, and sometimes both, but on a few occasions they just stop you in your tracks completely:

– – –

From: Emma
To: Marilyn Edwards
Sent: Thursday, March 31, 10:09 AM

My cat died four years ago and I don't think I'll ever 'get over it' properly and I can't face having another cat. She died in her sleep, on my bed – something awoke me early in the morning and I looked at her curled up by my feet. She was twitching slightly, so I stroked her, thinking she was having a nightmare. But she never woke up and I was, and remain, heartbroken.

However, I just thought I'd pass this story on to you, which I heard from an RSPCA worker called Diana Lewis who works (or used to) for the North Devon Branch. She was called to a house to look after a cat whose owner had died. The owner was an old man and he had collapsed on the floor. When the ambulance arrived they found his face was sopping wet and the cat was on top of him, frantically licking his face, trying to revive him.

As the cat was also old, the RSPCA lady took the cat home with her to look after him, as she thought it would be kinder. He was very subdued and curled up into a ball, and wouldn't respond to any attention. The RSPCA lady left him alone and the next day went to stroke him; except he had died in the night.

Isn't that sad? A cat who died of a broken heart.

Emma

Following the news from Caroline and Nathan that they really do want to buy Moon Cottage, Michael and I hardly know ourselves. To feel the tension lifting off us is like the best holiday in the world. We know we mustn't relax completely, as they will, of course, have to have a full survey done on it and it is a very old building so that could throw up any number of problems. It is so lovely, though, to know that they feel the same way about Moon Cottage as we did and do, and, before us, Janet and any number of other people to whom Moon Cottage has opened herself up. Moon Cottage chooses who lives within her walls and it never happens until she is ready. We make a date to go down and meet Caroline and Nathan in April.

I hear Michael addressing the cats as he lets them out into the sharp spring air for their first early morning romp of the day:

'There you go, you lucky lot, you don't have to be confined within the walls of Moon Cottage after all. Enjoy your paradise here, go on, run, run! And mind that traffic!'

'Oh, don't even joke on that subject!' I urge him, as I give him a hug. We both walk out into the garden. The hills are white with snow. Our end of the village is up on a hill but we are surrounded by even higher hills to the West, the North and the East and these have been covered with snow for some days now. Each time that the great Ingleborough looks as if its snowy cape is getting a bit threadbare and the dark stone starts showing through, there is another snowfall and yet again she is cloaked in immaculate white. I shiver as I look out at our splendid vista.

'Soon the lambs are going to be born and it is so hard when it's like this for them.'

'But Mo, tomorrow it could just as easily be sunny again, with a big thaw and you said yourself a few days ago that spring is well under way.' And sure enough that is exactly what happens. There is a switch in temperature, a thaw sets in, and lambs start popping out from everywhere. Five days later, as we look out over our gate into the field behind our little paddock across the road, we can see the newly born lambs wiggling their tails in that wonderful lambkin way as they head-butt their long-suffering mothers in search of milk. I had asked Richard Prickett, whose lambs they are, what breed they were and he replied mainly Texels but with a few Texel/Cheviot crosses and I think he also said Lleyns. I love lambing time; it is my most favourite time of year in the farming calendar, although in the old days hay time came a close second. The only trouble is that in the North there is almost always what they call 'lamb snow', which is the inevitable late winter snowfall that comes during lambing or immediately after they are born, and it is a terrible strain on the endurance of both the tiny lambs and their mothers, not to mention the harassed shepherds in whose care they are.

Today a group of 'pilgrims' turn up next door, at the Old Vicarage, to call on Annabel and Richard to borrow the key to the church, so that they may go and visit the place where

the Reverend Theodore Bayley Hardy V.C., D.S.O., M.C.[12] was the incumbent until 1918, when he was wounded on the Somme and died of his wounds in a military hospital in Rouen three weeks before the Armistice. The Reverend Hardy, with the beautiful face of a poet, was the most decorated non-combatant of the First World War. This man was very brave and very good, and it makes me ache to think that we live in the house which was his coach house, although his favourite mode of transport was his bicycle, which in itself says much about the man. Michael and I have cycled round here only once and it almost killed us! It is excellent that people do come to seek him and his living out, but I wish more people knew about him, he was a remarkable man.

Spring is now seriously under way. The dawn chorus

---

[12] For more info there is a very good biography called *It's Only Me*, A life of The Reverend Theodore Bayley Hardy, V.C., D.S.O., M.C. Vicar of Hutton Roof, Westmorland by David Raw (Frank Peter's Publishing, 1988) ISBN 0948511451.

which I had thought was at its most incandescent two weeks ago is now utterly overwhelming and I am awestruck at the performance that our feathered choir lays on in its collective passion for love and life. It starts before sunrise at around 5.30 a.m. and builds until it is near impossible for anyone to sleep on through it and, however cold the weather, or fierce the winds, the birds are in no way discouraged, but riotously follow their instinct to acquire and protect their territory and attract and keep their mate. I cannot remember a better one. On top of this there are the frogs. Well, more precisely it is the frogs who are on top of the frogs. For the last two days I have seen two pairs of frogs firmly attached to each other and letting go for nothing and no one. The last twenty-four hours have been very windy and wet and mild, which is a total change from the weather hitherto. Michael comes bouncing into the bathroom with a pair of field glasses, gurgling, because today there are no fewer than ten frogs in the pond. This is slightly mad as the pond is nothing like large enough to cope with ten frogs. By lunchtime there are three enormous clumps of frogspawn, almost covering the entire surface of the pond. It really is so much that I wonder if I should not take some out, but on investigation I discover that, however much is laid, such a tiny fraction of it will develop into adult frogs that statistically speaking I should leave the whole lot, so I do. Unlike last summer when the frogs in our pond would let us bend down and stroke them (for fun I did try, just once, to kiss one of them but he wouldn't let me), these frogs submerge the second we open the door, so I am sure that means they have migrated some distance for the spawning and don't know us. The volume and constancy of their croaking seem almost exotic. Further proof, should proof be needed, of spring's arrival is provided by no fewer than three bumble-bees flying slowly around the garden, low down to the ground, looking for nest sites I imagine.

We are keeping the cats in because someone told me that Bengals are particularly keen on frogs, but I suspect Bengals are keen on anything and everything. With great difficulty Michael and I have clipped Gilly's claws; they were lethal and so long they were beginning to grow inwards.

Fannie has started to sleep up on top of the bookcase which is the first time since we have been at the Coach House, but it is awkward for her to get up to it. She always slept on top of the high bookcases at Moon Cottage. Today, however, Gilly came into the room, saw where Fannie was and, although much clumsier than Fannie (her sense of balance is still not as good as that of the other cats), she managed to climb up and challenge Fannie. Fannie was distraught and although she hissed and spat, she finally capitulated and half jumped, half fell down. So far there is no indication at all that the hormonal change since her hysterectomy has made her any more relaxed. She seems to be progressively more nervous and withdrawn. Since this episode Fannie has discovered an old leather-covered laundry box that I use for filing things, which is sitting on top of my filing cabinet. She can get into it by leaping off the top of the library steps, as long as I remember to leave them in front of the filing cabinet – not very convenient – but I desperately need her to find somewhere she can feel safe and high. I have put her favourite blanket in it and that is where she has been sleeping ever since.

Gilly and Pushkin continue to play together quite a bit. Sometimes he runs away because they are playing chase, but comes back for more, but sometimes he runs away and hides. Often though I spot him just sitting very still, watching her, almost obsessively. She appears not to notice that he is doing this, but as she is both female and a signed-up member of the genus Felis Catus she is almost certainly aware of him. Michael shocked me the other day as he was watching her cross the garden towards the gate:

'Gilly is such a girl somehow – look at her!'

'What on earth do you mean?'

'She is just so feminine. She sort of wiggles knowingly as she struts out – look see she is doing it now!'

'Michael, for goodness sake, she's a blimming cat.' He laughed. All the same I do sort of see what he means. Pushkin now sleeps on top of the bathroom cupboard if Fannie and Titus aren't there – otherwise on the blue blanket inside the wardrobe in the guest bedroom and only when he is really cold on the vet blanket on the cushions on the floor in my study. Titus spends her time alternating between the top of the same bathroom cupboard, but not if Pushkin is there, and the armchair in my study. Gilly has now taken over Pushkin's old bed on top of the box on the floor in my study. Her baby igloo is in the box, but for the moment she is shunning that during the daytime, although I think she sleeps on it at night.

Of the four cats, I would say that Fannie and Pushkin seem to be the most unsettled. Gilly and Titus both appear to have pretty much the same agenda, which is to do it their way, where and when they want to and ideally in the warmest spot.

CHAPTER 12

April blows in cold and fierce and, true to form, we watch a few large flakes of snow come floating down, although not enough to merit the title 'lamb snow'. As I peer down into our pond I see the tiniest wiggling of the tadpoles flexing their tails still suspended in their jelly and some way off free swimming.

Anne, our sub-postmistress, has resurrected her scarecrow down in her field with her hens, her duck and her goat, and a very striking scarecrow she is. I am curious, though, to know why this elegant, dark-haired, slim but curvaceous 'lovely' with black hair and one eye open and one eye closed, hugely lashed, wearing a tight-fitting red polo-necked jumper atop a smart black and white checked skirt complete with black tights, has suddenly been put on duty in her field, so the next time I remember I ask her about the young wench in her scarlet top.

'Ah ha! Well, she's there because of those damned buzzards. I have some newly hatched chicks and those hawks are the very devil for going after them . . . and the kestrels are nearly as bad and it helps to keep them off the hen food anyway.' I also discover that one day shortly after Ms S. Crow took up her station in the field the venerable Jimmy, a veteran Hutton Roofer, passing by on his mobility scooter to start the long climb up the hill for his daily chat to his much-loved wife at her grave in the churchyard, stopped his vehicle at Anne's wall and with some concern in his voice called out across the field towards the scarecrow, which, was at this point standing, or rather sloping, at a bit of a drunken lean:

'Anne, Anne, are you alright? Anne, answer me, why are you leaning like that?' and the real Anne, hearing him calling, had to go out and reassure him she was fit and well, but she was delighted to see that her doppelganger had done her job so well.

'Mind you,' Anne grins wickedly, 'the scarecrow I had some years back was her, but in a somewhat different rig-out. Before she had more what I call the look of Dolly Parton about her and a bigger bust. She was blonde in those days. It was to scare off the foxes. This time round I dyed her hair black and made her slimmer.' I laugh but when I go back and really study the mouth and the eyes I realise that she bears more than a passing resemblance to Dolly Parton, she's the spitting image.

'So it's a busty blonde to scare off Mr Fox and a slim brunette for the mighty buzzard, is it?' Anne makes no reply, she just smiles enigmatically. Then she adds:

'Talking of that other scarecrow, did you hear about the foxes and what happened?'

'No, tell, tell.'

'It was awful – it was the middle of winter and very cold, and being out late I hadn't got back to shut the hens in and those foxes, they came and cleared off with all the fat ones, the ones that were laying. They left just six of the scrawniest behind. The remains of dead chickens and ducks were spread all round the village. You know, those released urban foxes are the bad ones: they come when it is only just dusk; the rural ones are much more timid and would wait until the middle of the night. That's why I made the scarecrow. I wrote a poem about it.' This is an extract:

Tales of a Postmistress
. . .
Oh! How did she remember,
One frosty night last December.
Her hens and ducks that fox did find.
How he and his pals had dined!
Headless bodies scattered throughout the village,
What a senseless, wasteful pillage.
. . .
Meanwhile the postmistress sits and thinks:
'That fox I must hoodwink,
Before its teeth in my remaining hens it sinks.'
Suddenly up she jumps and says, 'Ah! Yes I know.'
Off up to her husband's shed she did go
Busy with wood, hammer, nail and hay
Until the end of the long day.
A lady scarecrow was in progress

With blonde hair, black stockings and red dress.
Out of this shed the lady came.
With her winking eyes, she looked game.
In the postmistress's paddock she stood
Amongst all those hens, ducks and mud.
Now one day when the postmistress was away
A little game village folks thought they would play.
Returned she did when it was night,
To find the scarecrow's bloomers had changed from blue
  to white!
Her black stockings she was flashing.
Her position was one of inviting passion!
In her belt was tucked her dress.
Oh! She did look a mess.
Every day her positions changed
Till the postmistress nearly went deranged.

Meanwhile in the P.O. the village joker came to say:
'Now you will have Family Allowance to pay . . .
Your scarecrow is in the family way!'

© Anne Huntington, December 1995

Michael and I go down to Moon Cottage to meet Caroline
and Nathan and to show them all the little things in the
cottage that they need to know about. They are a charming
couple and I know they are right for this special place. It is
always horrible at this stage of selling a house, because you
never know if it is going to be all right or if something
terrible will still go wrong, but it feels so good being in the
cottage with them. Wonderfully, too, Shirley has really
warmed to them and they like Shirley, which helps no end.
We owe Shirley so much for all that she has done and it

would be so good if this couple turn out to be her new neighbours.

We return back North with our spirits high, but we discover that things are no better between the cats than they were when we left. Watching them closely suggests to me that the power is constantly shifting and they are all wary, I suspect mainly inspired by Gilly's explosive unpredictability. Pushkin seems to be losing a bit of weight and his fur has gone dull. He is such a timid cat that this could be a reaction to Gilly, or is he ailing? Unlike Fannie since her hysterectomy, he, since his castration, has become friendlier and much more touchy-feely with Michael, as well as me. I study him attentively. His eyes are bright and his nose is coldish. He seems alert enough, but this is by his standards of course – he still sleeps for four-fifths of every day. He has begun to chase Gilly more now. Usually he chases her after she chases him, but previously where he was inclined to run away and hide, now he simply turns around and gives back to her what she is dishing out. She seems to like it. I am sure that what is mostly motivating Gilly is a strong desire to play, but it seems not to be perceived in this way by the others. Pushkin still adores Titus but Titus, who is now gaining shocking amounts of weight since her spaying, seems to be on a short fuse with him and is quick to show her irritation. Titus will touch noses with Gilly but they never lie together as such. They will lie, by default, on the same large bed but not companionably. Pushkin and Gilly touch noses a little but Pushkin tends to be a bit jumpy which makes Gilly chase him and so he runs, although now he will chase her back again. Although I cannot say that it appears any better between Fannie and Gilly, Fannie does seem to be more relaxed with us.

Gilly really is one feisty cat. It would be anthropomorphic to suggest that she is deceitful when I don't know what it is that motivates her, but she appears to consciously lull the other cats into believing that she is in passive mode and is either paying them no attention at all, or certainly means no harm to them, but when they are totally relaxed she just goes for it. She will wait round the side of the sofa and then, when the others are displaying their wariness, she will look away, for really long periods. They will, eventually, visibly relax, at which point she swings round and attacks them.

Today she alarms me by jumping down the back of a large chest of drawers slotted into an alcove which is only 3¼ inches wider than the chest. The drawers are full and it is heavy and I simply can't move it. She gets stuck in the gap at the back and starts to panic and make a terrible fuss, but do what I may I'm unable to reach her. I try stuffing pillows down the back to try to get her to climb on to them and up that way, to no avail. I can hear her claws desperately scrabbling at the back of the slippery chest of drawers and eventually, in an almost morphing manner, she pulls herself in thin enough to squeeze through the crack at the side. I have no idea how she managed it and how her ribs survived it, but I am just praying that she will now leave it alone as a 'dangerous place'.

Caroline and Nathan contact us having had the results of their survey on Moon Cottage and, as expected, there is a long list of things that need attending to. The worst problem is damp which is inevitable in an old building, so we offer a contribution towards the cost of getting it fixed and agree a date for exchange and completion. We now feel able to take a longed-for holiday in France, but as usual I feel remorse and not a little apprehension about leaving the cats behind, especially not being certain of how Gilly is likely to react with the others over a fortnight. On the day we are to leave

I bring out the hanging clothes holder as well as the big suitcase, as we are driving down to the south of France in our own car, and Titus, to my horror, takes one look at it and goes into a terrible hunched position of grief. She plonks her fat little self down on the still empty hanging clothes holder and just stays there. She refuses to move and, even when she hears the outside door open, she still stays there and will not go outside or anything. I try to comfort her but she is inconsolable. Fannie retires to my study and climbs up into her box which seems to be the only place in the whole house now where she feels really safe, as Gilly has usurped both the top of the cupboard in our bathroom and also the top of the bookshelves in my study but at the moment cannot get into the box on top of the filing cabinet. She keeps trying though, so it will only be a matter of time. Pushkin stays asleep in the spare bedroom and his body language remains inscrutable, so I have no idea if he feels any concern or not at our impending departure.

Kalyacitta, my stepdaughter, has very kindly agreed to cat-sit the house while we are away and some of the time she will have a girlfriend and also her partner, Vajragupta, to stay with her too.

We start our holiday in France happily enough, but after seven days away I am so nerve-wracked and anxious for news of the cats that finally I succumb and, just before we all retire to bed, I reckon it might be OK to phone KC and speak, so with a deep breath I dial our number back in Cumbria. She answers the phone almost immediately and seems content enough in herself, which is hugely reassuring, and I am much relieved. Eventually I feel able to broach the subject of the cats and Kalyacitta indicates that there is ongoing friction between Fannie and Gilly, although I could have expected nothing less.

'You never told me about Gilly's obsession with water, did

you?' Kalyacitta laughingly chides me. 'I couldn't understand why near their water bowl in the conservatory I would mop up the puddle and then half an hour later it was as if the bowl was leaking, until I saw her paddling away in it, and today she went up to the pond and spent all her time in the corner by the rocks, and in the end she was standing in it.' It is so good to hear these small stories and after more in this vein I retire to bed comforted by the knowledge that they are in the safest hands it is possible to be.

While we are in France things suddenly start going wrong on the final stages of the sale of Moon Cottage, this time because the purchaser of Caroline and Nathan's flat is not prepared to exchange on the agreed date, and every other day we have fraught conversations with either Nathan and/or Caroline or our estate agent and the date is postponed yet again.

Under this cloud we make the long drive back home and finally we arrive back in Cumbria. Kalyacitta and Vajragupta say their farewells to us and KC assures us that she has loved being at the Coach House and tells us the cats are fine, which they self-evidently are. She tells me that Fannie killed a mouse, but that before she could clear it up it received a sky burial.[13] I laugh and hug myself with pleasure. She and

---

[13] sky burial is a ritual practice common in Tibet that involves placing the body of the deceased on high ground in a special place so that birds of prey will dispose of it, as many Tibetans believe that birds of prey are the carriers of souls to heaven.

VJ are both ordained Buddhists and so it is appropriate that a sky burial should happen for a mouse while they are both here.

Immediately we get back from holiday I receive an email from one of the youngest readers who has yet written to me. She deliciously signs herself 'From your biggest fans Kirsty and Merlin XXXXXXXXXXXXXX'. Harriet aka Kirsty has a cat called Merlin and she gives me regular updates on his doings which are various and often very naughty. She has won a competition at school for a brilliant poem she wrote when she was eleven, which has now been published in a book she tells me. She is now twelve. I reproduce her winning poem 'A Wild Hack' and oh how I felt like that when I was eleven too and utterly horse-mad:

A Wild Hack

Cantering, galloping, racing, trotting,
Over fields and through woods,
Flowing mane, flapping nostrils,
Through a puddle,
Over a log,

Stop for a picnic,
Run around, pick some flowers,
Calm down,
Lay on your back, stare at the clouds,
Wonder why??

Back to the stables,
Time to muck out,
Wished you were still out and about,
Got to go,

Back to the city,
Hoped it wasn't true!

© Harriet Garside

On 31 May we exchange contracts and on 9 June we complete the contract for the sale of Moon Cottage to Caroline and Nathan. We are weak with relief. We can hardly believe it has finally happened. Caroline and Nathan have two rabbits, one a female English Lop rabbit with those enormous ears, called Rosie, and the other, remarkably, a white Lionhead rabbit, called Scooter. I say 'remarkably', because Shirley also has a Lionhead rabbit called Buffy and saw this as a special sign that it was meant to be when Caroline and Nathan first saw the cottage. When we met Caroline and Nathan in Moon Cottage in April, Caroline had said:

'Let's raise a glass to Moon Cottage and also let's toast the Rabbits of Moon Cottage.' I long for Caroline to write *that* book. She writes me the following email in reply to my questions, and I am so glad I never knew about the Pinner property until now – phew!

– – –

From: Caroline Wallace
To: Marilyn Edwards
Cc: Nathan Richardson
Sent: Wednesday, June 22, 11:25 AM
Subject: RE: Moon Cottage

Dear Marilyn,
You asked about the cottage and the internet. I saw the cottage on the internet on 8 March and as you know we viewed it on 12 March. I had taken the 360 degree tour online but Nathan hadn't (he was really busy at work and tends not to get as obsessed as I do). I just knew I was going to love it. We arranged

to see a 3 bedroom house in Pinner beforehand (my plan was to show Nathan an awful property first so that he would love the cottage as much as I did). We took a drive round Pinner, which is absolutely stunning, and then drove to the house. The street it was in was so quiet – all you could hear was the birds singing – and a man was out washing his car. I was starting to panic in case Nathan liked this house but fortunately it was truly awful inside!

We arrived about 30 mins early for the Moon Cottage viewing. Nathan was concerned about the busy road so we went to the White Bear to watch the traffic go past. I was quietly cursing every driver. Anyway, off we trotted to Shirley's and she invited us in as the estate agents were in the middle of a viewing. It couldn't have been better because we got to see what the cottage would look like when really lived in – and of course Shirley is just a beautiful person.

As soon as I walked in the front door I knew that I had been right and that I was willing to fight to the death for this place. By the time we had got to the kitchen Nathan was also smitten. He didn't say anything but I could just tell from his eyes. After Shirley had shown us all the hidden treasures in the cottage, we went to her place for a cup of tea. We stayed there for an hour and a half. I think I already told you that Nathan forgot he was in a different cottage and kept opening doors and cupboards in Shirley's home! Luckily Shirley didn't mind one bit. The visit just ended perfectly when we saw that she had a rabbit too.

Talking of which, as you know our rabbits are house rabbits and we haven't got any further with letting them outside yet, but that's the next step.

Move over cats, the rabbits are here!
With our warmest wishes,
Caroline

Dr Caroline Wallace
Science Policy Advisor

CHAPTER 13

John has come to stay with us for the night and, in the absence of a permanent parish priest at our local catholic church, he offers to say Mass the following day. The three of us leave early in the morning for Mass (making sure that the cats are firmly shut in) and afterwards I do some shopping, so I don't return to the Coach House until 11.30. Meanwhile, Michael and John have gone on to the local town of Kendal to pursue other matters. As I drive back to the Coach House the rain buckets down – it is positively tropical in its force. It is the sort of rain that if you are caught in it without an umbrella, every stitch of clothing is soaked within seconds of exposure and you can feel it running down your skin. I unlock the front door and walk in calling out to the cats. Pushkin and Fannie come to greet me and I assume that Titus and Gilly are asleep elsewhere. I go upstairs and suddenly I hear Gilly's unmistakeable voice full of outrage and protest, but from outside! As I rush to the front door, there she is, trying to get in, looking like a moth-eaten drowned rat. I am utterly confounded. How could she have got out? I let her in and towel her down. She has been out for the whole of the downpour, I reckon.

'It's nothing more than you deserve, young madam,' I joke with her as she complains at the rub-a-dub-scrub going on. I go up to my desk and start my day's work and, suddenly, from outside my study, from I think the bathroom, I hear an almighty crashing noise. I go out to see what is happening. Fannie is lying on the spare bed with an inscrutable expression on her face, but not looking disturbed – if anything looking rather pleased – so I have to assume Gilly is not in this room. Pushkin and Titus are both lying in my study on the chair together, but of Gilly there is no sign. I look everywhere: in the airing cupboard, the wardrobes and the boxes she routinely hides in, but there isn't a trace of her. As I go into the guest bathroom again, I see that John has left the window open about six inches, but I cannot believe she has got down from there. It is very high up. But the more I think about it, the more I am persuaded that she must have escaped that way, which also explains how she was out when I got back from the shopping. I go outside and call, but to no avail, so I let Fannie out in the hope that she will stir Gilly up. At this point John and Michael return, and John goes off in search of her and spots her way across the field at the back and eventually, with John in hot pursuit, she returns to the garden where I

314

capture her and bring her in. We all go into the garden and look up at the bathroom window in amazement. There is a sloping drainpipe running down the side of the house just underneath the window and I suspect she must have tried to straddle that and fell off, hence the crash. I gulp, but she is fine and doesn't seem any the worse for wear. When she gets back into the house, as if proof were needed, she immediately leaps up onto the bathroom windowsill to try to repeat the performance, bashing her head forcefully against the now firmly closed window.

Talking of black magical things I have not yet envisaged Gilly as either a spider or a little black bear, but there is time for both of these incarnations. I receive this email from my agent in America, Melissa Chinchillo, who I have learned shares my love of cats. I beg her to send me information and pictures of her own cats after I discover that she gave a home to two feral cats from the 'wilds' of Staten Island – the picture of her cat LooLoo – a boy but he's cool with his name – wearing a pink feather boa is very special as you can see from Peter's drawing at the beginning of this chapter:

– – –

From: Melissa Chinchillo
To: Marilyn Edwards
Sent: Friday, May 06, 12:35 am
Subject: RE: The Cats on Hutton Roof

Dear Marilyn,
OK, I weaken. I am sending you a picture of my charming LooLoo (aka Buster, L'il Buddy, Rusty-Buster, Petey, and Sparkey). Not sure if I mentioned, but he's a male who was mistakenly thought to be female, so friends and family (particularly male ones) insist on giving him boyish nicknames.

But I maintain that he is LooLoo through and through and is quite happy with his name and to wear fancy costumes. He dragged that poor pink boa around the apartment until I finally had to throw it away – and he loves all sorts of necklaces and bow ties. Go figure! He is the cat I so yearned for as a girl when I tortured my poor cats with dress-up.

Spydah (aka Spydey, L'il Biddy, and SweetPea) is quite camera-shy so I have none to show you at the moment. Spydah got her name because she's all black and was so wild when I first got her that she would scurry around like a little black spider. She has now become more like a graceful little black bear.

It was quite an experience bringing them home from the wilds of Staten Island (that's a bit of geographical joke; it's quite a populated place)! They hid in my bedroom behind and underneath furniture and would only come out at night when I was 'sleeping' (not with them in the room!) and tear around the room. I wasn't sure if they were playing or just very freaked out. I worried for a long time because it took about 3–4 months for them to finally be affectionate, though they began playing with me after 1 month. But they would run away if I ever tried to pet them . . . But it was a fantastic learning experience on how to gain their trust – especially after their first trip to the vet when we had a little progress, and it was dashed because they were so torn up by going in their carry-cages and being driven in a car . . . Now, you'd never know they were feral . . . except a little with Spydah, as she can sometimes be shy. She was the runt of the litter, the woman who gave them to me said, and she still has a little of that mentality compared to her huge brother. He sometimes horses around with her too much for her liking and then she'll take to under the bed.

I try at all costs to give Spydey lots of one-on-one affection, separate from LooLoo, because he'll try to steal the show – and eat her food – at all costs. Right this moment, he's on my desk as I type and Spydah is patiently poised on my bed behind me waiting for me to give her a snuggle.

All the best,
Melissa

~

In early June France and Mark come up to see us, bringing with them the most wonderful drawing in crayons of Pushkin[14] that France has secretly drawn for me as a gift. I am astonished at the way she can capture the essence of a particular cat's personality and character. She is a talented artist. While they are here she takes a large number of pictures of the other cats, and later on I receive the most amazing portrait of Fannie, who has a special place in my heart as she knows. Over a long leisurely lunch France tells me about Spooky who has just had kittens. The litter consists of just two – a tortoiseshell girl with a lot of white and a mainly black boy, with a small amount of white. Mother and kittens are all doing well.

The actual birth happened at an especially awkward moment for her as she was involved in giving a private French lesson in her house with two of the children from her school. Spooky absolutely insisted that France should leave everything and go upstairs to be with her. I am very touched that her queen depends upon France each time to act as midwife.

'We all sat on the floor so I could keep close to Spooky while trying to teach French at the same time. I had prepared her a nest at the right end of the wardrobe, but she would have none of it. This time she had decided she would

---

[14] Both the pastels of Pushkin and of Fannie can be seen on my website under the names of the individual cats: www.thecatsofmooncottage. co.uk

317

have them in the left half of the wardrobe, over all the Christmas paper, bags, cards, other wrapping stuff and junk I keep there. So I had to empty it all (still trying to do my French lesson at the same time) and replace the bedding there. My lesson finished, the kids had to leave, and unfortunately for them, the first kitten was born only minutes after their departure.'

After France and Mark return back home to Spooky and her kittens (they had a neighbour cat-sitting while they were away), I get an update. The kittens have their eyes open at last. She has been quite concerned as kittens normally open their eyes between five and ten days of age, but Chester and Harriet, as these two kittens are called, didn't open theirs until they were twelve days old. She has just heard that they are to be adopted as a pair by her local butcher's wife, a lady called Kath, who plans to get a puppy at the same time. Kath lives locally, and this means that France will be able to see the kittens as often as she likes, which pleases her enormously. It also helps France to know that there is no point in allowing herself to feel broody, as she has the same weakness for kittens that I have. France gives me regular updates on their development over the next few weeks and then I get an email from her, explaining a particularly eventful party that she and Mark held over the weekend for assorted friends.

– – –

From: France Bauduin
To: Marilyn Edwards
Sent: July 11th 15:39

Well, so much happened yesterday, I had to write to give you an update on the kittens.

The kittens have now found out how to get downstairs. That,

on its own, was a good new experience for them. But once people started arriving for our BBQ, they suddenly discovered a new kind of human too, the kind that runs, yells, and carries you all over the place like a rag doll: Kids!!! There were 4 little girls (5, 7, 8 and 13), the 5 year-old being a hyperactive kid at that. Chester took it all very well; he accepted being carried everywhere without batting an eyelid, as if it was mummy doing it. Harriet, though, became increasingly spooked and would try to hide whenever she could to avoid being handled.

Well, I couldn't be everywhere so just had to take it on trust that the kittens would be alright.

A couple of hours later, just as the BBQ, complete with oven BBQ chicken, sausages, burger steaks and salads, was about to be served, the little girl came to see me worriedly. They just couldn't find the kittens. At first, I was not too worried. Obviously, they had found some place to hide away and get a bit of peace. Except that when I came upstairs, I noticed someone had fully opened the window and this is one of the places the kittens can easily climb to. Good grief, had they fallen off the window? With the kids, I looked again in all the known hiding places they had used since they were born. I couldn't find them anywhere. I looked at other possible places. No kittens. I gave a quick look outside but couldn't see either of them. The only thing that was keeping me from utterly panicking was that Spooky was in our bedroom and didn't seem worried. If they had fallen through the window, surely she would have heard them and be looking for them.

Well, in the end, I found them. They were in my wardrobe, sleeping between my shoes under the shoe rack. Thank God for that! I could finally attend to my guests and have some supper myself.

The rest of the evening passed smoothly enough. Both Grippette and Uni came to say hello but legged it soon afterwards finding there was too much activity for their taste.

By the end of the evening, however, I heard Spooky's worried calls: the ones she makes when she is looking for her kittens and can't find them. Someone had left the back door open, and both kittens were playing in the backyard in the dark. Talk about a day of discoveries, going from being penned upstairs to finding downstairs and the backyard all in one day. I got Harriet easily (being mostly white) but Chester was a little more difficult to spot (being almost all black). The little devils!

Today the back door remains closed as all the windows (well they are opened up 1 inch or so). Not great especially in this heat but I just don't want to have to worry. Yesterday was enough for the week.

Only 2 weeks to go before I give them away. Not long. At least I am on Holiday and can spare more time to play with them.

Love France.

I continue to get progress reports from France and shortly after this she tells me of an occasion when Spooky comes into the house carrying the largest dead mouse she has ever seen. Her account makes me laugh as it is clearly the all-important lesson that maternal cats give to their offspring at a certain stage in their development; it is exactly what Otto did when Fannie and Titus were only a few weeks old.

'When she saw me come to her, she put it down and just left it there. So right, I get the message. I am to bring the kittens to the mouse, I am after all their "auntie" and "kitten-sitter", so I must assume my responsibilities at all costs. This time the reaction was fantastic: proper kitten reactions at last. They fought for it, threw it in the air, and growled "MINE!" "MINE!" at each other.'

And so the kittens are growing up fast. France tells me that as the kittens get older, then Spooky's attitude towards them is changing, and she is much less protective towards them. At nine weeks old they are about to go for their first set of injections and she and Kath, who is soon to be their new human companion, both use the same vet which is useful. I know that France is dreading the moment of handover for herself and also for poor Spooky. She next contacts me as follows:

'For Spooky, she didn't seem to miss them too much in the evening but started miaowing and looking for them in the middle of the night, coming to lie on me three times to take some comfort from me. Spooky rarely does that. To do it three times in the same night shows how much she missed the kittens and was trying to find a bit of reassurance and love elsewhere. This morning she's been sleeping most of the time. Kath called this morning to give me an update on the kittens. She said they settled down very well, especially Chester who was very happy to flop on anyone's lap for a nap. Harriet seems very happy as well and they have been playing all morning.' France then confesses that she has felt the need to bike over to them and check them out for herself. She reports back that the kittens are fit and well and clearly being looked after supremely well in their new home. Spooky is still calling for them but less often and is on her way to recovery, ditto France I hope, but as displacement activity I suspect, I get this:

From: France Bauduin
To: Marilyn Edwards
Sent: July 30th 18:44

Here is a drawing I have done of Harriet and Chester together.

CHAPTER 14

The situation continues to be tense between Fannie and Gilly. I keep convincing myself that Gilly is only trying to play; sometimes when she sits and toughs it out with Fannie, Fannie does seem to be her own worst enemy. Fannie, on first seeing Gilly, will hiss whether there is any chase implicit or not, and as Gilly stares at her, Fannie always chooses a course of action which is doomed. She will half crouch, half lie on the ground, with her ears pinned back along her head, and hiss repeatedly, the hisses getting progressively louder. If she were ever to walk towards Gilly, as do Titus and Pushkin, then Gilly would back down, but she never does. Gilly will now creep closer and closer with her pricked ears quivering and her whiskers angled forward inquiringly as when a cat stalks prey, and as she gets closer, in the absence of retaliation the only action open to Fannie is for her to turn tail and run, at which point Gilly takes off after her in full pursuit. I comfort Fannie when this happens but realise there is a risk that it will encourage her to play the 'pathetic' card even more than she already does.

When Gilly tries the same tack, exactly, with Titus, Titus just thrashes her tail around violently and either stays still or walks slowly around the 'obstruction' of Gilly. With Pushkin, depending upon his mood, he either runs away or, now increasingly, he will half run away and then you can almost see him consciously change his mind when he stops abruptly, turns and chases Gilly, who in turn responds by running away. The cruellest thing of all now is that Pushkin has just taken to regularly chasing the woebegone Fannie, which is really harsh when all those months when she was on heat and calling to him, he would never go near her. He clearly doesn't chase her meaning to harm her, but she is so muddled up and disturbed by Gilly that her reaction to him is exactly the same as her reaction to Gilly. You can tell from his body language after he has chased Fannie that he actually thinks it's rather a good wheeze.

All four cats have been going out more frequently and for longer spells and indeed we leave Titus out for as long as she wants, as she mainly goes into the field at the back and then comes back on her own. The only downside of Titus's spells outside is that she eats a lot of meadow grass and then promptly comes in to be sick. Why do cats come inside to be sick? Maybe it's a need for privacy as vomiting in the open air would highlight your vulnerability? Fannie spends less and less time outside at the moment; she can't cope with being chased by Gilly outside, although mainly Gilly ignores her when they are in the garden. Pushkin, on the other hand, who held top position until very recently as the most timid of the three cats, now spends more time out because, sadly, he caught a blackbird fledgling and is clearly on the lookout for more. Of all of them, though, Gilly is the loose cannon as she spends her time anywhere and everywhere running wildly at high speeds and without any care for where she is going, so it could as easily be the road as the field at the back. She runs round our garden, round Richard and Annabel's garden, in the road, anywhere she pleases, and I just pray. Michael has a theory that Fannie sends her out there on a daily basis.

Today I go to see my dear friend Brian, who lives over in Richmond at the eastern end of Swaledale. He is valiantly confronting recent widowhood and the aftermath of what he refers to as 'a dyno-rod job' on his prostate. While sitting on a rickety bench outside his house, glass in hand, Brian regales me, against the sound of tractor-drawn hay-wains thundering past, with a tale of how he and Valerie, setting out on a long research visit to New York, had arranged to stay with two old friends who had an extremely chic apartment on Roosevelt Island in the City's East River. Hospitality was always unstintingly offered, but Valerie used to recount how full residents' rights were only granted after she had been interviewed by no fewer than five cats who lined up on a sofa to inspect her and assure themselves that she would pass muster. (The trip proved a great success and the book that emerged from it was dedicated to 'Ray and Peter and the Famous Five' – although one of those five went some way towards derailing things near the start when Brian – last man out in the morning departure – failed to check the whereabouts of everyone and found, returning that evening, that the Cat Frederick had been shut in a bedroom with serious consequences visited upon a swan's-down duvet and he, Brian, now in receipt of a yellow card as a result.)

The following day Brian and I take a gentle walk with Jessie, his much-loved Cairn terrier, in the grounds of Easby Abbey.

As we walk I am moved by the sense of complete quiet and tranquillity that emanates out of every block of stone of these ancient ruins, and its surrounding woodland, where the loudest sound is the soft coo-coo-cooing of a plump woodpigeon calling to its mate. The ruins of the Abbey lie alongside the River Swale and it was originally inhabited by Premonstratensian Canons known locally as the White Canons (because their habits were white). At the time Easby was built, there was also a Benedictine priory, St Martin's, a mile upstream on the other side of the river, whose monks wore black habits. The mind conjures up a delicious monochromatic image of these two groups of religious facing each other across the river like pieces from a living chess set. When I make this observation to Brian he chortles:

'A bit like "Alice" – but did you know that her progenitor was at school in Richmond before going to Rugby and would have known the valley and Easby and all!'

'Hey, you don't think that when he wrote . . . No, it would be too much of a coincidence?'

Quite why the Abbey feels as tranquil as it does I am not sure as it has had a fairly tortured existence. The White Canons, like the Benedictines, followed a simple and austere life, but they were in constant danger of being raided by the Scots and were obliged to call in the English army for protection. They got it, but at a fearful cost. In 1346, an English army, on its way to the Battle of Neville's Cross, was billeted in the Abbey. The soldiers spent most of the time in drunken brawling and inflicted as much damage on the Abbey as the Scots would have done. Eventually the Abbey suffered further looting and destruction with the Dissolution of the Monasteries and was finally abandoned;[15]

---

[15] this historical information from A *look at Richmond* by John Ryder (Welbury Press) ISBN 0 905826 00 0.

a sad place, but all the same, breathtakingly beautiful.

After saying farewell to Brian and Jessie I drive back from Richmond taking the low road home which comes winding down through the thick woods beside the Swale and am enchanted by the slanting golden sunlight of this late spring/early summer and it melts my heart. The varied green of the leaves is almost throbbing in its intensity and the colour everywhere is violently bright. I have a sense of long shadows and golden light and as I drive through it I feel an ardent allegiance to it – this particular light, this precise lie of the land, could not be anywhere else. They are unique to this hemisphere, to this continent, to this island. This is where I belong.

~

Today is Midsummer's Day and today, Hugh, our great nephew comes to visit Michael and me for the first time. Hugh is the eleven-month-old son of Claire and grandson of Catherine, Michael's sister, and he was born shortly after our grandson Oskar, whom we both miss terribly because he lives far away in Sweden, so we are enchanted to get a baby-fix.

I am bewitched by the interaction between Hugh and Gilly. Gilly has never met a small child in her life before and is not at all sure how to take him, but Hugh is utterly trusting of Gilly, as he has a much-loved and loving cat at home with whom he plays happily for hours. Gilly watches him and soon he starts to crawl around the floor chasing her. She adores this but keeps running away from him – it is very funny to see the chaser being chased for once, but she keeps peeping out round the corners of her hiding places when she deems that his progress is too slow to make sure that he is still in pursuit. Over lunch Claire straps Hugh into his pushchair and Gilly, sitting above him on the cat platform, suddenly puts out her paw, claws fully retracted, I gratefully observe, and pats him lightly on the head, several times.

'I reckon she is trying to work out what exactly he is,' Michael observes. 'Is he fish, is he fowl, or is he good red herring? Oh silly Gilly, he is none of those things; he is just a human kitten, only younger even than you.'

As our lunch progresses Catherine entertains us with her tales of Baldrick, their fifteen-year-old ginger moggy who, rather like Titus, has always had difficulty in jumping and climbing and, when he feels the time has come to ascend onto their bed, spends several concentrated seconds swaying his backside from side to side in the manner of a sumo wrestler psyching himself up in order to make that effortful spring which will, in Baldrick's case he hopes, result in his landing four-square on top of the bed.

Dear old Baldrick who, when he first arrived in the Hughes household having been named 'Baby' by the RSPCA as the smallest and scruffiest of several siblings who had temporarily been homed there following the death of their mother on the road, was greeted with enthusiasm by Ray, who announced:

'I have just the name for you, my boy. "Baldrick" it is from now on', and so it has remained. Baldrick, who at the age of eight weeks, was greeted by their long-resident queen, Nellie, with a hatred and irritation that she never wholly lost and which she manifested by removing a piece of Baldrick's ear, and it remains a notable battle scar to this day. Whether it was Nellie's personality or not it is hard to say, but while she lived Baldrick remained silent. However, following her death at the venerable age of twenty years, Baldrick has now taken on her role and has found his voice and noisily miaows his greetings and demands for food, which he would never have done while Nellie was around.

Since writing the above I have had the sad news from Catherine that Baldrick has rejoined Nellie, but one hopes, with his voice intact. Baldrick, please rest in peace.

CHAPTER 15

I confess it, a new love: the bumblebee! I am captivated by them and feel so guilty that I have never before understood why they are so wonderful. They, more than any other insect, have become for me the harbinger of spring. Although it is now midsummer I here record that from mid-March onwards our garden was host to many slow and lumbering bumblebees and I was alarmed for them as the frosts were not yet finished when first I saw them, although the days I did spot them early were always mild and sunny. I didn't then know why or what they were about, only that they were astonishingly early, until I came across a completely wonderful book which is now my bumblebee bible.[16] From this book I learned that the early bees that I was seeing were all queen bumblebees, newly awakened from winter hibernation, having been fertilised by their chosen male in the autumn, and now desperately trying to replenish their lost body fats with pollen and nectar from suitable plants. The reason they seemed so slow is that they were just able to generate enough body heat to get off

[16] *Field Guide to the Bumblebees of Great Britain & Ireland* by Mike Edwards and Martin Jenner (Ocelli, 2005) £9.99, ISBN 0954971302. Their argument for using only the scientific names is very persuasive.

the ground, but only just. Their solemn and solitary task from late February until early May, depending upon the species, was first to feed up in order to develop their fertilised ovaries and then to find a suitable location for a nest to start the new colony. The bumblebees that I spied in those first spring days were probably the common *bombus terrestris*, although they are very similar in appearance to *bombus pratorum* who are also widespread early bumblebees, but I am sure that it was one or the other, and for both species their chosen nesting sites are in undergrowth or even underground. I discover from my bumblebee mentor and namesake (but sadly no relation) Mike Edwards that these feisty queens, having chosen their nest site, would have formed a ball of pollen within it and made a nectar pot and, surrounded by these home comforts, would then have set out about reproducing their first offspring, which would be worker bees, and these workers would all be *female*. Worker bees can only produce male bees themselves and, at this crucial early stage, the queen then 'instructs' them that they may not produce bees; they must go out and bring in food, and this they do, their function being to forage and care for the colony, although if death and destruction were to deprive them of their queen, without aid of fertilisation they could produce males.

In March and April our garden had many early flowering plants, some early heathers,[17] crocus,[18] cowslips,[19] rosemary,[20] flowering currant,[21] rhododendrons,[22] clematis[23] and gorse[24]

---

[17] erica
[18] crocus
[19] primuls
[20] rosmarinus
[21] ribes
[22] rhododendrons
[23] clematis
[24] ulex europaeus

I have also just found my pressed flower album and on 10 April, coming back from church, Michael and I picked from the hedge-row just down the road some bluebells,[25] primroses,[26] cowslips,[27] aconites[28] and black-thorn,[29] all beloved by bumblebees, and there they are, looking a bit squashed (and Gilly has eaten most of the bluebell) but a true relic of our early spring.

This being nature, and red in tooth and claw, I discover that there is a group of bumblebees called cuckoo bumblebees who are parasitic on social bumblebees and in May the female cuckoo bumblebee, *bombus psithyrus*, who is large and powerful will usurp a social bumblebee's nest and will either 'hypnotise' (subdue her chemically) or kill the queen and take over the workers to care for her own off-spring. For more information on true and fake bumblebees do seek out this wonderful tome. It is a great work of painstaking observation and says more about bumblebees than any other guide I have seen.

In late May and through June the bumblebees were unbridled in their desire for the nectar contained within the tight little whitey-pink flowers of the cotoneaster[30] that clambers rampantly up our gatepost and over our gate and

---

[25] endymion
[26] primula veris
[27] primula
[28] aconitum
[29] prunus spinosa
[30] corokia

also spills over the dividing wall from the Old Vicarage. However diminutive a flower it may bear, it seems to make no difference at all to the busy bumbling bumblebees, as it seems it's the all-important elixir contained within that must be sought out at all costs. I am intrigued by how bumblebees will visit the same flower again and again, supping only a little on each visit, as if in exacting obedience to some predetermined directive of 'little and often'.

The cats through this early summer are continuing to hone their hunting skills and Fannie catches and partially eats, with great flamboyance, two mice on consecutive days. Pushkin, although less successful than Fannie, spends long hours staring at one hole in the ground and presumably has in the past been successful using this technique, otherwise surely he would give up on it. Titus tends to just lie and twitch her tail and join in any other successful rounding up of prey that the others have engendered. Gilly, twice, rather sweetly brings in curled up brown leaves with great triumph, which she bats around, jumps on, holds aloft in her paws while lying on her back, exactly as if they were small mice and which, initially, fools the other cats who gather round expectantly but who then wander off, disdainfully, as they realise the whole thing is a complete humbug. This morning, however, it is a different story. Gilly catches her first mouse. It is alive and well and has no teeth marks on it, but it is very frightened. Michael and I gently remove it from her, and Michael takes it away into a field the other side of the road where she never goes, but after we remove it from her, she goes rigid with rage in my arms, like a two-year-old with temper tantrums, and in the end I have to put her down as I am fearful she will start biting and clawing. She so clearly understands the difference between the real thing and her former little brown leaves. Shortly after this, within just a few days, she catches and kills a blue tit, which I find her with in the sitting-room, tossing it around as if it were a toy, although the truth is, I suppose, that cats toss toys around as if they were dead birds. As before when the cats caught a blue tit, I am astonished that such a tiny bird has so many thousands of feathers. She then catches a greenfinch and after that a dunnock. I am beginning to be worried now. The bird kill has been comparatively low so far and part of the joy of living here is the wealth of birdlife, which I am anxious we do not unbalance. Gilly isn't very efficient at killing them, but just brilliant at catching them – she seems to have an instinctive sense of self and is skilful at concealing herself. She, like Pushkin, will sit it out for hours, but in Gilly's case she makes sure she is hidden under a bush, whereas Pushkin usually remains visible to all.

Fannie continues to garner and kill shrews, field mice and field voles. Her greatest number of catches recently has been field voles, with their tiny round ears and short tails. It is said that a vole's innards taste bad to cats. Fannie eats part of them, the head usually, but leaves the rest, although she seems to eat all of the mice she captures, so perhaps this is true.

The hayfield behind the Coach House is growing higher by the day and nestling among the tall grasses is an abundance of wild flowers. Predominant among them is meadow buttercup,[31] but red clover[32] runs a close second followed by ribwort plantains.[33] Buried amidst this profusion and lower to the ground is the delicate bluey-violet of tufted vetch[34] and meadow crane's-bill[35] and today, walking carefully near the edge so that I don't flatten it, I find the wonderful tall yellow rattle or hay rattle,[36] and tradition dictates that when its seed pods rattle it's time to mow the hay, but at the moment it is still in glorious yellow flower. This hayfield is a wonderful species-rich meadow and looking out from the kitchen window over its butter-yellow, pink and blue flowers bobbing and dancing amongst the lush grasses makes me ache with pleasure. We find ourselves laughing every time we let Gilly out because when she finally squeezes herself through the fence and into the field at the back she unfailingly begins a series of enormous springy jumps, which enable her to cover great distances over the meadow grass and the wild flowers. Unlike Gilly, with her energetic

---

[31] Ranunculus acris
[32] Trifolium pratense
[33] Plantago lanceolata
[34] Vicia cracca
[35] Geranium pratense
[36] Rhinanthus minor

leapfroggings, all three of the older cats force their way through the long grass with apparent reluctance, and when it's been raining and there is a danger they might get wet they just turn tail and give up on it. And then, one dry and sunny day, the field is mown flat in preparation for a group of campers as the grass is now far too long for the comfortable pitching of a tent and it is dry and sunny at the moment, but rain is forecast. As we watch them lay low the grass and flowers with a powerful tractor and scythe attachment I am just a little afraid for the bumblebees that their vital supply of clover nectar has been cut short, as although much of the clover has died back there are still some healthy blossoms in there. But I need not have worried as, immediately the hay-meadow is flattened, the bumblebees appear to move en masse to the tiny bell-shaped pink flowers that almost invisibly (to us but not them) adorn the hedgerow on all the boundaries of the field, and completely surround our house. This thick hedgerow, so irresistibly attractive to bees, consists mainly of the dense shrub called snowberry.[37] As I turn towards the house, the hedges are positively thrumming with the low buzzing of many tens of fat furry bumblebees and from time to time I spot a few of Richard's delicate slim honey bees balletically darting around their heavier distant-relatives, reminding me of a scene from my late childhood, when a gang of us girls, taking part in a gymkhana on our pint-sized ponies, caused disarray by mistakenly cantering into a field in which two sets of shire horses were performing a sample ploughing, to our chagrin and the mirth of the many onlookers.

As soon as the farmers leave the field, having baled and wrapped the silage, I let the cats out to see what they make of it. Fannie and Titus rush into the field with their tails up,

---

[37] Symphoricarpos albus

clearly more at ease now that they have their old familiar long-distance view back, although Fannie stops short, suspiciously, as soon as she sees the big bale just outside the kitchen window. Gilly, on the other hand, is agitated by the whole thing as her only memory seems to be of the tall grass which she liked and this new, long vista dotted with giant black bundles and its overpowering scent of mown hay is most worrying. She stands and sniffs repeatedly and then, perceptibly trembling, she quickly turns about and runs through the fence back into the garden. She is still only a little kitten at heart, for all her spirit.

It is now high summer and the weather for days on end has been sunny and beautiful – indeed, it is exceptionally dry for Cumbria. I have taken to writing out in the garden, under the shade of the giant Scots Pines, and both Gilly and Fannie come up to me from time to time to check that I am still at it, just as Michael does! I work at the big garden table and have a chair by the side of the one I am sitting on, which has a cushion on it. Fannie curls up on it proprietorially and writing at the table with her beside me in my domestic wilderness does properly make it 'Paradise enow'. Very quickly, however, I realise that this is going to mean trouble when I get checked out by Pushkin and Titus as well, who eye her keenly, so to avoid noses being put out of joint I surround myself with four chairs each with its cushion, just in case. Settling down to write outside is now a huge kerfuffle as I carry out the laptop, the extension lead, the dictionary, the chairs, the cushions, added to which periodically I have to move around to avoid the sun sneaking through the overhead branches and dazzling me. It is also entertainingly distracting, not least because I am concealed from the road, but can hear the ardent conversations and sometimes arguments of the hot sweaty walkers, having just climbed the hill from the village, as they innocently tramp past on their way up to the Crag. Life is hard! As I sit here I luxuriate in the mellifluous bird song coming at me from all angles and in particular that budgie-like chitter-chattering of swallows that is both extraordinarily comforting and at the same time exotic. Another prevalent exotic sound around here is the tinkling-bell call of the goldfinches.

Not all is peaceful, however. Gilly sometimes just goes too far in her assaults on Fannie and today she attacks Fannie in the guest bathroom, causing her to shriek with terror, although it isn't a real fight, Fannie is overreacting as usual. I am so cross that I tap Gilly on the nose, although I know full well that physical discipline and shouting is not the way to coerce cats into better behaviour, and say very sternly: 'Naughty, naughty cat' and push her outside the bathroom. She really glares at me as I do this. She turns away from me and I watch her flounce off downstairs. The whole way down she complains with her coarse baritone 'miaow, miaow, miaow' and I can hear her carrying on with it right through the conservatory and along into the other part of the house and up the stairs into our bedroom. My sense of remorse (she is after all only a very young cat still) makes me go and seek her out, after first comforting Fannie and settling her down in my study. When I reach Gilly she doesn't want to be cuddled and is very cross with me. We talk a bit about it all and although I don't believe she ends up thinking I was right in what I did, we part on better terms.

All that took place yesterday, but today she has a really bad fight with Fannie and Fannie is so jumpy that she just retires to her little box on top of the filing cabinet. Although Gilly has now usurped every other resting place that Fannie has hitherto slept in, this box, although she could get into it, she has left alone. I tremble for Fannie at the thought of what she or I will do when Gilly finally hijacks that one as well. Sometimes Fannie still gets up on top of the bookcase, but she feels less secure up there as Gilly often climbs up there too, although Gilly has fallen down at least twice while in the process of climbing up.

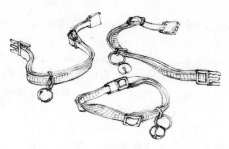

CHAPTER 16

The bird kill that I have witnessed through the summer is worrying me and although I have mixed feelings about cat collars, I did have one on my former cat Otto, complete with bell, and she killed, I believe, only one bird in her life. I study the RSPB website and find an article headed:

COLLAR THAT CAT TO SAVE WILDLIFE!

A correctly fitted collar and bell can reduce cat predation by a third, according to new RSPB research. The study, undertaken by volunteer cat owners from across the UK, tested the effect of different collar-mounted warning devices in reducing cat predation within gardens. Results show that cats equipped with a bell returned 41 per cent fewer birds and 34 per cent fewer mammals than those with a plain collar. Those equipped with an electronic sonic device returned 51 per cent fewer birds and 38 per cent fewer mammals, compared with cats wearing a plain collar.

I decide I should try what the RSPB advises as this summer four birds have met their end who would not otherwise have done so without the benefit of the Coach House cats, not to mention numerous small mammals, perhaps ten in total, mainly shrews, a few mice and one or two voles. Gilly manages to force her collar open (it has the safety fastening that Claire Bessant recommends on the RSPB website) twice within half an hour of first wearing it, and it does reassure me that it is easy to open on the safety count, but perhaps just too easy? Pushkin is appalled at the invasion of his body and his hearing in this way and slinks away tinkling his bell loudly to some hiding place where a cat might sit and mope who has been subjected to this indignity. Titus sits and takes it like the cat she is, but looks up at me with an expression of dignified hurt on her face that I am doing this horrible thing to her. Fannie rushes away and manages to rip it off five times in the first hour of her wearing it. When I do put it back on her after the fifth time of her removal, she just looks at me with large eyes filled with fear and in front of me scratches the safety lock open within ten seconds with what I take to be a combination of iron will and pleading. At this point I capitulate as she is so stricken by her relationship with Gilly that I feel she just doesn't need more grief in her life at the moment. I find the other cats and it is clear that the tinkling bells (they are surprisingly loud) are causing them considerable stress, so one by one over a period of twenty-four hours I remove the bells, but leave the collars as I have now paid for engraved identity discs which will be coming shortly and need the collars from which to hang them. Through each of the subsequent two nights I wake at intervals to hear one or other of the cats scratching, scratching, scratching, but all three now keep the collars round their necks for all their efforts. I do need to find a different collar for Fannie, when the discs arrive, but am still worried about her reaction. I will wait to see whether the others get used to them.

Honourably, I will try to record all bird kill from now. I do realise that without bells to ward off the victims of their hunting sprees their collars are useless, other than to identify them if they get lost, but I would like to hope that their kill rate is sufficiently low not to merit the ding-a-ling harassment these bells would otherwise give them. The mind boggles at the effect the sonic devices must have on the sensitive hearing of cats. I am encouraged in my pursuit of a bell-less course when Sue Fallon, a new email friend and cat-lover, replies to my question on bells with:

– – –

From: Sue Fallon
To: Marilyn Edwards
Sent: Friday, July 29, 1:32 PM
Subject: RE: Bells

Hello Marilyn,

Cats and bells – my cats wear collars (apart from Syddy who always gets them in his mouth and gets the collar stuck in his teeth). I remove the bells, though, as I read many moons (excuse the pun) ago that cats have such sensitive hearing that even a little bell is like having a cow bell clanking in their head 24/7. If they are going to catch birds it seems that cats are clever enough to be able to stop the bell (I have observed this myself from the days when they did have bells). It is amazing that they can do it, but bells that have been tinkling away suddenly stop as they begin to stalk. On average I think my lot take about 4 or 5 birds between them the whole year and I have a lot of birds in my garden. The ones they manage to catch are either sick or, sadly, the youngest who have not realised you're supposed to take off rapidly when a cat is spied. I even have a Robin who quite happily bobs around close to me while I am gardening and we have a meaningful conversation. (Did I mention that I was quite mad?). Obviously your cats are enjoying their new-found freedom?

Best wishes,

Sue

Sue is pretty good on cats. She has a remarkable nine, every one of which she adores. The oldest is Muffin at eleven, followed by Whatsit at seven, and mother of Syddy, Tymmy, Dympy and Mischief, all aged six, and the others are the brood of another – sadly missing – cat, who Sue continues to hope will one day come home, also six years old, and they are Butty, Jiffy and Flash.

One of Gilly's most appealing party tricks since her very first introduction into the Coach House has been to retrieve a small furry dark-blue bird on an elastic string (which lost its plastic eyes within the first five minutes of meeting Gilly). She will not 'fetch' any other toy, but if I sit on the sofa in the sitting-room and throw it into the kitchen she will race off, pick it up in her mouth and return, dropping it at my feet as if she were a small black Labrador. It provides me with endless fun, although when she was much younger she would gallop off to bring it back in what seemed then a tireless pursuit of it. Now in her older age (all of nine months) she sometimes rather arrogantly strolls off after it and, if she is really bored, just looks at me and drops it down again in the kitchen. I thought this was unique, but then I got this email from Suzanne and realised I was one of thousands who are bewitched by the talents of Bengals:

— — —

From: Suzanne
To: Marilyn
Sent: Thursday, July 14, 9:15 PM

Wait until my mum hears that you have a Bengal! She will be thrilled! Let me tell you, they are hard work. Cute as a button when they are kittens, but as they get older they turn into children! My dad isn't the biggest fan of cats. We've had so many over the years, and with these two around it drives him crazy! They literally run the household. They have such strong personalities. I think that is a Bengal's nature. I could tell you a million funny stories about the two of them . . . but the best one of all is how much they are like dogs! Seriously! Our youngest one, Luca, plays fetch! We didn't even have to teach him. He has a little green mouse that he plays with and one day we threw it for him and he brought it back. And he will do it over and over again until it drives you insane! He will only do it with that particular green mouse, strange.

So there you go! Gilly is just a clone of every other Bengal. No, of course she isn't, but there are clearly traits in Bengals that are specially theirs. (Since writing the above, two different cat-lovers who do not have Bengals have told me their cats retrieve, so I withdraw the statement that this is peculiar to Bengals!)

The relationship between Gilly and Fannie continues as uncomfortably as ever and I worry, as Fannie now seems to spend her entire time in my study or outside, but certainly doesn't seem able to live with us in the rest of the house. On the rare occasions now that she and I do share a cuddle in the morning after the bath, I actively have to seek her out and bring her into the bathroom and shut the door, so she can be assured that Gilly will not disrupt it. What on earth is going to happen in the winter and once the rains start in earnest and she cannot escape into the garden and the surrounding fields? Gilly is, however, an enchanting cat to have around the place, and both Michael and I adore her being part of our household and just long for the relationship between her and Fannie not to escalate to any more of a problem than it currently is. Michael continues to call her his 'Black Magic' and he is utterly besotted by her. Talking of which, Bengals of course, I receive an email from Beth, Treacle's carer and companion, who tells me that her move to more northern Scotland (she currently lives in an exquisite but remote part of the county of Dumfries and Galloway which is just reachable by us, but any further north and we are talking real cross-country journeying) is imminent and I realise that if I am to see Gilly's half-brother before he becomes inaccessible, then it is now or never. She adds the following at the end of her email:

– – –

From: Beth
To: Marilyn
Sent: Wednesday, August 03, 10:52

A blog entry
Yesterday, young Treacle went out at tea-time. It was a grey and miserable day, with a heavy drizzle. Shortly after tea, we realised that (a) Treacle wasn't around and (b) it was raining heavily. Mr L went to look for the cat; he wasn't at any of his usual entry stations, but could be heard crying pitifully. Mr L braved the storm and went outside to look, saying, 'Treacle is distressed' as he went out of the door. I was hunting for my shoes when I heard

Ted shout. Two single cries, both the same. A very loud and harsh cry – 'OW!' I read it as a Bengal language version of 'Don't worry – I'll get you!' SuperTed flew out of the front door, metaphoric cape streaming in the wind created by his rushing. He stopped outside the porch. His head whipped first to the left, then just as quickly to the right. No Treacle! Then he looked up. RAIN!! – and indoors he bolted. What a wuss! Treacle was hiding under the veranda – and would not come out. Oh no – it's wet out there! Cajoling him would bring him forward to the edge of the decking, but as soon as he saw the big drips, he backed up again. I lay on the floor, getting soaking wet and muddy. He just looked at me with those huge yellow eyes, and mewled an anguished 'I'm wet!'

It was Mr L's long arm that reached in and pulled the cat out. He was quickly popped back through the kitchen window and ran into the sitting room to be with his mate. A bone-dry Teddy, cool as a cucumber, offered up his services to help dry Treacle off, with a smug look on his face that said, 'See? I told you I would come and get you!' No matter how bad things get, the cats can always make us smile.

Beth

Beth commands a wonderful blog on her website about all manner of things, which often includes great stories about her cats, and it's well worth a visit by any cat lover. This is how you find her: http://www.woolgathering.org.uk. So without more ado Michael, John and I set off to the very tip of Dumfries and Galloway. Because I want to talk black cat with Beth and meet Treacle, I leave the men in a nearby small country town, to watch one of the first football matches of the season and, waving them merrily goodbye, I drive off into the Lowther hills. Treacle sure has got an idyllic place to hang out and lots of sheep to play with. Following Beth's immaculate driving instructions I finally find the village of Wanlockhead which, it proudly proclaims on a boundary board, is Scotland's highest village at 1,531 feet above sea level. That is high. I arrive at their house and am warmly welcomed by Griff, a very friendly mongrel collie, and Suzie, a Border collie, and Steve and Beth, and as we walk into their house, there I spy the illustrious Treacle. He is an astonishingly handsome cat. He has Gilly's looks but is more masculine and definite somehow. His blackness is as impenetrable as Gilly's and his silky-soft Bengal coat glistens as it catches the sunlight. As he turns side on I am able to admire his strong masculine profile. He swings back and stares steadily across at me with his penetrating yellow eyes. I very briefly meet Treacle's beloved feline companion, Teddy, a stunning brown marbled Bengal, but he hates me and my camera and runs away. I sadly never catch a glimpse of Lulu, Beth's Bengal cross, but she had warned me that Lulu was a complete recluse. Where they live is paradise, so where they are going to must be quite extraordinary. But after we talk for a bit I feel I really ought to let her get on with her dreaded packing, so I take my leave and drive off to find the boys.

Just before the close of August I hear, to my great pleasure, from Christopher Gordon, the brother of my dear deceased friend, Giles.

– – –

From: Christopher Gordon
To: Marilyn Edwards
Sent: Monday, August 22, 6:23 PM
Subject: Contact

Dear Marilyn
I will get back to you shortly about George, and I write with Cleo (sexy grey half-Burmese moggy) sitting on my desk and purring

loudly. Somewhere I remember reading that Cardinal Richelieu usually had a cat on his desk when working, although I have to say I find it too distracting.

Best wishes,

Christopher

From: Marilyn Edwards
To: Christopher Gordon
Sent: Tuesday, August 23, 4:35
Subject: Re: contact

. . . PS Oh and do send my best to Cleo, and I am intrigued by what element in her you find sexy. You men(!) – Michael said something similar to me the other day about our black Bengal kitten (born around Halloween last year – she is a girl so we couldn't call her Giles – but we have called her Gilly in honour of your bro). She is sleek and slim and long legged and, as he was watching her sashaying towards the gate, he said, 'Oh, she is such a girl, she is so feminine' and there was a real yearning in his voice for her girlishness, it made me laugh.

Marilyn

From: Christopher Gordon
To: Marilyn Edwards
Sent: Tuesday, August 23, 6:11 PM
Subject: Re: contact

We all clearly have a need for displacement activity! August is not a great month in which to try and work . . .

What is so sexy about Cleo? Hmmm . . . being Cleo. I have a deeply unscientific theory that cats predominantly embody the female principle, dogs the male. Which is why I don't much care for dogs, I suspect. I mean, who wants to waste time or affection on a permanently attention-seeking animal with extrovert arrested teenage mentality, desperate for constant reassurance that it is loved? Ugh! It's demeaning, embarrassing and irksome – with the possible exception of collies. Dogs are just so boringly uncomplicated and predictable! The cat's introverted feminine self-sufficiency and moodiness, its need to be wooed, on the other hand . . . Was it something I did? No response. Was it something I said? No response. Was it something I didn't say? No response. Was it something you think I might have thought, that could have hurt your feelings if I'd ever got round to putting it into words? Maybe . . . Ah.

No, no, I never stereotype. I think that the combination of those cat eyes in an intelligent haughty face with its slightly smug self-contained expression is a big factor. It's a constant challenge. Cats flirt outrageously and tend to play hard to get. And when they don't, but flop down on the ground on their backs just for you, well, how can one resist? Dogs don't even know what flirting is. Not all cats are sexy. George isn't, although he has quite a sweet face, but it's just not very intelligent (but Cassandra, his black and white Persian predecessor, was). Cleo's predecessor – also grey Burmese – Scipio was dead sexy. He was very much a boy, and had those long legs (whereas Cleo, to be frank, having failed to do her post-natal exercises is now somewhat low slung). Dogs smell – although their owners always seem to deny this. Of course, cats don't. Though that reminds me people sometimes comment (with alarm!) on a habit I have of sniffing cat's paws as they lie in the sun – the combination of slightly warm sweaty pads/tufted fur is 100% redolent of being in a mosque in Istanbul – well, OK, I suppose it does come over as slightly weird. Whatever turns you on.

But enough of this – all the best,
Christopher

And following that Christopher then sends me this wonderful story about George, his cat, properly called George

Pompidou, not because of any statesmanlike behaviour he manifested but because 'as a kitten he looked rather like a pompom'. Here is George's story as told by Christopher:

George is a black – with white paws, nose and bib – Persian moggie. He is not very bright. His life has always consisted mainly of sleeping outside in the sun, with two daily visits to the house for food (which you can set your clocks by – 7.30 a.m. and 5.00 p.m.). Despite being such an 'outdoor' cat, he is a completely hopeless hunter. Since his emergence from kittenhood, I can't recall him ever having moved faster than a slow stroll. He never threatens anything. Once when he was quite young and we lived in the Meon Valley, he did manage to catch a baby rabbit in a neighbouring field. Alex, our eldest boy (who has always had a sort of empathy with George, because this cat's rather pathetic nature amuses him), saw it happen. George miaowed – although the noise he makes is not impressive at the best of times – to draw attention to his prowess with the rabbit between his front paws and looked sideways to seek approval from Alex on the road. The rabbit escaped and hopped off – and George ignominiously failed to catch it again despite trying really hard. Nowadays in our more urban location in Winchester he doesn't even bother to try. He sits on the grass surrounded by pigeons and blackbirds, which feed contentedly only inches away from his nose. This can, however, be misleading for the odd pigeon which deduces a false syllogism: George is a wimp, George is a cat, and therefore all cats are wimps. Other black and white cats in our neighbourhood now take advantage of the pigeons' thinking they are not a threat – so pigeons must have even smaller brains than George.

Typically, the one 'event' in George's laid-back life wasn't really an event at all. The location was the village of Meonstoke where we then lived – or more accurately Meonstoke and Corhampton, the adjoining village which straddles the A32 road. It was in the

351

middle of a hot summer spell. Sue had just collected Adam, our fourth and youngest child, from school during the afternoon when she received a phone call to say that someone had reported a dead cat lying on the side of the bend on the A32 road near the village shop. It was a black and white Persian, and it sounded very like George. Sue and Adam duly went off to the scene of the accident, with Sue doing her best to protect Adam from seeing the result of the horrors of a head-on collision between a cat and a passing vehicle. The face was, indeed, a complete mess – but the small black spot on the predominantly white rear left leg clearly identified the corpse as George's.

They quickly returned home to seek out a winding sheet and box for the corpse, and then the two of them, with considerable effort, dug a grave in the hard soil at the bottom of the garden, alongside the final resting place of Chloe – another beloved family cat – who also came to grief on the road. The funeral service over, Sue and Adam returned to the house, where the latter began to inscribe a piece of slate with a suitable inscription to mark George's tomb. It was now 5.00 p.m. That hour that George never missed and sure enough George sauntered in demanding his tea . . . Never, until that moment, claims Sue, had she literally known what it meant for the jaw to drop. By a process of elimination we think we identified the true owner of the dead moggie in Corhampton, but the woman – who was not even in the habit of feeding her cats properly or regularly – denied it, so we will never know for sure who the cat who lies next to Chloe is.

Since telling the tale above of the Resurrection of George, just as this book is going to press, I receive the following email from Christopher:

- - -

From: Christopher Gordon
To: Marilyn Edwards
Sent: Thursday, March 02, 5:30 pm
Subject: End of story

Marilyn:

Just for the record, this is to report that George(s) (Pompidou) failed to appear for his food on Sunday last, and his body was found today in a shrubbery by one of our neighbours.

We'd been searching around and asking people in the locality over the past two or three days to check sheds etc., in case he had been shut in when they were working in their gardens on Saturday/Sunday.

He was 15 + and seems simply to have expired.

With best wishes,

Christopher

CHAPTER 17

It is now the end of the first week in August and it has been very dry for several weeks, and since the introduction of the collars on the cats at the end of July the scratching has continued. Gilly has stopped removing her collar, but oddly enough Titus, who had not mastered the art of escape at the beginning of the collar regime, now removes it every night, but rather artlessly leaves it on the end of our bed, so of course I replace it each morning. Michael is fondling Titus – minus collar – in bed early one morning when out of the silence he suddenly declares loudly:

'Marilyn, Titus has nasty lumps all round her neck.'

'Mnn – I know,' I mumble, trying desperately hard to hang on to that exquisite state of unconsciousness known to those not suffering from insomnia as 'sleep'.

'But they're really nasty. They have blood round them.' I rouse myself and have a look and rather than just scratching marks they do indeed possess the qualities of angry and painful lesions. Later on that morning I have another look and decide I must take her down to the long-suffering Gerard. I inspect all the other cats minutely. Fannie has a couple of small lumps but not angry and she hasn't been scratching, so she gets the all clear for the moment. I look all over Gilly and cannot see anything, so I reckon she is fine too. I find Pushkin asleep on the pillow on the spare bed and I gently remove his collar. To my concern he too has lumps where the collar had been, two or three and, although they are not livid, when I gently put pressure on them they are clearly irritating to him. I bundle him up in a cat cage and then go in search of Titus. Pushkin makes his petrified and unhappy girlish mewls. They are surprisingly falsetto and are getting higher and louder and under other circumstances they make me giggle, but today I am empathising with him and so they make me sweat slightly. I find and squash Titus into the smaller cat cage, which should properly have been Pushkin's, and she makes one protesting miaow and then falls silent. As I drive off with them together I realise that yet again poor Titus is being accompanied whether she likes it or not by the omnipresent Pushkin. When I arrive at the vet's and haul them out, I hear another feline patient's carer say, above a loud protesting racket coming from a carrying box:

'Can I just go out and get some rubber gloves, as I think he may bite and scratch when we get him out?' Ah, the joys of being a vet! We are called in and Gerard looks at Titus first. I am convinced that it must be the collars that are causing it, or possibly Titus is now allergic to the Metacam I give her for her arthritic legs from her earlier operations, and I baldly announce this. Gerard smiles at me benignly and lets me carry on and then, after carefully examining Titus and especially the area round her neck, he says quietly:

'Marilyn, this looks to me like a typical reaction to harvest mite.[38] It is the larval stage that does the damage – they are almost invisible to the human eye, but they swarm up the cats from long grasses in late summer and early autumn and typically they get in between the toes. I was bitten myself on

---

[38] Trombicula autumnalis

my back this weekend and it itches like mad.' He carefully studies both Titus and then Pushkin in minute detail and shows me exactly where they are irritated. I can see that the collars in themselves didn't cause the lesions, but rather the heat generated by the collars on the cats and the fact that their fur is thinner in that area was responsible for the attacks around their necks. I had noticed the cats attacking their feet too and this is more of the same. Apparently upland areas are especially prone to infestations of harvest mite, who love chalk and limestone and who proliferate in hot dry summers, and this has been unusually dry for Cumbria with its normal annual rainfall of between 60 and 100 inches. The larvae sneakily wait in large numbers on long grasses until a passing cat (apparently preferred) or human (next best) comes into their zone, when they swarm over them and feast off their tissue fluid for three or four days before dropping off again on some other patch of grass to complete the rest of their life-cycle and to go on to produce more lovely harvest mites for next year. The cats are so irritated by the result of these infestations that Gerard decides he must inject them with a corticosteroid, but we both agree that if their reaction continues to be bad we need to find some other way of treating the problem.

Meanwhile I have a small project bubbling under, which in the way of small projects is turning in my mind into something more major. Michael and I have talked on and off about my keeping donkeys. I long for a little affectionate long-eared donkey, but the paddock we have across the road simply isn't big enough and, anyway, I know that if I had a donkey I would want two as company for each other. There is the small problem of who might be persuaded to rent which field to us as almost all the fields are used year-round by sheep farmers who either own them or rent them from other farmers. On top of this the donkeys would need to be provided with proper shelter and I have talked in rather vague terms to Richard and Annabel and also to Ian in the village, but I keep stumbling upon various forms of resistance and I can feel my resolution breaking down. I did mention to Annabel that I might keep hens instead, as I used to keep hens when I lived in the Dales. Not the same thing at all as donkeys, I know, but they do at least have a practical purpose: one can eat their eggs. Annabel is rather keen on the idea which possibly means I could ask her to lock them up if we are away or out late which would make it workable: it is during the winter that keeping free-range poultry becomes most difficult. I now have the problem of persuading Michael.

'But what *is* the point of having hens? I simply don't get it.'

'They're hugely rewarding, they're funny and they're the only pets I know where you can eat their output.'

'But I can buy eggs, free-range eggs, from Anne down the road anytime we want them, you know that!'

'Yes, that's true, but I want the pleasure of watching hens and talking to them and being with them and, oh, just having them about the place. It is an amazingly tranquil and lovely thing to hear their little clucks and so good when you hear that triumphant chortle of "I've laid an egg! I've laid an egg! I've laid an egg!" and you would so love going to collect the eggs in the morning, you know you would, and anyway we need to do something with that weed-ridden paddock.'

'Marilyn, you told me you were either going to make it into a wild-flower meadow or a herb garden and you have had over a year to do it.'

'Oh I know, but go on I have made one bed into a herb garden already, and I've cleared a load of weeds away . . .' As I trail off, Michael clears his throat in a theatrical manner, so I gird my loins and continue:

'I'm not just making excuses, honestly, but the more I read about wild-flower meadows, the more I understand that it is a sort of battle and that usually the deep-rooted indigenous weeds triumph over everything else,' and more in that vein until our exchange fizzles out and the dust gently settles again.

Annabel, however, heroically comes to the rescue. Every time she meets Michael she bravely urges him to consider the efficacy and pleasures of hen husbandry and slowly I watch him yield. I realise only now how really very alarmed she must have been at the donkey idea, and it is true that some donkeys can disturb the peace mightily. I go down to see Anne at the Post Office to confess that I might be about to embark on the poultry route – Anne has a colourful collection of hens and bantams consisting of several breeds including Rhode Islands and Marans and she sells the eggs, so I am anxious to allay any fears she might have that I am setting up in competition. In the course of explaining where my hen-lust has sprung from, I tell her that I had really wanted donkeys and she tells me a wonderful story about a local farmer who used to give a group of donkeys from Morecambe Bay a winter break in a local field and that they regularly used to go into full unending bouts of braying that were enough to awaken the dead. However, their holidays in this part of the Lune valley ended when it was discovered

that either in order to procure themselves a view of the crag or for the sheer hell of doing it or even I suppose inspired by their bellies, they had collectively eaten an enormous hole in the hedge. After that particular winter the Morecambe Bay donkeys were never to be seen in the village again.

For the last three Sundays John has been staying with us as he has been acting as supply priest to the catholic church in Kirkby Lonsdale in the interregnum between Fr John Turner leaving and the new priest, Fr Luiz Ruscillo, who is to take over some time in early September. Today John and Michael attack the little paddock in a way that I confess I had not managed on my own and, within a short space of time, the wildest of the weeds and their plastic carpets, which had been laid down by Pamela when she was operating her plant nursery, have been stripped out and the paddock reveals wonderful dark fallow soil just waiting for my wild flower meadow seeds to be sown. As the men collapse in exhaustion back in the garden of the Coach House I eagerly go into battle with hoe and fork and start to prepare the seed bed. (John, who for many years was a priest in Zaire, comments that that is exactly how it is out there, the men do the heavy labouring on the land and then the women move in afterwards to sow the crops.) My meadow grass consists of various grasses including chewing's fescue, sheep's fescue, hard fescue, slender red fescue and crested dogtail, but alongside these grasses is a separate bag containing a glorious litany of wild flowers. Included are lady's bedstraw, ox-eye daisy, ribwort plantain, yarrow, wild carrot, self heal, red campion, viper's buglos, St John's wort, musk mallow, yellow rattle, meadow buttercup, primrose, B. knapweed, cowslip, rough hawkbit, ragged robin, and then additionally there is corn flower, corn chamomile, corn marigold, field poppy and black medick.

So after some toiling on my part, during which I exude a convincing display of sweat, blood and tears (of effort), I finally get my seeds sown and join the boys over a bottle of wine to celebrate 'a job well done'.

'So all we have to do is sit back and wait for this wonderful wild flower meadow to just spring up, is that it?' Michael teases me.

'Well, I reckon if the weather stays as it is – warm and alternately dry and wet in the right quantity, there is a good chance of it growing before winter . . . well, the grasses will and the flowers should come later.'

We talk for a while about the different breeds of hens and I explain to John and Michael why I'm especially keen to acquire pure Marans. I have always loved the so-called utility breeds of hen and for the size of eggs prefer larger hens rather than the little bantams which are great fun but tend to be rather flighty. But Marans, with their smart dark cuckoo colouring, are especially appealing as they lay the darkest brown eggs in the world.

'So when exactly are you thinking of getting these hens?'

'Oh, as soon as possible, but I have tried various sources on the internet, and pure Marans are hard to get, especially at this time of year, so I'm beginning to get a bit worried.'

'Oh, I know you, once you're on a "project" like this, there'll be no stopping you, I am sure you will find your hens before the autumn is out' and, sure enough, with the help of the Poultry Club of Great Britain and an exceptionally helpful hen breeder called Edward Boothman, I am finally directed to a master Maran breeder called Maurice Jackson, from whom I am able to reserve my point of lay pullets.

The cats continue to be troubled by the ubiquitous harvest mites and Pushkin attacks his feet regularly. Titus scratches periodically but not obsessively, and Fannie seems to be least afflicted, although from time to time I have seen her delicately chewing between her toes. Poor Gilly is the one, however, who seems to be suffering most. She has the most beautiful silky glossy fur and whether it is the quality of her

fur that makes her skin so sensitive, who knows, but she licks compulsively and recently has taken to nibbling out the fur from her back legs, a little from her front legs and now her stomach, so she is rapidly assuming the mantle of one very moth-eaten cat who seems to be trying very hard to climb out of her fur. I take her back to Gerard, again, and he presents to us an elixir in an aerosol which contains a concentrate of Evening Primrose Oil which he hopes will help to encourage regrowth of her fur and perhaps help her itchiness.

'I rather think that Gilly has a very low threshold of itch,' he laughs and adds: 'I'm afraid this is what happens when you live in what appears to be the world's epicentre for the dreaded harvest mite.'

'I know, it's really terrible up in Hutton Roof and Michael is covered in bites all over his torso and his legs. It's funny but I never remember the estate agent mentioning this as a possible reason for not buying.'

'Yes, most unreasonable. You feel they should say something along the lines of "idyllic surroundings but completely uninhabitable between the months of August and November", do you?' he ribs me. I subsequently discover, though, that at least two of the women in the village cover themselves with Autan-Active insect repellent spray all day every day and again at night through the summer and autumn months to ward off the little devils. Next year, I

promise myself, we will use the
Autan and I will spray
Frontline all over the cats
before the mite cycle
starts, which means
beginning in July.

Pushkin has recently
started a very bad thing
when we let him out in
the garden. He is now
jumping on to the
gate and running into
Richard and Annabel's
garden next door, and I
have invited them both to shout
at him forcefully to discourage
these visits. Worst of all, Gilly, who greatly admires Pushkin
and watches him closely, has found her own way into their
garden also and is less intimidated by loud shouts.

Unconnected with the harvest mites, I think, I cannot fail
to be aware of how the cats have yet again had a strange
shake-up about where they are lying. I have noticed in the
past that places that are their habitual resting places for
months on end will suddenly go completely out of favour.
Titus, for example, now spends most of her time sleeping on
the landing at the top of the stairs, which is dark and
draughty and hard. Pushkin sleeps on the floor in the spare
bedroom which is almost as bad a place as the one chosen
by Titus, and Fannie just stays up in her laundry box on top
of the filing cabinet. Gilly sleeps mainly these days back on
her igloo from her first home, which is in a box in my study.

On 5 September Maurice Jackson, his lovely smiley wife
Ruth and a couple of their friends come over to the Coach
House to deliver the eagerly awaited six Maran pullets which

are now sixteen weeks old. They won't in fact lay until around twenty-three or twenty-four weeks, Maurice warns me. I am ridiculously excited. It is wonderful to take delivery of them. I have prepared for weeks, although the grass in the extended paddock is still growing and needs to be fully enclosed with chicken wire, so the first few weeks of their existence they will stay in the outer bit with access to the covered tunnel. A farming family in the village, the Armisteads, have very kindly sold to me for a very reasonable price two old-fashioned chicken coops, complete with slatted floors and sliding pop-hole doors that are around fifty years old and have been stored safely undercover for many a year and also an aluminium food storage container, and my old mate from the Dales, Thomas Raw, who helped me all those years ago with my Rhode Island Reds, comes over to help me again in adapting the coop with a perch and nest boxes. Wonderfully, he has never thrown away the original round-edged perches, the buckets, the water container, the dustbins for feed and my precious milk churn in which I stored the corn. Thank goodness for farmers and their hoarding instincts say I.

Maurice and I together unload the precious cargo, and as we carefully transfer each of the pullets from the two cat carriers that have acted as their means of transport into the hen coop, Maurice, who clearly knows everything there is to know about hens, suggests that I keep them penned up in their coop until 6 p.m. in the evening, then let them out and by 8 p.m. it will be near enough dusk for them to want to go back in to roost. Michael and I do that, but Michael is very uncertain about the whole thing.

'What on earth are you going to do when it gets dark, and you can't catch them?'

'Maurice swears it'll be alright, so I'm sure it will.' And sure enough, come dusk, at 7.50 p.m. exactly, they all walk back into the coop that they had been shut up in for most of the day and, when we lift the side lid, there they all are, neatly roosting up on the perch in a little line, except that Michael holds the lid open too long and two of them jump out again, but eventually it is fine and we all settle down for the night.

The following day we let them out and watch them with all the pride of newly adoptive parents. They are so cute and very curious. Their combs and wattles are still very small and pink rather than red, so they have a bit of growing to do yet awhile. In our time-honoured tradition of naming cats in a literary manner, we have decided to call the hens after women writers, all but one that is, who is called Alex, because Alex asked us to as she can no longer have a kitten. She will just have to write a book that is all. So they are, alphabetically, Agatha, Alex, Charlotte, Emily, George and Jane. Agatha was the name that Michael chose and from this time on, whenever he praises any hen, he always calls her Agatha, regardless of whoever it is.

Shortly after this, although I have every confidence in my fescue meadow grasses, I worry about one non-productive part of the paddock and whether the hens will have enough grass, so with the much-appreciated help of Anthony Chaplow and his feisty two-year-old daughter Josie, from down in the village, turfs are neatly laid on the slow-growing section so that the hens will definitely have some fully developed grass before winter sets in.

The one dark shadow that hangs over us in all of this is that between the date I phoned Maurice and reserved my Maran hens and the hens arriving, worrying outbreaks of Avian flu have occurred in China and some gloom-mongers are saying it is bound to come across the whole of Europe and all free-range poultry will ultimately have to be culled.

CHAPTER 18

The phone goes early one evening as I am sitting at my desk staring at the computer screen. Stretching across to answer it, I look up out of the window and register dark storm clouds rolling down over the hills and see the branches blowing in the wind. It is the end of the first week in September and England has been enjoying a late summer heat wave, but the weather has turned suddenly and it's now distinctly autumnal. As I cradle the receiver to my ear I hear Michael speaking – uncharacteristically quietly – and over his voice I can hear the sound of a woman sobbing. As I listen, my stomach contracts. There is a particular form of weeping that is unique to the newly bereaved that is distinct from all other forms of sorrow and I know this is what I am hearing.

'Mo, I am in the village. Little Oliver, the black kitten, is dead.' The sound of the adjacent sobs intensifies. Michael continues in a low voice:

'I am here helping Peter dig a grave, I am with Hilary. He was run over.' I gasp in horror and then ask:

'Michael, you weren't involved?'

'Of course not,' he remonstrates.

I feel wretched for the poor little cat who was so adorable and utterly desolated for the family who loved him so much.

'Should I come down?'

'Yes!'

I start to run down the hill and then, getting a stitch, have to slow down to a walk. I can feel tears dribbling down my face and am ashamed as what I feel must be as nothing compared with what the family who love him feel. That little black cat was the cutest cat in the world. He was special over and above the way that all cats – particularly loved cats – are special. He engendered affection in all who met him. He was extrovert, affectionate, purrful and a talented footballer to boot with a love of corks – when first I saw him I reckoned he was a Georgie or a Becks of a cat and then I teased Peter Warner that he may even have been a reincarnation of his beloved black cat Pelé and at one time he so nearly came to live with us.

As I approach Hilary and Phil's house I can see the outlined figures of Michael and Peter in the back garden digging with rugged determination and two young female figures standing close by with heads bowed down, who I realise must be Peter's sisters, Elizabeth and Catherine. I walk round the back of their house and there, in the middle of the lawn, is the forlorn figure of their once beautiful cat lying stretched out on a towel, bedraggled from the rain and stiff in death, and Hilary is kneeling on the grass next to him, crying quietly. The girls look utterly broken-hearted and Peter and Michael just keep their heads down and dig, dig, dig. Phil, their father, is still travelling home from work but Peter has phoned him to forewarn him of what awaits him on his return. Slowly, each of the family members in turn talks of Ollie and how special he was and how much fun they had with him and Elizabeth says, laughing bravely through her tears, that Ollie is playing even more now in his cat heaven than he did here on earth as he won't any longer have to stop for sleep. Peter had already called Thomas, their other older cat, over to inspect Ollie's body so that he wouldn't mourn, as a previous cat of theirs, Bethany, had mourned for her dead feline companion Toby. Thomas doesn't hang about though; he scuttles over the wall and into an adjacent field. Just before the committal of Ollie's body into the hole in the ground Peter says he must get something. Because I am worried he is going to wrap the cat in a shroud of some kind which will slow up the process of decomposition, I ask him warily 'what?' and he just replies quietly:

'A cross.' I am embarrassed by my brutish intervention for even asking. Ollie is buried with great dignity in the ground wearing a silver cross round his neck and with a catnip toy between his paws which he had played with in the ten happy months that he had spent as a member of this loving family. As the final turf is replaced over the mound under which he lies, Thomas suddenly reappears on the wall, and watches, sphinx-like, the final stamping down of the grave. No one present is really sure whether Thomas has or hasn't 'registered' that it was Ollie and that he was dead – time will tell. Thomas and Ollie were not always the best of friends but that doesn't mean that Thomas will be free of grief for his housemate. As we talk I bewail the frequency of road death for cats, but Hilary then tells me that of the five cats they have lived with over twenty-two years, Ollie is in fact the first to be killed by a car.

'We have a cat flap and they are free to come and go as

they please, day or night. We believe that this village is a safe village.'

I discover from Michael afterwards that Ollie's body was found just by the bridge on Gallowber Lane,[39] the quietest single-track road out of the village, which is only a few hundred yards from where he was first discovered as a kitten on Halloween last year and that Peter bravely carried his stiff little body home cradled in a towel.

As Michael drives me back up the hill I hear once more in my inner ear the anguish in Hilary's voice as she whispered:

'I cannot believe I will never again receive that Ollie welcome that he gave us every morning.'

The very next day I have an appointment to take Gilly to see Gerard, the vet, as I have been concerned for some time that her chronic diarrhoea may be harmful to her, even though I am aware she has always had a sensitive stomach, and now she is having loose bowel movements *outside* the cat litter tray rather than in it, but a further cause for concern is that her back legs are noticeably lacking in hair and her front legs are nearly as bad and so is the area under her tail. As I bundle up my black (and now white in parts) moth-eaten 'fluff ball', who is still so innocent of trips to the vet and other hated car journeys that she is actually sitting on the cat-carrying basket, eager for an adventure, I feel a sharp, albeit pointless pang of guilt that my black Halloween cat is alive and Ollie down the road is not and as I pass over the bridge where he was run over I feel an overwhelming sense of sadness.

---

[39] known as Gallowber as, at one time, sheep rustlers were hanged from the gallows at the lane end as an appalling example to their fellow men of their wrong-doing.

Gerard gives her an antihistamine injection but also takes a slide of her hairs to confirm under a microscope that it is 'self-abuse', i.e. she is tearing out her own fur, rather than it just spontaneously dropping out, and the following day he confirms to me that she is, but by this time I know that too as she is licking and licking repeatedly, something I should have realised myself earlier. On our return home I let her out into the garden and go off to attend to the hens. As I am refilling their bucket of water I hear from across the road a series of furious and oft-repeated wails, almost bellows, from Gilly from somewhere right in the middle of the garden. The noise she is making is extraordinary. She is really yelling and I can hear Michael talking back to her. I return to the garden and find Michael shaking with laughter.

'She is completely outrageous. That noise you heard was her shouting from plain bad temper.'

'Why? I was transfixed when I first heard it; they could have heard it up at Lupton!'

'I came out when I first heard her racket: she was standing looking down at a dead shrew and just yelling at it because it wouldn't move, and then she moved forward and flung it up in the air with her front foot and let it drop down and got even crosser when it remained where it fell. I'm afraid it has had a bin-burial!'

The next day I go back to the surgery as Gerard is enthusiastically committed to eliminating everything that can be wrong with Gilly. He is doubly concerned about her chronic diarrhoea and her 'self-abuse' which he still feels are unrelated, and this trip is for me to collect the antibiotic for her bowel. Because Gilly is a difficult patient we have agreed to administer the antibiotic in liquid form to be squeezed into her mouth via a small syringe without a needle.

When Michael and I attempt to administer the antibiotic it is nothing like as simple as we had imagined and in the end we have to resort to the time-honoured tradition of wrapping Gilly in a towel to stop her clawing us and between us squidging in the antibiotic. She hates it and spits it straight out again so I am covered in it all. The next day we try again, and very slowly we get the medicine down her. She makes a wonderful, loveable, gulping, half-drowning noise which disarmingly sounds like the noise she makes when she really loves some good food – a sort of loud combination of 'yum, yum, yum' followed by a gulping plea for help, which this time, when we put her on the floor, is followed with 'yow, yow, yow' and then followed by violent vomiting which in its turn is followed by more baleful complaints. After this she shuffles off to her bed with a tragic air and I follow her and watch her go into a deep sleep.

I come back downstairs and Michael nudges me: 'Look at this.' I turn round and there is Fannie trotting, yes trotting, up and down the conservatory with her nose in the air and full of confidence.

'I can't remember the last time I saw Fannie bouncing round like that inside the house,' I observe mournfully.

'That's true, but there couldn't have been a cat in the village, never mind the house, who didn't hear Gilly's "dying swan" performance, and Fannie has come down to celebrate.'

'That's awful,' I giggle, but it is spot on. She comes up to me quietly making her special miaow and I pick her up in my arms and cuddle her, mumbling into the top of her head:

'Fannie, you don't have to be quite so shockingly buoyant.' She just purrs, deeply.

The next day Peter Warner comes to stay for a few days. His aim is to reacquaint himself with the cats and in Gilly's case to meet her for the first time; to do feline life drawings;

to meet some of the people in the village whose own cat tales have become intermingled with the tales of the Coach House cats; to become more familiar with the surrounding lie of the land and to work out the new jacket.

Early on in his visit he watches Michael and me wrestling with Gilly in the feeding of her antibiotics and he quietly shows us a better way. He gently bends both her ears back under his hand which he holds there: this successfully distracts her and after squeezing half the dose of medicine into her mouth, he stops and strokes her throat to help her swallow and then continues. It works. She still gulps and makes her yum, yum, yum noises, but she has taken it all and hasn't spat it back and isn't sick. However, as soon as we release her she shuffles off, in case we decide to give her more, and yet again we are regaled by the sight of Fannie strutting the length of the conservatory in triumph at Gilly's indisposition.

I am beguiled by Peter's observation as an artist of the extraordinary shine of Gilly's coat. He says that the shine and the blackness is like ebony and it has the density of treacle, which is, I realise now, of course why Beth must have called her beloved black Bengal boy 'Treacle'. He is amused at her feistiness also, and of course, being the human-loving Bengal cat she is, she plays to the gallery. However, on his second day here I hear him murmuring to Pushkin:

'I think, Pushkin, you really are my favourite, you know.' Pushkin responds warmly by head-butting Peter's hand a couple of times.

'Peter, I am shocked at you, you're not supposed to have favourites.'

'Oh, I know, but he's so friendly. There really *has* been a remarkable change in him since I last saw him.'

And I reflect that when Peter was last here Pushkin was still in the last stages of his trauma from the move and he hated being here, and now he loves it probably more than any of them and he is more and more adventurous and wandering further and further away all the time. We achieve much in Peter's visit and after he has gone I think that I sense the cats missing him around. He is almost certainly the only houseguest they have experienced who openly welcomes their lounging around on his bed so that he can sketch them from early morning until late at night.

One small incident that happens while Peter is here makes me catch my breath. While I am showing him some significant landmarks in the middle of the village and we are standing just outside Hutton Roof Hall, I suddenly turn round, having talked about the tragic death of Ollie, and there is a black cat sitting bang in the middle of the road in defiance of all traffic. As I stare at him the cat gets up, shakes a leg and walks off.

It is, I discover, Samson who, together with his female companion Delilah, lives with Anthony and Jacky Chaplow and their two children, Josie and Scott.

Shortly after Peter drives away on his long trek back to the South-east, Gilly has a noisy 'woe-is-me' bout of diarrhoea around my newly planted rose (Rosa New Dawn, a lovely fragrant pale pearl-pink double climber, which I am longing to see spill up and over the wall) and, in a rather emphatic display of relief following it, she races out from under the rose and halfway across the garden, just for the hell of it, stops and instead gives Fannie a comprehensive chasing.

Fannie runs into the house, ears flattened and hissing madly, and Gilly chases her upstairs, whereupon she flees into my study. Pushkin and Titus are both downstairs and have watched this performance in that peculiarly feline manner of being only mildly interested, but as Gilly chases upstairs, Pushkin becomes more animated and chases on up after her. I don't see what happens, but quite shortly afterwards Pushkin comes downstairs again and Gilly follows. Pushkin, realising he is being followed, lies down on his side on the bend in the stairs beating his tail animatedly and watches her, wanting to play. Gilly with consummate grace sidesteps him and moves into the kitchen to eat. After she has refuelled sufficiently she comes back and starts to walk upstairs past him. He bats her gently but playfully on the head with his right foreleg. Surprisingly she backs off, but then he starts to chase her and she runs upstairs, but she stays up there and won't join in his quite clear invitation to play.

The relationship between them changes all the time, as do the places where they rest. It depends on climate, ascendancy and mood; whether I am in front of my computer where three of them sleep usually and, most significantly of all, whether I have lit a fire in the sitting-room. We have the central heating on low in the evenings now and really do not need a fire as well, but it is such a cheerful thing to have and, if anyone is staying and it is remotely cool, I light a fire and then the status quo is radically altered. Gilly is the first to grab it, stretched flat out, full length on the rug slap in front of it like a small black dog. Fannie and Titus will then take the sofa opposite and Pushkin joins them on the arm of it. I love it when all four cats are in there like that. Then it is perfect. Not much room for people but great feline karma!

CHAPTER 19

The field immediately opposite our house, behind the hen paddock, is owned by Ian and Elizabeth, who live at the bottom of the hill. Shortly after we first moved in, Ian and Elizabeth came up to visit us, and as Ian was admiring the view from our window in due deference to our ecstasy at what we overlooked, I will never forget the following exchange:

'You do realise that that field out there is mine.'

'Yes, I do. But hey, Ian, why are you saying it in that funny way?'

'Well, it's really good we've seen you tonight because I wasn't sure when I would catch you to tell you that we're seriously thinking of growing a leylandii hedge along the back boundary of your little yard and our field as a wind break.'

I looked up at him in horror. His field is what we look straight over towards Ingleborough and the Yorkshire Dales. It was only when I saw the sparkle of laughter in his eyes, and his mouth twisted up in barely controlled mirth that I was fully reassured that he was winding us up. We were easy meat for him that night!

For some years Ian has leased this field to Harold[40] from

---

[40] who was at one time the official village cat grave digger and who also once told us that when he was younger he dreamed about getting enough money to buy the house we now live in 'but it just went and got too big' as subsequent owners added bits to it!

the other end of the village, who in fact built the sturdy dry stone wall around the hen paddock as a commission for Pamela when it was a plant nursery. Harold kept sheep on it at various times of the year, but now he has semi-retired and moved away and so for most of this year Ian has been letting it out to Sue and Richard, who farm land all around us and who live right in the middle of the village. I have enjoyed watching the, to me, unusual assortment of sheep and sometimes cattle that have been steadily grazing it. I am used to the old Dales way (pre-Foot-and-Mouth) of sheep-farming, which typically consisted of flocks of hardy Swaledale ewes with their black masks and white muzzles and curly horns, who every November were put to the larger, but much more tender roman-nosed Bluefaced Leicester tups. The lambs they fathered would be born from April onwards, to be sold at the auction marts if they were male as 'fat' lambs, or 'store' lambs from July on or, if they were gimmers (female), to farmers 'from down-country' for breeding in the exclusive Mule Sheep Association gimmer lamb sales in September. Although these lambs are called (confusingly) 'Mules', they are fertile and not at all mule-like in any

way and are good breeders, good mothers and make good meat. Now, however, as I look out at Ian's field opposite I see it is full of Texel tups, a breed completely new to me, with deliciously funny faces. Their heads are completely white, but they have black nose leather and black lips and they always peer at you slightly myopically along their noses, which somehow gives them the appearance of grinning – this is enhanced by their stiff ears which hang forwards at slightly skewed angles, giving them a rather disconnected look somehow. It is lovely to be surrounded by smiling sheep, even if it is only an illusion! As I watch them for several days I become galvanised and decide I must find out more about sheep farming this side of the hill as it is clearly a whole different ball game from how it was east of the Pennines. I phone the Pricketts up and rather cheekily persuade Sue to allow me to go farming with them one day and thus begins my instruction in animal husbandry in the Southern Lakes as, in common with most other farmers around here, they farm livestock exclusively, although Sue does have another string to her bow, which interests me greatly.

I drive down to the Prickett farmstead in the middle of the village, recognisable from a distance by its oval hanging sign rather like a pub sign, which on one side shows a Texel tup in bas relief surrounded by the inscription Hutton Roof Hall and on the other side the name again but this time encompassing a Limousin bull. Over the front door of the beautiful stone-built house is a Victorian date stone above the lintel stating 1869. I walk round to the side door and am greeted by a bonny, slim, smiling young woman who, with her glowing cheeks, is the very embodiment of health and who is the mistress of all that I survey. Sue, who has pulled the short straw labelled 'teacher' as Richard is busy baling, takes my lesson in hand immediately and I learn from her, and then more later from my Dales friend, Thomas, that everything has indeed changed on both sides of the hill since the country was swept by the scourge of Foot and Mouth Disease in 2001. The new trend in sheep farming, even in comparatively high pastures like the Cumbrian fells, is to concentrate on producing stock that can go straight to the market for meat rather than risk the process of breeding and passing on to other farmers in milder climes to fatten up the stock. During the Foot and Mouth epidemic many sheep farmers, those who managed to stay in it, were forced by the restriction of movement of stock to breed from their own Mules, rather than stick with the traditional Swaledales or Rough Fells, and this led to a diversification of stockholding, which is why I am now all at sea when I view the sheep around me. Sue takes me round some of the many acres that she and Richard farm and shows me with pride their Texel tups, which are terminal sires bred for their exceptional carcass qualities. I discover too that the Texel ewe is hardy and exceptionally thrifty and her lambs have a tremendous get-up-and-go attitude, seeking milk as soon as they are born.

Richard and Sue will also put their Texel tups to Lleyn, Rough Fell and Texel ewes and their Rough Fell tups to Rough Fell and Blackface ewes. As I am digesting this inform-ation Sue points out a Texel gimmer which they have decided they will put with their 'Klintup' as they have just one of these amongst their gang of Texel and Rough Fell boys.

'What on earth is a Klintup?' I ask.

'A Lleyn tup? Well, it's a breed which originated in North Wales. L-L-E-Y-N!' Sue spells out for me patiently. 'We use that Lleyn tup to produce the Lleyn/Texel crosses I was talking about.'

I had seen the name on paper but never heard it pronounced. This learning business is difficult for both parties! But Sue is wonderful and is not off-put by my daft questions and continues her tuition with a litany of other sheep crosses that they produce. Originally they had produced Mashams before they started to breed their own Texel tups – in fact her father had crossed a Charollais tup with a Texel Ewe to use the tup lamb with his Welsh Mule ewes – but now with their own flock of Texel tups they cross Texels with Rough Fells, Hill Cheviots, North Country Cheviots, Texels and all crosses in between. They did cross a Border Leicester tup with a Texel ewe for several years to try to get a sheep that produced more lambs – although Border Leicesters don't live as long as the hardy Texels. At the end of this long list of crosses I ask Sue about Herdwicks and she says, predictably:

'Ah, yes, we also have a few Herdwicks crossed with Texels.' It is the Herdwicks in particular that I want to know about as they are unique to the Lakes – with their white faces and browny/grey exceptionally waterproof fleeces – having a legendary instinct for 'hefting'[41] – although there are a few around here in other farmers' flocks. Every year out of the lambs that are born Richard and Sue will keep around 120 gimmers as replacements for their current stock and they will aim to keep those gimmers that were born as one of two or more so that the multiple birth 'gene' might be passed on. They have used Blackface tups too but have given them up since they suffered cruelly from Toxoplasmosis passed on, supposedly, from foxes on the crag, or possibly feral cats. I know that it is a parasite that afflicts cats but hadn't realised it could be passed to other mammals and have since discovered that *Toxoplasma gondii* can infect all warm-blooded animals but an essential stage of its life-cycle occurs only in cats. In sheep it causes abortions.

During this tour we have travelled from pasture to pasture in Richard and Sue's Jeep. We now drive down the single-track Gallowber Lane, over the little bridge where poor little

---

[41] a northern hill-farming term for sheep who stick to the same hillside, who know precisely what bit is their home patch without aid of fences. Herdwicks are particularly likely to become hefted into an area and the cull during the Foot and Mouth epidemic is said to have destroyed 40 per cent of the national flock of Herdwicks.

Ollie was killed and turn right through a field gate and bumpily make our way up into a high pasture, which climbs ever higher up through woodland and beyond until we find ourselves on top of a grassy hill in the middle of nowhere. The views from there make my eyes fill up for the pure pleasure of being alive and being able to stand and stare at this rural paradise. As we climb out of the Jeep on the summit we hear above us a skylark[42] singing his heart out in wonderful liquid trilling chirrups and my soul soars the skies with him. The perspective of all our neighbours and their land and their houses is completely different from this angle and I spend a happy half-hour while Sue patiently points out who is what and where.

As well as all the sheep, Richard and Sue also keep a suckler herd, which essentially means that they are involved in beef farming, rather than dairy farming, which these days is increasingly thankless. Their stock consists of Limousin bulls, some pure bred cows and some crosses, including Angus and Angus-x-Friesians, Belgian Blue-x-Friesians and Salers, originally from the mountains of the Auvergne – and like some of the continental sheep this last is a new breed to me, but they are well suited to the rain-swept hillsides of the Westmorland Fells.

We finally return to the large welcoming farmhouse kitchen where I meet one of their five cats. This one is called Wunky and she is a four-year-old neutered female, mainly white with patches of tortie colouring, who has a disarming wheeze that Sue thinks might be the legacy of some flu she

---

[42] Alauda arvensis

contracted when a very small kitten. It never gets worse and it never goes away. She and her neutered sister Tigger, a white-bibbed tabby, are the two cats that sleep in the farmhouse. The other three, called in ascending order of age Tabby Tom (two years old), Big Tom Cat (five years old) and The Fast Cat (very, very old and very, very unfriendly), are completely outside working cats and are nowhere to be seen because they are no doubt busy. Their two Border collies, Bev and Misty, are also absent, but almost certainly they are with their master. Just as we are sitting down, in wanders the missing Tigger who takes one look at me, decides I am no threat, and curls up on a cat bed in the corner. Tigger looks the picture of innocence but Sue wrinkles her nose.

'I've had to stop feeding the birds. Tigger, in particular, is just a devil with them. She's the only cat we've ever had who regularly catches swallows.'

'Blimey, fully grown ones?'

'Fully grown, out of the nest, young, old, you name it. She gets fat in the winter, but in the summer she is lithe and thin, from chasing after swallows. And when she goes out into the yard, they swoop down on her, and you can always tell from the alarm calls they make that Tigger is around and it is only Tigger, none of the other cats!' I look across at the gently sleeping feline with not inconsiderable respect. Cats are hunters and some are very good at it.

I now manage to get Sue to explain more about the other 'string' to her bow of being an ace farmer and midwife to cattle and sheep. The string in question started when she joined the WI and began to make marmalade and jellies. I presume she started this because she had such long lonely hours to fill or more likely because one of the truths in life is if you want a job done, ask a busy person! She went on from there to make more and more different jellies, chutneys, jams and other preserves, always whenever possible from locally grown produce and always seasonally, and started slowly to sell them through a local farm shop called Kitridding[43] in Lupton and then at Lucy's bistro in more distant Ambleside and Country Delights in Settle. In September 2004 she was awarded the highly prestigious and much-coveted award of North West Producer of the Year by the North West Fine Foods sponsored by Defra and Booths and she also won a Silver Award in the Great Tastes Award in the same summer. From an article in *Cumbria Life Magazine* she gained the title of 'The Blackcurrant Queen' which has rather charmingly stuck. I have eaten some of her Tomato Chutney and her Seville Marmalade and they are indeed absolutely scrumptious. Often in the summer evenings I have seen her and Richard walking together with their two sheepdogs, laughing and talking, and from time to time Sue will stop and pick a plant from the hedgerow, which is presumably some useful ingredient to be added to one of her delicious home-made preserves. I do wish Richard and Sue and their sons Jim and Peter all the luck in the world with their enterprises.

---

[43] http://www.kitridding.co.uk/New/

CHAPTER 20

Michael and I are hoping that the signs we see of Fannie gaining in confidence are not just our own wishful thinking, but even though we both feel we recognise this, she clearly continues to have a distinct fearfulness of Gilly which never seems to leave her. Today as I am sitting in the downstairs cloakroom Fannie squeezes round the door companionably and jumps up on to the boiler and from there to the drier, which is atop the washing machine, and as I look up to the little mirror above the washbasin I see her eyes staring down into mine with a dark intense softness. I murmur: 'O Fannie, darling girl. I love you so much . . . so much.' My voice is low and meant only for her, but by that utterance and the manner of its delivery, I make my mistake. As I look back into her eyes in the mirror her head suddenly goes down, her body stiffens and her ears come forward at the most acute angle possible with an awesome concentration, and I know with complete certainty that, although out of my sight, Gilly has emerged and is coming round the door somewhere. Gilly, having heard my dulcet tones, has decided to see what gives. Within seconds we are both assailed by the fierce hissing that is Fannie's immediate reaction to Gilly on all occasions and, with a thump and a cry which morphs into a half-groan, Fannie leaps down and races out, chased closely by Gilly. Up they thunder, into my study overhead and I hear Fannie scramble up the filing cabinet, alternately hissing and squawking, and I know that she will have clambered into her little box. Gilly then promptly trots downstairs again and comes back into the lavatory, tail waving victoriously. She looks up at me and blinks twice, owlishly, and then miaows demandingly in her deep strident voice. In deference to her wishes I turn on the cold tap in the basin and up she jumps to drink the running water she so enjoys. She shows no sign of remorse for her bad behaviour towards Fannie, although I have seen cats – in particular Fannie – feel such an emotion, but then from her point of view she, Gilly, was only playing a game, wasn't she?

It is late September and with a stab of remorse I realise that all the swallows have gone and that yet again I have failed to see the great migration of those intrepid travellers, although if I look around hard enough I will probably still find the tail-end charlies, the second brood, hanging on till they have fattened up enough for the long haul. Truth to tell, I miss it almost every year; only one year did I actually observe the day they flew – early that morning they were all there chittering away on the telegraph wires and by the afternoon I realised that they had gone, but even so, I still missed the precise moment of take-off. At the beginning of

September I remember Sue Prickett shivering as she looked up and saw them gathering on the telegraph lines four deep like so many crotchets and quavers (only with the fifth stave missing).

'Why are you shuddering?' I asked, although the sight of them assembling in greater numbers, day by day, always saddens me too.

'Oh the earlier they go, the tougher our winter is going to be, they always say,' she laughed, but I understand full well her melancholy. In spite of our climate change and the long hot and intermittently damp summer, it is indeed early for our swallows to have gone, so we shall see what sort of a winter is to hit us.[44]

I have recently introduced another bird-feeding station into the garden with all manner of seeds, nuts and fat balls, although top choice is sunflower hearts, and am amused to see an extraordinary mixture of birds sitting on the splayed-out upward pointing boughs of the yew tree, like so many Christmas tree decorations clamped to the branches, blowing up and down in the wind. They are almost certainly checking to make sure there are no cats around. As I look now from my window I can see four chaffinches, three greenfinches, two thrushes, two blackbirds and a constantly changing number of great tits, blue tits and coal tits, and on the telephone line immediately outside the window are four goldfinches, who especially love sunflower hearts. The thrushes and the blackbirds, although they do visit the flat seed tray, are really in the yew because they are defending the ripe red berries which they are in the process of systematically devouring as they become soft enough. Yesterday I was thrilled to see two nuthatches on the nuts: their visits are spasmodic and I had thought seasonal, but I

---

[44] For information, it *was* a long cold winter.

discover they are in fact actually resident here, year-round, but nesting up in the woodland. They are timid, and certainly visit less frequently than their equally bashful larger cousins, the great spotted woodpecker, two of which regularly 'hit' the nuts, for a few brightly coloured seconds.

This should have been a good year for insectivorous birds as the insect life has been abundant – not only has there been a surfeit of the now detested harvest mites but also scourges of mosquitoes, midges, gnats, moths, blue-bottles, horseflies (aka clegs) and, of course, the common housefly have all been ever-present. Although not fodder for most garden birds, bumblebees this year have abounded and indeed they continue to bumble around even today, although our ears are no longer filled with the comforting sound of their heavy hums: you have to lean closely to them now to catch even one note of their diminuendo-hymn to autumn. That quiet hymn could be thought of as a requiem as the queen bumblebee, having produced unceasing numbers of workers since February or March, will recently have produced new queens and male non-workers who will by now have mated and, that having been done, all the males will die, as will the old queen, and the new queens will shortly go away to hibernate in order to produce next year's 'bike' of hardworking bumblebees. Although with bumblebees, as with so many other species, there is new evidence to suggest some colonies now are able to work over winter due to the warmer climate. On Monday, which turned into a glorious warm sunny day, Michael and I were enchanted to witness two sleepy bumblebees being joined on their nectar-hunt by no fewer than four red admiral butterflies[45] on the long white bottle-brush spikes of the

---

[45] Vanessa atalanta

fragrant autumn-flowering white pearl bugbane[46] so perhaps this kaleidoscopic quartet is going to risk hibernating here in Cumbria rather than migrating to Europe or North Africa. Hibernation for red admirals is common in the south of England, but I am unsure this far north. Their caterpillars love nettles and there are certainly plenty of those in the nearby hedgerows, although the adults now are nectar hungry and are supping copiously from not only the white pearl, which seems to be their preferred host of the moment, but also from the late-blooming dark violet buddleia[47] over by the gate, added to which they have the blackberries that are knitted into the hedge around two sides of the hens' paddock across the road from which to feast and, when all these are gone, they will be able to move on to the flowering ivy[48] that blankets our garden wall. I am constantly in awe at the considerable nursery skills of the former owner and creator of this garden, Pamela, who has relinquished to us a garden that is not only wildlife friendly and extremely attractive, but which also flowers almost year-round.

Thomas, who did such a fine job of rendering the chick coops into housing for laying hens, very generously offers to come and help Michael with the fencing around the paddock, so that I can at last let the hens out into a bigger space. The day that Thomas chooses is frustratingly for me

---

[46] Cimicifuga simplex
[47] Buddleia davidii
[48] Hedera helix

one when I will be out doing signings at bookshops all day, but both he and Michael claim that they are glad that I won't be able to interfere with their day's labouring, which they call 'man's work', and I am also told that when I do come back I must on no account come in and behave like the foreman. What a hard brief! I organise a cold lunch for them both and, just before I leave, Thomas pulls up in his Land Rover laden down with sixteen large round 6-foot-6-inch-long stakes, two sledge-hammers, nails, screws and other accoutrements for the job in hand. As he starts to unload he is laughing:

'Nay, I saw some sheep yonder using a thur'ole. It's a gey lang time since I saw one of them!'

'What's a "thurrell", Thomas?'

'Why a "thur'ole" or "thirl hole"[49] is a hole in a wall low down for sheep to pass *through* from one field into another, when mebbe the farmer doesn't want larger stock going through. You can block them up with a paving slab if you don't want the sheep passing through.'

As I take my leave of them they are already stuck into their day's work and when I return in mid-afternoon, they have just finished. There is a curiously conspiratorial air about them both, but the fruits of their labour look superb. I thank Thomas effusively for his toil and he replies:

---

[49] also called hogg hole, thawl, smout hole, sheep creep and sometimes cripple hole.

'It was a great pleasure working with Michael, and we did a good job together.'

After he has gone Michael says in a wistful sort of voice:

'Today was a good day, you know. It was really nice working with Thomas, he's very good company. And blimey he's one strong man.'

When I get into the house there are two or three empty beer bottles on the side and the food has disappeared, so I presume that Michael looked after Thomas properly. With great ceremony we remove the dividing fence between the hens' coop, the tunnel and the extended paddock and the hens are now free to roam. They spend most of their time flying up on to the internal wall and back down again, but although they could fly up and over the fencing that Thomas and Michael so laboriously erected they don't, and seem content enough to settle down in their larger quarters.

Today is sparkling and bright and the sun is already warm. I rush out as soon as I am awake to open up their ark and, sliding the door up and to one side, I talk the while to reassure them in response to their cackling and clucking protests coming from within. There then follows the usual unseemly scramble through the pop hole and down the ramp to get out, accompanied by the flexing of wings and running circuits round the ark to check all is as it was before they went to bed. This morning a couple of them captivate me by adopting, with great seriousness, the fighting posture of mature cockerels facing each other square on, each standing fully upright with neck stretched up to its tallest limit and at the same time pressing their puffed-out chests to each other, and touching the end of their beaks, so it is really quite hard for them to peer at each other from that angle. They hold this position for about thirty seconds before breaking away and scratching about as if nothing has happened. Sometimes as they pass each other I have noticed that if they feel threatened, they will fluff out their neck feathers at the base, which I recognise from Victorian paintings of fighting cocks and which is also reminiscent of hostile cats with their bottle-brush tails. I have had to buy corrugated plastic to cover the roof of the coop as in the torrential downpours we have intermittently been having, in spite of my earlier creosoting, rain has been leaking in. Today continues to be mild and sunny and I carefully inspect the 'green manure' for any signs of growth. I had planted out Hungarian rye,[50] Alsike clover,[51] sprouting clover organic, field beans,[52] giant winter spinach and winter cress. The turf which we laid three weeks ago is beginning to put down long white roots through into the soil so soon it should be well anchored, and my wild flower meadow is growing reasonably well, although the fescue grasses do look very delicate so I fear how they will stand up to the hens' foraging.

Today I receive a sad email which has an extraordinary follow up to it.

---

[50] Secale Cereale
[51] Trifolium Hybridum
[52] Vicia Faba

From: Amanda Jane
To: Marilyn Edwards
Sent: Monday, October 03, 10:28 PM
Subject: Re: New reader

Dear Marilyn,

Your book certainly got to me, yes, because I lost my cat called Dali a year ago . . . Dali was 3–4 years old when I got him from the Cat Protection League (he was mainly black with white socks and neck). He lived with me, as an indoor cat, for 6 years in total. He was never a sickly cat, slept with me every night (head on pillow and covered with the quilt or curled up in the arch of my back) and that is where he would stay until morning.

He was an unassuming cat but very affectionate and especially good at knowing when I needed a cuddle.

The last couple of years of his life he was prone to getting small, benign cysts just above his eyes (I think 4 in total); he would have quick, routine operations and have them removed without any problem.

In October last year I took him to have another lump/cyst removed. I took him to the vet's on the Monday night so he was there to have the operation first thing on the Tuesday morning. It was a new vet who I had the consultation with and who would be carrying out the operation – I took an instant dislike to him as he seemed over-confident and even a bit 'cocky'.

As I signed the consent form for the operation I had a sick feeling in my stomach. I then said goodbye to my gorgeous Dali and returned to my car where I sat and cried, having second thoughts about leaving him there.

I didn't feel any better on the morning of the operation but was patient and telephoned the surgery at 12.00 p.m. as suggested by the vet. I was told that Dali was still 'under' and to ring again at 1.00 p.m. The next hour seemed to last a lifetime. When I telephoned I was told by the veterinary nurse that Dali had come to nicely and that I could collect him in an hour (I was so relieved he was okay and excited about collecting him).

I reached the surgery and rang the bell (thinking it slightly odd that nobody was on reception). I was then met by the vet who was trying to tell me that Dali had collapsed 2 mins before I had arrived (after coming to completely from the anaesthetic). He was almost hysterical, making very odd laughing noises. In shock, I understood him to be making Dali better and that he had everything under control – I was clearly not hearing what he was really saying – Dali had already died!

You will not believe it, but a year has gone by and I still haven't been able to collect Dali's ashes – cannot bring myself to do it (if indeed they are still there) . . . they carried out a postmortem as they have to in such a situation but they found no reason why he died when he did . . . I was simply told that it's something that can just happen, although extremely rare. I also cannot find it in myself to forgive the vet . . . So, that's the story behind the tears . . .

Best wishes,
Amanda

Amanda, in her email, goes on to say that she has and loves dearly two British shorthair females called Hegel (someone else with a sexing problem!) and Ruby, but that does not, of course, heal the wounds of no longer having her beloved Dali.

A few weeks later I email Amanda, urging her to try to collect the ashes and asking her permission for me to use her email in the book. Twenty-four hours after sending the email I receive this amazing sequel:

‒ ‒ ‒

From: Amanda Jane
To: Marilyn Edwards
Sent: Wednesday, November 09, 7:52 PM
Subject: Re: An extract?

Hi again Marilyn,
Just had to tell you that following our communications yesterday, my partner Paul rang me at work today to let me know that he had received a telephone call from the vet's, about Dali's ashes!!!! After a whole year! They were apparently very nice on the phone and just wanted to get a message to me to let me know that they still had the ashes and that I could go in and collect them if I wanted to!

I find the whole thing very strange, especially after your email (and as I said I was sure they had probably got rid of them). So after work I collected Dali and he is back home, albeit in a less than impressive box! Although I wouldn't share this with just anyone, I am convinced that it was a message from him . . . almost that he approves of his story being included in your book. It's just all so bizarre, but wonderful at the same time.

Just thought you would like to know . . .

Amanda

CHAPTER 21

It is early October, I am on my own and I am being unremittingly assailed by Gilly. She is on heat. She has been calling loudly for the last two days and, more to the point, for the last two nights and Michael, lucky chap, has missed it all by dint of being in Scotland with Johnny and Oliver. This is the first time that Gilly has come into season, and on the first night I was rather bemused as I thought she was yowling for Michael, as she divides her favours between us equally and will lie as often stretched out next to him as to me. It did disconcert me that so brief an absence was causing her this amount of distress. But as I lay in the dark being plagued by her wails, the sounds changed key and became more guttural in their pitch and more urgent in their delivery. Total recall of how it was with Fannie's last heat overwhelms me, and I realise that this is no feline anxiety for a missing human companion: this is far more primeval and driven. Gilly's 'normal' voice is a rasping one, but her 'calling' voice has to be heard to be believed and sleep is quite impossible when she is in full cry.

When I told Michael about it on the phone on Sunday morning I think it is what tipped him into staying on an extra night with his boys. Anyway now I am stuck with it. I email the breeders and ask them if they still have their stud

available and whether I can bring her up to them. They phone me back to say that although normally they would prefer that it be a second heat for a first mating, as she is nearly a year old and therefore presumably close to fully grown and developed, this heat should be OK and that, yes, their stud is available. Although they are aware that I know that Gilly has not been mated they still require that I take her down to the vet's and get her fully tested for FeLV and FIV. I explain about her allergy to harvest mite, but they don't see that as an impediment, and since her course of antibiotic when Peter Warner was here (and also since restricting her diet to either Hills Dried Adult Cat or Burns Dried Adult only) her bowels have sorted themselves out, so that is no longer a problem. I make an appointment at the vet's and discuss her health with Paul when I take her down, and he agrees with the breeders that everything is fine and the breeding can go ahead. He shaves a great big square patch of fur from her throat to do the blood tests, which gives moth-eaten little Gilly an even stranger look still, and after a suitable waiting time he reports back that the results of the test are negative.

Michael returns home from Scotland and we discuss all that is happening at length. We are both really excited at the prospect of Gilly's impending family. I am due to take Gilly to the breeders in forty-eight hours' time. I phone Peter Warner and tell him that this is all taking place, just to check that he still wants a kitten from her. He enthusiastically confirms that he does. It has always been agreed between us that if there is a choice of gender, Peter should have a female kitten who would be more likely to get on better with Blue, his neutered tom. As we are talking Peter then adds that, in time, he would quite like to breed from the kitten himself. I repeat to him that the deal I have with the breeders is that the offspring of Gilly may not be bred from, but he still says he would like the possibility of considering it, and so I tell him I will talk to the breeders. I duly phone the breeders and because I mention the active list they are immediately very unhappy that I am even asking them. I quickly say I understand and that I will go back to Peter and explain that it is not going to be possible, which I do, and Peter takes it on board and agrees completely with all that they ask, although he is of course disappointed. I go back assuring the breeders that all will be well and so it is with extreme dismay that evening that I find an email from them, the main message of which is:

'We are very sorry but we have decided that we cannot go ahead with the mating.' Michael and I are devastated. Michael in fact becomes quite angry. I just feel desperate and let down, but, stirred up by Michael's anger, I email back, really upset, saying I feel betrayed. I receive a reply saying that they will pay for Gilly's FeLV test if that will help, but that for the moment their answer is still that they would rather not do the mating, but that they are prepared to consider some time in the future 'some arrangement that is amicable all ways round. What that may be at present, we just don't know'. It is all so vague and it doesn't resolve the problem of the here and now, and so I feel I need to take time out to think about it all. When I was first looking for Gilly there was another breeder further south who was really helpful and he said to me then that if I ever needed a Bengal stud I should consider approaching him. Michael and I talk long and hard about whether we should do that.

Gilly is still rampaging around and calling fit to wake the

dead and for two nights I sleep very little. On my second sleepless night I find myself praying intensely for guidance and for peace and suddenly at around 4.30 a.m. I fall asleep, very deeply. When the light wakes me in the morning inside my head I know the answer. At breakfast I say to Michael that I've been thinking. He groans. He always groans when I say that, it's strange!

'How many cats do we have at the moment?'

'You know jolly well we have four, why are you asking daft questions like this?'

'Oh, because this is an exercise, go on indulge me.'

'Huh, when don't I? Alright, next?'

'If Gilly has kittens, how many do you think we would keep here?'

'That's like how long is a piece of string: it depends on how many she has, but I imagine you would want to keep at least two knowing you.'

'Which would mean how many cats would we have here then?'

'Six, by my reckoning.'

'And three of them would be Bengals. How do you think Fannie would react to that?'

'She would probably have a nervous breakdown, pack her bags and leave home, or top herself, but what is daft about your questions now, is that you knew all this all along.'

'No, what is different now, is that I've seen, we have both seen, how really bad it is for Fannie with Gilly, in a way it never was when Pushkin came, for example.'

'Yes, that's true,' he says thoughtfully.

'I just feel, Michael, sometimes things happen, or don't happen for a reason. I couldn't understand why that couple, who are basically good people, have gone back on their word in this way, even when I assured them that Peter would adhere to everything they asked, but now I feel it's as if it is for a reason. If we had been going to have kittens from Gilly, it had to be this year for the kitten to be any companion to Blue for Peter, and the same was true for Janice – she wanted the kitten sooner rather than later – and for us too. We've been trying to have kittens for over three years now. And it feels to me, right now, as if this is God directly saying, "Don't do it."'

Michael goes quiet for a little while and then very gently he agrees. It is strange but for him too, as for me, it is as if there is writing on the wall. I email the breeders and tell them that I will get Gilly spayed and I phone the vet as soon as they are open. Gerard is on holiday so we have to wait a little while, but I book her in.

Gilly calls for nearly two weeks and her voice becomes daily hoarser from her abuse of it, so that she now sounds like a feline equivalent of Edith Piaf emitting that wonderful guttural cracked rendering of 'Non, je ne regrette rien', only in Gilly's case it is exceedingly difficult to determine what she may or may not regret. And she is so different when she is on heat – not least because she stops threatening Fannie. To begin with Fannie doesn't trust this change and continues to hiss whenever she sees Gilly, but finally they are able to be in the same room, on the same sofa, without friction. The truth is Gilly is barely remembering to eat.

I remember how desperate it was for Titus and for Fannie when they both came on heat, and in the last stages for Fannie it was almost unbearable, which triggered my searching out her stud boy and then finally resorting to having her neutered. Now, here, for Gilly it is again so hard for her. I can hardly bear seeing her distress. As I pick her up in my arms and try to cradle her, instead of her lying flexibly on her back staring up at me, as she would normally, she stretches out her body full length, in a strange, rigid pose and her eyes have a distant look while she makes a rasping moaning cry. She is so altered from how she is normally. The date for her hysterectomy is in the diary two weeks from today.

I am in my study working away at my desk and have let the three older cats out into the garden but have carefully shut the door so that Gilly cannot join them, as while I am sure there are no full toms around it would be foolhardy to risk her becoming pregnant at this stage. Suddenly, through my study window I can hear Gilly's cries, rasping and raucous and very angry-sounding coming apparently from outside. I rush downstairs and I can still hear her carrying on and then it goes quiet. I run up the other flight of stairs into our bedroom and see her walking across the bed, scratching repeatedly at the duvet. The window with the cat guard is wide open and that is why it had sounded as if she was outside: she must have seen the other cats in the garden and was expressing her frustration with some force. I look at the duvet cover and realise, suddenly, that it is soaking wet. In her disturbed state she has urinated, with an apparently full bladder, right through the duvet, through the sheet, the undersheet, the mattress cover and the mattress. I strip the bedding down as fast I can, wash the mattress and cover the bed with a series of long strips of bubble-wrap. We have an enormous bed so washing the enormous duvet requires an industrial washing machine, for which we have to go down to the town. The following day we are out very late and on our return crash into bed and sleep heavily. In the morning we sleep late, but suddenly Michael shouts out:

'I don't believe it, she's at it again, right now!' And sure enough she has just left another huge puddle right where Michael was sleeping. Again we strip the bed down and this time I am able to wash the smaller temporary duvet at home. I remember how much anxiety Hilary had when her little Ollie did this a couple of times on their bed, and it is, indeed, very disturbing. Our added problem is that there is no door to our bedroom and no way of blocking out any cat who wants to come in. Needless to say, on the third morning she attempts to do the same thing again and we just manage to stop her. Her ardour seems to have lessened a little, as she is only waking us twice during the night now, whereas before she was calling every hour or so. Michael asks me:

'Will the neutering definitely stop this impossible behaviour?'

'Oh Michael, I just pray it will. I'm sure it's because she's so frustrated, but the only trouble is the hormonal change takes a while before it kicks in and she has been spraying outside. She's the first female cat I have seen who sprays like a tom, although I always knew they can do it.'

The following day I wake up early and am nervous that she may repeat the performance and to crack 'the syndrome' seems to me paramount, so I take the risk of impregnation and let her out. I open the door wide and the air smells wonderful. It is a glorious mild sunny day and the hills look magnificent in their purple and gold livery. All four cats go bounding out joyously. After about an hour Pushkin, Titus and Fannie return and lounge around the conservatory happily, idly watching the birds at the feeders, but 'Black Magic' remains out for a good four hours. Michael goes to help Richard with his mammoth task of leaf clearance next door,

when he learns that at some point in her travels she has been sighted by Richard round the back of his garden, which we are all trying to teach her is strictly forbidden. 'Forbidden', however, is a concept which seems quite alien to young Gilly.

Gilly wakes up the following day, at exactly 7.15 a.m., having lain next to me all night without stirring. I hear her go downstairs and I assume she is using the cat litter tray. Lying in a state of semi-sleep, I become aware of her quiet return as she springs lightly onto the bed and I open one eye to see her surveying Michael's sleeping form and then, before I can stop her, she forcefully empties a full bladder all over him, the duvet et al. Things are uttered by us both which no human should ever say to a companion cat, much loved or otherwise, and the washing machine and the dryer are brought back into full eco-unfriendly operation yet again.

Then, the next day, although she is still doing her feline imitation of Piaf in a half-hearted way when she remembers to, she visibly goes 'off the boil'. Fannie trots past her in her new reassured confident manner, and Gilly slowly hunches her shoulders, puts her head down and does 'the stare'. Fannie is transparently horrified – and in a different way

so am I. Before I know what is happening Gilly has chased Fannie upstairs, and all is as it was before. Indeed, it is worse than before. Later in the day, while sitting at my computer, I hear an unfamiliar scratching noise. I turn round to look. To my horror I see Gilly just disappearing into Fannie's special box on top of the filing cabinet. Fannie, while this is happening, is downstairs eating.

'No, Gilly! That's the Holy of Holies. You cannot go in there.' I climb up the library steps, reach in and pull her out and plonk her on the floor. Immediately she starts her ascent again. She does it by climbing up the bookshelves rather than springing up from the top of the steps as Fannie does it, so at least for now, by moving books around, I can make it impossible for her to repeat this.

Gilly, post-heat, now seems to be asserting territorial rights. She singles out whichever chair is Titus's favourite and lies on it, in front of Titus. If Titus isn't in the room, then she doesn't bother. Pushkin still tries to sneak round the back of the stairs in Michael's study where he hid when we first moved here, and the other day I found Gilly lurking in there too.

One thing that Gilly does that is quite beguiling is to lie on top of the cat platform in the conservatory staring out of the window, but when you go up to her, she gives you what I call her veiled look. Although on other occasions she does give you direct eye contact – she even does the dreadful stare, which is seriously threatening – when she is in her modest mode she seems to go to some lengths to avoid holding direct eye contact, so as you approach her on her platform she holds her head down in the coy manner of a woman from a culture where she has been taught never to make eye contact – Gilly the bashful. Gilly the modest. Gilly the games player.

CHAPTER 22

It is now the end of October and over the last few weeks the rain has been intermittent, but when it has come, it has been torrential and the polythene tunnel has come into its own as the hens' shelter. I have recently introduced a deep litter of wood shavings into the tunnel, which they adore and they spend more time in there, dust bathing in the shavings and in the compost, than they do on the open grass in the paddock proper. I had imagined that once I let them out into the main paddock they would never come in, but the tunnel is definitely their favourite place even on dry days. They feel safe in there too, I think. As well as hating the rain, they are not keen on having their feathers ruffled up too much either, and although it is still astonishingly mild the autumn winds are gusting almost every day now, bringing down the leaves from the many trees that surround the house. The gutters keep filling up and overflowing with leaves so that the rain spills over the edges and pours down the windows of the conservatory like a solid waterfall. Michael has already been round the whole of the outside of the house with his stepladder clearing them out, but there are still many more leaves to fall, and fall they do. As we look out through the windows they come spiralling down, some seemingly so desirous of making their landfall that they

407

 jostle and somersault past others which are on a more leisurely trajectory. This unrelenting 'confetti', which has been happening for days, just reinforces to me the truly staggering number of leaves each tree produces. The leaf-fall is deeply attractive to worms, who take cover beneath the mounting piles, and today as I walk out with the hens' food in my hand, having kicked a pile of leaves to one side, I spot a particularly large and juicy looking specimen and put him on the hens' warm mash to give to them as a treat. When I get across the road and into the tunnel where I feed the hens, I am belatedly overcome with remorse at the fate I am delivering to this harmless creature, so I hastily toss him away into the now quite long grass in the paddock, in the hope that this will enhance his odds of surviving. The hens fail to notice their 'treat' flying through the air, so at least for this day he does indeed get away.

Although I have kept hens in the past I am astonished anew at the bullying that goes on between them and it is so unfair too, as the biggest and the strongest gang up on the smallest and youngest, with no one hen prepared to defend her coop mate in distress. It is said that cockerels keep their girls in check and prevent this bad behaviour, but I have never owned one so I cannot vouch for it. The youngest and most got-at hen I call Emily and her tail is tattered and scruffy, which I was putting down to the moult they have all been going through, but I have just recently noticed that two of the others pull her tail feathers out each time they are close to her. Rather like Fannie with Gilly she is her own worst enemy, however, as whenever she comes near the others she goes on autopilot and starts to squawk and rush around attracting enormous attention to herself, so even the hens who would have ignored her are almost compelled to give her a passing tweak or stab. They adore raisins and all of them come over to eat out of my hand. They also do that hen curtsey, which they properly do for the cockerel, so he might mount them, but which in the absence of a cockerel they do for the alpha being. It is useful that they do it, as it means it is easier to pick them up and give them an examination or, more likely, a cuddle from time to time.

It feels terrible that Avian flu might be creeping closer and I get so depressed by the prevailing view that it is simply a matter of when rather than if. Tonight I was standing in the tunnel just putting the feed away for the night and outside a blackbird was singing that long lyrical dusk song of eventide and the thought that all this rich bird life could be under serious threat is unbearable.

Yesterday, the eve of Halloween, I received this email from young Kirsty aka Harriet, the young poet with a cat called Merlin, who, she tells me, has just fully recovered from a near fatal car accident. She then, adorably, sends this email birthday card which is the first and only one that Gilly has received – oh, I am such a bad mother! ☹

From: Kirsty Wheeler
To: Marilyn Edwards
Sent: Sunday, October 30, 1:51 PM
Subject: Gilly's Birthday

To Gilly,

HAPPY BIRTHDAY
From
Kirsty and Merlin

>^-^< 'meow' Xxxxxxxxxxxxxxx

Two days later I hear from Kate who, writing about her deceased cats, uses the magical phrase 'my Three, plus a previous sealpoint, now all live in my heart'. Her writing moves me so much. I write back and she replies:

– – –

From: Kate Clarke
To: Marilyn Edwards
Sent: Tuesday, November 01, 9:31
Subject: Re: BRILLIANT!

Dear Marilyn,

The ashes of The Three are in their box in my bedroom and will be stirred into mine (not quite yet I hope!) before being sprinkled in a beautiful Glen in Scotland, where we spent three VERY happy years. Each one died in my arms.

Within a week of Harry's death 'The Computer at the Surgery' demanded I attend for my annual MOT and Doc asked, 'What's up, Kate?' I heard myself telling him that at that moment there was a huge jagged rock living just under my heart, but as this had happened before I knew that with time it would turn into a precious pearl. I waited for him to certify me, instead he agreed saying that the loss of an animal is a huge bereavement; we have to love animals to understand the hurt . . .

. . . I am honoured to have had them in my life. We are truly blessed, we who love The Glorious Cat.

Kate

That description of the pain of bereavement, which in time will turn into a precious pearl, even now, as I write, makes my eyes fill up. All of Kate's cats deserve more of a mention but for reasons of space I concentrate here on Harry. Kate writes:

HARRY: Cream Pointed Siamese, born 8 April 92, died 16 January 01. When I went to 'view' him, having been told his three sisters were chosen but he was left, I could understand why. In front of the large farmhouse fire curled up in a neat row lay three perfect little socks – his sisters. On a human knee lay the nearest thing I have seen to ET in my life. Long neck, HUGE feet, even bigger ears and the sapphire blue glorious eyes should have been swapped over as they appeared to be opposing each other. His coat at that stage was all pale cream, the glorious reddish caramel developed as he grew. Well, my dear, had to buy him, didn't I, no one else would – surely? Even my closest friends agreed, he was ugly. He grew into THE most dashing, gloriously handsome, big-hearted and kindly Gentleman ever. All three were fed together, Harry would sit back and wait for the girls to eat their fill before he approached! And a note for Michael, Harry was the best football player born, every article became a football . . . unless he decided that for a wee while it would be a rugby day! Sadly Harry developed thyroid problems, then my first experience of a cat suffering from the dreaded kidney problems. I will forever remember the Vet showing me the final results sheet saying, 'Unfortunately there is no Dialysis Treatment for animals.' Harry, a kind-hearted and true gentleman to his end, God bless him. I spent days clutching my red dressing gown – his favourite 'bed'. The girls missed him, so I had to get them over this by being 'normal'.

~

The time for Gilly's operation is now approaching and since early yesterday evening all four cats have been deprived of their food and have been restless most of the night as a result. Gilly is especially active, and so I weaken and arise. And then what a petitioning starts up! As I enter the kitchen to make some coffee Pushkin, Fannie and Titus all sit in a sad line, miaowing and making small plaintive moans. They are positioned in the precise places that the food bowls normally occupy. Their eyes are large and trusting and never leave me for a second. I bustle around and try not to hear or see them. Gilly, somewhat obligingly, has come down and positioned herself on top of the cat carrier that is to take her to the vet, so one way and the other the four felines have communicated emotional blackmail on full voltage. Gritting my teeth I grab Gilly and unceremoniously bundle her inside the carrier and off she and I go.

Why do I always feel this dreadful sense of doom? I have been extraordinarily lucky and nothing untoward has ever happened to any of my cats at any of the vets that I have taken them to, but I keep hearing such sad stories about things that go wrong under anaesthetic or in recovery. Recently, when Michael and I stayed in Bristol with our French Canadian friend France and her partner Mark, she showed me a picture of her very first cat, Smoky, a beautiful gentle long-haired black moggy, with a tiny white patch on his chest, and as she talked about him, her eyes misted over. At the time she is speaking of she was still living in Canada.

'I had to take Smoky to the vet because he had an eye-infection and the vet took the opportunity to give him a thorough examination and mentioned the poor state of his teeth at the time. Smoky was prescribed an antibiotic cream for his eyes and I then made an appointment to have his teeth cleaned.'

'How old was Smoky at this time?'

'He was ten years old and in fact I remember signing a paper where it was clearly stated that there was a risk for cats over the age of ten years old to be sedated, and I presumed this was a standard paper they were giving to everyone to cover themselves and I never thought that the risk was very high.' As she looks at the picture of Smoky, her eyes fill up, but she continues in a low, steady, voice:

'It was 13 October 1993, and I was at work. At around 5.00 p.m. the phone went and the vet, a woman, started to explain to me that Smoky had died at the very end of the cleaning process.'

'Was she contrite, did she sound upset?' I gasp, in horror.

'I think she was sincerely sad at what had happened. She described the whole cleaning process and told me how she had just extracted his rotten teeth and was preparing to take him out of anaesthesia, when his heart just stopped beating. She explained all the methods she tried to resuscitate him and gave me a tentative explanation for this accident. She thought he might have had a heart murmur and she could perform an autopsy if I wanted to know for sure. I said it didn't matter, it wouldn't bring him back. She also asked me if I wanted his body back, but I said she could dispose of it – have it incinerated. I had to go back to sign a few papers and she gave me the tooth she had extracted at the end.

This I have kept as a memento of Smoky.' France looks at me, grinning, in her matter-of-fact way. I touch her hand sympathetically. Her voice changes:

'While I had kept my cool speaking to the vet, once I'd hung up, I remember sitting heavily on the chair near the phone, moaning out loud, "Mon chat est mort!" "Mon chat est mort!" A friend drove me back home and I remember crying my heart out all evening, all night and part of the next morning. I must have gone to work, but when I came back home I remember just frantically looking through the newspaper for kittens for sale. I found a place – the same friend drove me there – and the very next morning, a Friday, I came back home with a new kitten, who turned out to be the terrible Misty. My mourning of Smoky had been very intense but only lasted twenty-four hours or so.' France's use of the adjective 'terrible' in relation to Misty, who because of his bad behaviour ended up at the vet's almost monthly needing repairs of one kind or another, makes me laugh, but I gently suggest:

'You say "intense but only lasted twenty-four hours or so". . . France, looking at you now, you still miss that dear little cat and you remember him with so much love and affection. Your grief lasted much longer than just those intense twenty-four hours of agony'. France in her turn laughs and adds:

'I do remember him very clearly. Smoky was rather a timid cat, especially with other cats, and he was very sweet. I can still picture my nephew Gabriel, then about two years old, carrying him upside down (rear paws and tail up in front of his face with Smoky's head and front paws trailing near the floor between Gaby's two spread legs as he was trying to bring Smoky to us without tripping on him). Held this way, the cat was almost as tall as him and sweet Smoky was not saying a thing about being mishandled like that, although he did climb up on some high furniture afterwards to get out of reach from Gaby when he finally let go of him. He was not an especially bright cat. More than once we ended up sitting on him because we had not seen him, and yet he always seemed to think we would never hurt him and would stop before we squashed him. He was that kind of cat with a total trust in humans, even young children, and in some terrible way you can't help but think, if it wasn't for me, he would still be alive. In the end, I feel it's "live and learn". I'm never going to have another of my cats operated on unless it is absolutely necessary and otherwise, I'll make sure they're checked annually so problems with teeth and all else can be prevented.' As I survey her sleek and content-looking cluster of cats, consisting of Apollo, Grippette, Spooky and Uni, I have no doubt at all that I am in the presence of a very well-nurtured group of felines.

In fact Kate, who emailed me at Halloween, told me that one of her beloved cats, Chloe died on 8 July 2003 after a dental cleaning operation 'went wrong' and she had to have her jaw wired:

The following seven weeks were HELL. You may think me totally and incurably nuts, but Chloe 'told' me with her eyes 'Come on, Mum, it's time, you must do it.' We went to the vet the next morning.

With all these gloomy thoughts in my mind I enter the surgery firmly gripping Gilly's cat-carrying cage, and as I announce myself at reception I notice another woman sitting down nursing a large long-haired cat in a cage on her knee, and while she is awaiting her turn to be seen, I realise that she is close to tears. She is called and leaves the cat in for surgery, and I long to ask her what her charge is there for, but her body language tells me she wants to be left alone, so I don't. As she has not taken the cage away with her I interpret that as probably positive. My turn arrives and after signing the dreaded 'consent form' for the operation and discussing the logistics of what is to happen, I leave Gilly to the tender mercies of the veterinary nurse Alison, who is very understanding. The whole process of surgery is so hard for the lads and lasses who have to carry it out, as they have to minister to the human end as well as the animals, and that is a hard call. The saintly Gerard phones me three hours later to tell me that Gilly has come round from the anaesthetic and he is happy with her progress. I feel a massive surge of relief. He is such a good vet, added to which he has a big heart, bless him. He remains concerned about her neurotic nibbling of her hair from her back legs and stomach, but as this is not life threatening, he says he will get back to me when he has spoken to a dermatologist friend, which he duly does. They are both pretty much in agreement that her initial hair loss had most likely been caused by a reaction to the itchiness caused by the harvest mites, but since then she has continued to nibble turning it into a psychogenic alopecia. 'Great,' I speculate gloomily, 'that should be easy to cure.'

The Yorkshire nature artist Richard Bell and his wife Barbara, whom Michael and I have met a couple of times over the last two years, arrive on their way back to Middlestown in Yorkshire from a holiday in the Lakes, just as I am about to depart to collect Gilly and bring her home. Richard does some superb sketches of Fannie, who is relaxing with Titus in the conservatory in her newfound freedom of a world without Gilly and they can be seen on his website, which is www.willowisland.co.uk and you then go into his Nature Diary for November 2005. In fact, he has written and illustrated many books, one of which I have sitting on my desk now, called *Rough Patch* which is breathtakingly beautiful, a really inspiring book packed with wonderful black and white sketches, crayon drawings and paintings and subtitled 'a sketchbook from the wilder side of the garden'. However, I have to leave Richard and Barbara in the capable hands of Michael while I set off through what seems like a never-ending wall of rain to collect the girl.

I jauntily bounce into the surgery to collect 'Black Magic' and Alison brings her into the consulting room in her carrier. I am gently pulled up short when I peer inside and find a very forlorn, somehow really small black ball hunched up, with her ears down like Yoda, looking very sorry for herself, indeed. As we talk I take in the exceptionally small neat scar that Gerard has managed in his deft surgery and the tiny area of fur that Alison has shaved off and am hugely grateful to them both for their joint effort in keeping the ever balding Gilly as intact as possible. After receiving some gentle post-operative advice from Alison, I bundle her up and put her in the car and drive the mile and a half home as carefully as possible. She is completely silent inside the cage until we come up the hill near the side of the house and about twenty feet away from the gate of the Coach House she lets out a long single but astonishingly loud wail, which I take to be a recognition sound at the smell of HOME. When I get her inside she is extremely wobbly on her legs so I carry her into the kitchen and let her eat and drink a little. The other cats watch her but keep their distance and at this stage there is no hissing from them at the smell of anaesthetic on her breath. She starts to walk towards the stairs and I follow nervously. As she starts to climb the first stair she is so wibbly-wobbly that I fear she will never make it, so I carry her up. I shut her in my study and stay in there myself. This is unheard of from the point of view of the other resident cats and I hear both Fannie and Titus making their protests outside the door.

'Sorry, guys, but this time it's her turn for TLC – you don't have to be in here, there is a fire lit downstairs, go on down', and eventually they do take themselves off. By early evening I reckon she is strong enough to take the presence of the other cats, so then I open the door and let them in, and she gets up and weakly tries to play with them. I have got an uncovered cat litter tray in my study to save her walking the stairs, but to my surprise she just lies in it for a while, so I swap it for a covered one from downstairs, which she eventually uses for the purpose it was intended. Titus is the only one to get really close to her and she gently hisses as she gets the first 'whiff' of anaesthetic, but that is all. Gilly considerably below par is a very strange phenomenon and tonight I would say she is definitely more knocked out than were either Fannie or Titus. She is a smaller framed cat than the other two girls so that may be why, or it could be the Bengal thing of being a 'drama queen'. She sleeps in the study on the armchair that is really the one that Titus and Fannie used to sleep in, but they both allow it unchallenged. We leave her there and eventually retire to our room to sleep. At about 4.15 a.m. I feel the gentle weight of Gilly jumping up on to our bed and she quietly nestles into my back. As I feel her relax against me I experience a huge twinge of guilt, but as I stroke her she purrs that all forgiving purr that cats have.

CHAPTER 23

Gilly has recovered well from her operation, and has calmed down when she is outside, her former rampaging far and wide is now, thank goodness, at an end, well for the moment at any rate. She continues to terrorise poor Fannie though, and Fannie has not regained any more confidence. If anything she is more uncertain than ever of where she stands in the hierarchy of the Coach House. Generally, it is more or less all right between Titus and Gilly. Sometimes there is just the shadow of irritation from Titus, but Gilly is respectful of Titus and at night on occasion they will both sleep on our bed, although not close to each other as would Fannie and Titus, and that leads me to the night time ritual and how it is now. The glorious and superb thing about cats is that there is no standard status quo, there is no normal, there is no absolute. As soon as you think you know where a particular cat likes to lie, it will shun that place and find another much less suitable sleeping spot, and this goes equally for their loving rituals. There is no such thing as a 'usual' hello, or goodbye, or I love you. You may think there is, but it can change at a moment's notice. On the Coach House cats and their rituals, the current night-time ritual is that Gilly sleeps on the floor in the sitting-room in front of the fire, stretched out full length on the rug with the ease

and territorial ownership of a small black Labrador. Titus
and Fannie will have been curled up together in the
armchair in my study for most of the day and/or evening,
but as I turn out the lights, Titus will come down and follow
Michael and me up to our room, and soon after that
Pushkin will emerge from whichever strange hiding place is
his current chosen spot. Gilly will stay in the sitting-room
and Fannie will stay in the study. We both stroke Pushkin
and Titus and then put out the lights. Pushkin immediately
leaves the room and returns to an unknown place within the
warmer part of the house. Titus sometimes stays on our bed
and sometimes doesn't. After about an hour Gilly will
appear and lie stretched out next to either Michael or me,
depending upon her mood. But then sometimes she
doesn't. Fannie never comes near us. Well, having said that,
last night Fannie came in the middle of the night. None of
the other cats was in our bedroom at the time. She quietly
lay down on the bed between Michael and me and was there
at dawn, and so for the first time in months she and I had
our cuddle in the bathroom after my bath, but the sacred
cuddle is now rare, although since writing this it has
happened a few times, so again things are on the change a
little perhaps?

George is ill. It was bound to happen that one of them would get ill sooner or later and it is poor little George. Yesterday, when I opened the hen coop and let them all out, I noticed that one of them was limping slightly, but I thought it wasn't serious. Then this morning I open the pop hole and she comes out last limping very badly. Every time she puts one leg near the ground she pulls it back as if she is touching hot bricks. As I am watching her she suddenly keels over and flumps down on her side. The other hens immediately gather round her and start to peck her, nastily, like they do. I phone the vet's and demand, rather rudely, to know if whoever is on duty knows anything about hens. It turns out that it is young Paul, who lives on a large mixed farm, and although only newly qualified he is brilliant with livestock of all kinds. On the phone there is loads of gloom about possibly Marek's disease, which rings all sorts of bells to do with the Herpes virus and the onset of tumours, but he says to bring her down and he'll have a look-see. After I have been waiting for a while the door opens and a young, good-looking farmer with a black Labrador with his tail in plaster comes in and sits next to me. We are both there as Saturday morning emer-

gencies. His Lab sniffs inquiringly at my solid-sided cat carrier and the young man says:

'What's wrong with your cat?'

'It's not a cat.' Suddenly abashed, I go quiet.

'What on earth is in there, then?'

'A hen.'

'A hen? A hen did you say? But for goodness sake you would only have paid a couple of quid for that and think what the bill at the end of this lot will be!' I laugh, and mumble something about the quality of life, but as he continues to tease me I protest:

'But hey, you wouldn't have ignored the plight your dog was in, even though the vet's bills might eventually mount up to more than you paid for him, would you?'

'Well, no, but he's a dog. Oh, alright, fair enough then.'

It all becomes slightly embarrassing as it's my turn first and I take her into the surgery and by this time – it had been really cold overnight, the temperature had dropped at one point to –5°C – George is beginning to perk up a bit and look quite bright-eyed again in the unaccustomed heat of the car and now the warm surgery. Paul asks me if I know her weight and, of course, I haven't a clue, so we have to weigh the cat carrier with her in it and then, while his young assistant holds her, without her in it and all this time the young man and his dog are looking on askance as we pass him to get to the scales. Paul examines her and pronounces her to be free of the dreaded Marek's disease.

'I am fairly confident that it is a neuromuscular injury she has suffered. She has somehow damaged herself, flying into something possibly.' With that he deftly injects her with Rimadyl which is used for arthritis in dogs. The reason he needs to know her weight is so that he doesn't over-dose her, and as he plunges the needle into her she never makes a sound. We pack her up into her cage and I sneak past the young farmer wishing him luck with his dog. He grunts, but smiles back. That one felt like a baptism of fire. It is the first time I have run the gauntlet of a vet's surgery with a hen.

I get George back to her little paddock and open the cat carrier, and to my complete amazement she runs, yes, actually runs across the yard to join her coop-mates. She appears to be totally recovered. This time they just welcome her back and don't peck at her. As I am watching my little flock I suddenly become aware of them all switching their fixated gaze from me – always along with Michael a good touch for a treat of some kind – to the sky behind my head. I swing round to see what they are watching – they have gone completely silent – and there I see two huge buzzards[53] riding the thermals in slow, large circles. To begin with they are over the woods behind the house, then they glide over the house and now they are directly overhead. As they get ever closer I can hear that haunting 'pee-uuu' noise they mew to each other. The hens appear almost hypnotised but also a little apprehensive. Would a buzzard seriously be a predator for a large hen, I wonder? But also how do these hens, who have only known Maurice Jackson's farm near Keighley and more recently Hutton Roof, have such a finely honed instinct that they can recognise a possible predator so quickly and absolutely? We do get buzzards here, year-round, so perhaps it is from their time here and, for sure, a small chick would be vulnerable. Shortly after this sighting, rather disconcertingly I receive the following email from Mary White about her Bengal cat

---

[53] Buteo buteo

Purdie, which sets my alarm bells going on the subject of buzzards and not just in the context of chickens:

– – –

From: Mary White
To: Marilyn Edwards
Sent: Sunday, December 10, 11:11 AM
Subject: Re: Purdie the Immortal Bengal

Marilyn, let me tell you quickly about another Purdie life being used – I think she has 19 not 9.

During the summer Richard was doing some work in the garden – it was a lovely day and Purdie was just hanging around. Directly to the rear of the garden we have acre upon acre of farm fields, mainly used for hay, and a haven for little creatures such as voles, shrews, etc., and BUZZARDS–bloody great enormous birds that circle around looking for mice, that have a wing span of several feet.

On this day, Richard was working and Purdie was sitting on the path. Richard suddenly looked up the length of the path to see a buzzard swooping directly towards Purdie, claws and feet extended for the catch! Purdie just sat there looking completely unbothered. There was no time for Richard to do anything apart from watch in horror. It came down and the ONLY thing that stopped it taking her was that the 2 chimney pots on the path with my fuchsias in it seemed to be in its flight path and it had to swerve to miss them and misjudged its angle on poor Purdie, still sitting there nonchalantly! Richard said it came within inches of him and her . . .

So she is very unlucky this cat, or perhaps very lucky?
Love,
Mary

PS In case you ask, I did say to Richard that Purdie is quite a small cat (very small for a Bengal) and that perhaps the buzzard thought she was a large rabbit . . . or maybe we are kidding ourselves. Birds of prey, after all, do have the proverbial 'eyes like a hawk' and are supposed to be able to see for miles with 20/20 perfect vision! You'll remember Purdie's colouring, tabby with different kinds of browns and blacks.

I should mention that Mary White was the breeder from whom I acquired Pushkin, and I remember well, three years ago, meeting Purdie, who is a predominantly brown and black tabby. I then lost touch, and thanks to Ruth, who emailed me about her Pushkin earlier this year, we are now in contact again. Some time ago she told me the remarkable story of how Purdie had gone missing for ten days and when she did arrive back she was severely lame, with one hind leg held up from the ground. She was assumed by the vet to have been run over and by the time she hobbled home she was close to starving. On examination she had a severely fractured hip joint and following surgery was prescribed cage rest for a whole month. For a Bengal and her human carers that is such a long time! Imagine the noise. Her leg was nerve damaged, and the vet and everyone else said she would never regain the use of it. Mary massaged the leg every night and Purdie kept pulling the leg away; Mary persevered in spite of Purdie's protestations and, nearly four months after the accident, Purdie is now walking almost perfectly. When she wants to run she still uses the three legs, but can walk on all four. The good that has come from all of this is that Purdie is now a changed cat. She, who used to go off regularly for days at a time, now never goes out at night and she never strays far from the house, even in daylight.

∼

Kevin Dean, whom I first had contact with two years ago, is a young composer, instrumentalist and cabaret performer who confesses to spending 'all my wages on cat food for the strays when I work abroad'. When I first knew him he told me, with much excitement, that he was about to move house and was yearning to adopt two cats from the Country Cat Shelter in Lowestoft.

'There are many cats in the cat shelter, but there are two older girls with sadness in their eyes. Nobody wants them. They are overweight. I will get them sorted out. Lovely girls they are, Marilyn.' These two sisters had had a tough time because a couple who had originally cared for them, split up and, unable to look after them any more, took the cats to the shelter, then made up again and took the cats back home, and then sadly split up again, so the cats were returned to the shelter. When Kevin first sees them they have been in the shelter for five months, getting sadder by the week. He commits to sharing his home with these girls and names them Abbey Moon and Angel Moon. He visits them regularly while he is waiting to move, sometimes as often as three times a week for the next couple of months.

'Also I would "do the rounds" and give fuss to all the other cats. Kittens and pregnant mothers would come and go. The three-year-old dark tortie "Trixie" was still there. She was a very nervous cat. She had been at the shelter for the same amount of time as the sisters. Trixie was found in a barn mothering her litter and was often seen going out hunting with a fox. How could I not give her a home too? I told Elaine (who runs the shelter) that Trixie could come to Pixie Cottage as well. I re-named her Petal Rose. She walks like a fox.'

When Kevin first gets them back home Abbey and Angel immediately start investigating the cottage. Petal just hides under the kitchen table. Everything goes wonderfully well at the beginning and they all eat and learn to use the litter trays as Kevin hopes:

'I put their trays in the utility room. A cat flap leads from the kitchen to the utility. And for the first few days there were no problems. They knew where the toilet was and they seemed to be very content! But . . . one night I watched Petal go through the cat flap to the toilet. Within seconds she was back in the kitchen! She was one very shaken cat. What on earth happened? I just thought it was Petal being silly. A few minutes later Abbey wandered into the utility. Déjà vu! She zoomed back in too! What a commotion. I grabbed my keys and ventured into the utility. Nothing! I then opened the utility door to the garden. I had a wander around. Nothing. The outer utility door is partly patterned glass. Was it a fox peering through? Or maybe another cat? Or what? The cats remained nervous and shaky, including Angel, who hadn't even gone through the cat flap at the time. Petal hid herself. The two sisters just sat and nervously look towards the utility area. I went to bed. Petal normally sleeps on my office chair in the studio. Angel kips in the corner of the studio. And Abbey is Daddy's girl who sleeps on my bed. The night of the utility scare, Petal hid all night. Angel and Abbey slept in their usual places. The utility was not used again. The next morning I found a deposit on the rug in the front room. That following day I never heard the flap go again, but they just kept staring at it nervously!'

In fact, Kevin never does find out what it is that so upset all three cats, but they do settle down and become very contented cats in their new-found freedom with someone they can trust. As the time approaches for them to be let out of doors I become fretful, because their former traffic-sense may have been dulled and also for Petal Rose who is a near feral cat, will she revert to her wild ways?

He does let them out, of course, and they are fine and

become visibly happier and more relaxed, as they realise they are properly 'home'. Wonderfully, the nervous Petal becomes especially close to Angel, who looks out for her. All three of them get on remarkably well.

I continue to follow the tales of Kevin's cats with some interest. One day Kevin asks me if he ever told me about his 'vortex experience'.

'It first happened a few years ago. I arrived home from doing a cabaret show, totally sober. I lay back on the sofa with a glass of wine and put on the TV to catch the last half hour of a Bond film. Tigger-Mu-Mu was on the coffee table between me and the TV. She was facing away from me towards the large window with the curtains drawn. Tiggs was having a good wash in true Mogology style. Suddenly something caught my eye way left of the TV against the curtains. I looked and it was unbelievable . . . a swirling purple/blue vortex. That's the only way I can describe it. But what caught my eye even more was Tiggs, stuck in mid-wash, looking at the vortex. This vortex looked like something was trying to manifest. The episode lasted only a few seconds. When the vortex disappeared Tiggs continued to look at the space for a few seconds longer and then carried on washing. This sent shivers down my spine because Tiggs was not influenced by me at all and yet she clearly saw what I was seeing. It wasn't caused by a light shining through the window because the bungalow is in a cul-de-sac with no passing traffic; it has a large front garden, and thick curtains! What I saw was in the room.'

I am disconcerted by this and ask Kevin lots of questions. He says that he only experienced the 'vortex' once but on several occasions he saw a 'ghost' cat and so, he discovers recently, did his mother. However, both of them only saw it in this particular bungalow. It would be visible to him out of the corner of his eye and it would seem to be walking in that way that cats do and that in some strange way it looked like Tigger-Mu-Mu, which is odd as she was alive then, but the moment he turned round and looked at it square on it would fade.

'Sometimes I wondered if it was Barnaby Lilly, my first cat, but she wasn't a tabby. Sometimes when I saw it, I would then see Tiggs kipping on the chair. Could it be Tiggs astral projecting?'

All I feel able to offer is the Bard of Avon's immortal: 'There are more things in heaven and earth, Horatio, than are dreamt of in your philosophy.'

One day Kevin astonishes me by telling me that having read *The Cats of Moon Cottage* and been roused by the account of the deaths of Otto and Septi, he has written a piece of music to their memory. The track is called 'Otto and Septi's Tune' and it features on a CD called *Mogology: Music for Cats and Cat Lovers*.[54] When he sent it to me he said:

' "Otto and Septi's Tune" tells a story, musically. The general "hook" is their tune. The two electric guitars are the two cats: the main guitar being Septi and the replying and harmonising guitar being Otto moving her way into Septi's life. Often the two guitars are played together in harmony expressing the two cats in harmony together. The slightly haunting sinister middle section represents the two deaths; firstly Otto's, then Septi's, and then it's back to that main hook – their tune celebrating their lives and them being together again in cat heaven.'

When I first heard it, it made me cry. Three-quarters of the way through there are three very subtle heart-stopping distant cat calls over a near purr. The music is very beautiful. I suspect that that first book moved Kevin so much because

---

[54] *Mogology* by EOL/KDM Productions Cat No: MOG7318

of the experiences he had with his cat Barnaby Lilly, to whom he pays tribute with the piece of music, also on this CD, called 'The Tortoiseshell'. Barnaby Lilly was the very first cat in Kevin's life and was a beautiful white-fronted tortoiseshell. She became ill with tumours and Kevin, heart-broken, had to have her put to sleep. Tigger-Mu-Mu, a Cypress tabby, was his next cat. She had thyroid problems, but the pills his vet gave her seemed to sort her out. But slowly the passage of time took its toll on his little tabby cat.

'Tiggs would have days when she wouldn't eat at all and would just kip. These days started to happen more often. On the morning of 6 June last year I walked into the lounge and she was having trouble breathing. I knew this was it. I stayed with her and she died within half an hour. I think she was just waiting for me to get out of bed to say goodbye. She was always a spoilt cat, and still is! She is buried under a fountain feature with mist and lights that I bought for her the next day.' Kevin's music for Tiggs is a haunting melody called 'Purrs in Heaven'.

CHAPTER 24

Annabel comes across this morning for a quick chat and tells me, laughingly, that her brother Henry, a retired farmer, told her I mustn't - just mustn't - kiss the chickens. She says that she has been told to come and tell me this as it has been issued as a serious government warning.

'I mean honestly, Marilyn, as if you would.' I grin sheepishly. The truth is that all the hens are now extremely tame and will allow both Michael and me to pick them up and give them cuddles, and as most of them jump on to the wall when we go in to see them, they greet us at head height. Not that I actually do kiss them, beaks are strangely off-putting, but if they wanted to kiss us, or we them, it would be very easy so to do. The hens are now laying eggs daily and they are a beautiful deep brown colour with dark yellow yolks and truly delicious.

Annabel and Richard are off to Australia to spend Christmas with their daughter and just before they go they give us an enchanting present. It is a small glass pot of honey, the size and shape that Pooh Bear was especially fond of and the colour of the honey it contains is pure gold. Around the pot, designed by the fair hand of Richard himself, is a white label with the words:

AMBROSIA
Food of the Gods
from
Hutton Roof

Underneath this bold statement is a copy of Shepherd's wonderful drawing of Pooh hanging on to the string of a balloon surrounded by faintly hostile bees and underneath the drawing the phrase 'You never can tell with bees'.

As I thank Annabel effusively I observe:

'But they never swarmed on us this summer, they behaved impeccably.'

'Ah, but you never can tell,' she affirms.

Eating the food of the gods from Hutton Roof spread thickly on buttered bread is truly divine.

~

In this book I have attempted to observe and record the lives of the cats in the Coach House as accurately as possible and here, as the year end is reached, I give the reader a quick update.

Gilly has not only recovered well from her operation but also from her allergy to the harvest mite; all her glossy black fur has grown back on her legs and her tummy and over her scar and she looks sleek and shiny and well. Even her wonky whiskers are better than they have been before, although they will never be anything to write home about!

Fannie and Gilly continue to be full of aggression or fear towards each other, although on some days several hours will pass without any sign of tension between them and each day that happens I hope against hope that the dynamics of their relationship is sorted out, but in reality I don't think a day has passed without there being some explosive outburst between them both. Fannie has just learned recently how to be brave enough to come into the bathroom in the morning for her cuddle, and I think that is helping her; it is certainly helping me.

Pushkin and Gilly are friendly in a mutually fun-loving, chasing sort of way, although they never lie together. The only one Pushkin lies near is Titus, but then that is true of Gilly: she will lie with Titus too, but none of the others. Pushkin spends more of the day awake now, playing with Gilly and checking out where she is. He does seem to be quite infatuated by her. Gilly enjoys being with Pushkin and rampages around with him more than any of the others, and they always 'kiss' each other when they meet up in the hallway, or anywhere else. But of all the cats it is Titus whose company Gilly actively seeks out and, it appears to me, whose approval she seeks.

The bond has considerably strengthened again between Titus and Fannie and Titus to some extent protects Fannie from Gilly. They spend much time each day lying together in the chair in my study now, and Fannie seems to gain reassurance from this.

A small drama has just unfolded before us, which indicates something I had not previously known about the relationship between Titus and Fannie. Michael and I are sitting on a sofa in front of the fire watching television and Gilly is lying very close to the stove on the floor stretched out. Titus is resting, in a slightly uncomfortable-looking pose, on the empty sofa. Fannie comes down from upstairs and peers through the banisters to check where Gilly is lying, sees she is stretched out with her eyes closed and so squeezes between a pair of the balustrades, along the back of Titus's sofa and down into the kitchen to eat. Gilly hearing her eating, gets up, stretches, throws her one of her stares and, with all the normal accompanying hissing and spitting, chases her with great force back upstairs to my study. Gilly then saunters back down as she always does after she has 'despatched' Fannie in this way. Titus gets up off the sofa, slowly stretches, and walks over to Gilly who is sitting upright looking at the fire. Gilly turns her head round to look at Titus who then hits Gilly, three times rapidly, each one a really hard thwack with her front foot and then, without a backward glance, Titus goes upstairs to find Fannie. She rather disconcertingly has an expression on her face like my father's when he was in a rage.

'Did you see that, Michael?'

'Yes, I did. She did that for Fannie.'

'Do you *really* think that is why?'

'There was absolutely no other reason why she'd have just got up and clocked Gilly like that, it must've been because she didn't like what Gilly did to Fannie.' I look across at Gilly. She is looking into the fire quietly. I guess she is thinking, but what *is* it that she's thinking?

To complete this tableau Pushkin meanders into the room via the window from the conservatory courtesy of the cats' scratching post, climbs across the top of the bookcase, walks over Michael and me and our sofa and subsides gracefully in a leggy sprawl across the coffee table between us and the television like a small Russian Blue Emperor. He is now obscuring half of the screen from us but he, on the other hand, has an excellent view. The clock ticks, quietly and the logs crackle, merrily. I sigh, happily. I reckon this is as good as it gets with the four Coach House cats.

ACKNOWLEDGEMENTS

The author and publishers are grateful for permission to reproduce the following copyright material:

France Bauduin: Sketch of Harriet and Chester, reproduced on p. 322 (© 2005)
Doreen Dann: The Kitten House or Why not a Black One? (© 2000)
Harriet Garside: A Wild Hack (© 2004)
Anne Huntington: Tales of a Postmistress (© December 1995)
Beth Loft: Woolgathering: Ramblings of a woman who really ought to know better – Treacle archive blog (© 2005)

POSTSCRIPT

To contact Marilyn Edwards via email and for an update on the Moon Cottage cats please visit her website: www.thecatsofmooncottage.co.uk or write to –

The Coach House
Hutton Roof
Kirkby Lonsdale
Cumbria LA6 2PG

Peter Warner, the exceptionally talented illustrator of the Moon Cottage cat books, died following a short illness on 22 September 2007, which deprives the world of a uniquely gifted feline artist, musician, bon viveur, wit and lovely man. He will be greatly missed and I hope these books will help to be a memorial to him, as they displayed his ability to draw cats from life at its absolute best. For more information on his work do visit his website. www.peterwarner.com

Marilyn Edwards, January 2008